KT-172-972

Mary Warnock

A Memoir

Mary Warnock

A Memoir
People and Places

Duckworth

First published in 2000 by
Gerald Duckworth & Co. Ltd.
61 Frith Street, London W1V 5TA
Tel: 020 7434 4242
Fax: 020 7434 4420
Email: enquiries@duckworth-publishers.co.uk
www.ducknet.co.uk

A catalogue record for this book is available from the British Library

ISBN 0 7156 2955 7

Typeset by Derek Doyle & Associates, Liverpool
Printed in Great Britain by
Biddles Ltd, www.biddles.co.uk

Contents

For Kitty, Felix, James, Fanny and Boz,
with love and gratitude.

A Mistake Avoided

I meant one day to make
A bonfire of the past,
To set fires backward running
Riotously to slake
In time their malignant thirst.
What had been was to be
Unbuilt from the beginning,
Battered stone by stone
To true mortality,
Until at last we had
At our backs but the dead
True innocence of the moon.

I could have burned the past
In my magnificent fire;
How could the dead forbid
New flames to stir their dust?
But one day my desire
Slipped out of my fingers –
At that one thing you said
I saw a crowd of strangers
Come close suddenly: saying
'We were the past, are these
Strangers to blame? What use
To you would be our destroying?'

G.J.W.

Acknowledgements

I would like to express my gratitude to all those who have helped me put together this memoir. I must especially mention George Clayton, Peter Conradi, Jean Crossley (née Wilson), Michael Gerin-Tosh, Brian and Imogen Rose, Liz and Peter Shore, and Susan Wood. I must also thank Jean Austin, who read a first draft and who was as always, kind and encouraging. Of course all the mistakes and distortions are my own. At Duckworth, Martin Rynja has been unfailingly patient, amiable and enthusiastic.

List of Illustrations

Introduction

An introduction must be read first, but written last. In the chapters that follow I have tried to be honest about their subjects, people I have known, some well, some hardly at all, but to whose significance in my world I have given some thought. The accounts I have given of them are partial in every sense of the word. I have not attempted to describe them completely; and I have written of them as they appeared to me, from my particular point of view.

Each of the chapters contributes a kind of story; and a story must have a narrator, who may or may not play an active role in the plot. The narrator, whether the author or a fictional character, may be an Ancient Mariner who buttonholes his audience, or a bloodless figure like Nicholas in Anthony Powell's *A Dance to the Music of Time*. I have not remained so impassive as he in my stories; indeed I have been positively egocentric and often intrusive. All the same, some less episodic account of this narrator is perhaps required to fill in some of the temporal discontinuities, and to provide some continuity for the 'I' who has observed the others with less than perfect vision. It is easier to be alert to partiality if you know whose voice you are hearing.

The supreme difficulty of writing about one's self, however, is the risk of self-deception. It is of no help to decide to stick to the facts, because, notoriously, one may describe the facts to suit one's self. One may misremember; or, more disastrously, may obscure by words rendered meaningless by repetition, how things actually were.

Nevertheless, I am pretty well certain of some things, and one is that I had, on the whole, a supremely happy childhood, which has never lost its hold over me. This may seem surprising. My mother had an unhappy, though affluent, childhood and adolescence. She was the eldest child of Sir Felix Schuster Bt., a banker from a Jewish family who had come over from Frankfurt to Manchester in 1869 in pursuit of their wool-trade interests, and had converted to Christianity, even before leaving Germany. He was a figure straight from Osbert Lancaster; he could have been the model for Sir Ephraim Kirsch Bt. from Draynefleet, who wore hairy tweeds in the country, and incongruously attended shooting parties. My grandfather held such parties in the huge ugly Victorian house in West Sussex which he acquired in later life as his country seat. The Schusters were, on the whole, a melancholy lot. Sir Felix, with his pale, sad face, black beard and hooded eyes, was at heart a musician, and played the piano as if his heart would break. They had a rich mythology concerned with the frustrated brilliance of all their relatives. My Aunt Evelyn, for example, would, we were told, have been a world-class violinist, only she became deaf (that much at least was true; and it was true also that after her death a valuable violin was found among her possessions). My Uncle Bob, later Sir Victor Schuster, who had been at school at Winchester, and had gone on to New College, promised to be an extraordinary classical scholar, only he fell off his bicycle and damaged his brain. (For this there was less evidence. In later years, when I got to know him, he seemed to me charming, musical, extravagant and rather disreputable, but showing no sign of brain damage.) Only my poor mother, the eldest child, was thought to have no talents. Her engagement to my father, Archibald Wilson, of Scottish and Irish extraction, and though of quite distinguished family with no money to speak of, was opposed; they were permitted to marry only when he got a job teaching the newly instituted subject of Modern Languages at Winchester (Winchester was thought to be a cut above other schools, teachers there being 'dons', not regular schoolmasters). So my mother had enjoyed fewer than twenty years of happy marriage before my father died in a school epidemic of diphtheria in 1923. Their eldest child, Malcolm, suffered from what would now be known as severe autism, and lived nearly all his life in institutions; then came three children, Jean, Duncan and Grizel; their third son, Sandy, died of pneumonia in 1921, shortly before the birth of my sister, Stephana. I was born in April 1924, seven months after the death of my father.

It sounds a gloomy background. Moreover my mother, who made no secret of her preference for boys over girls, must have been greatly disappointed that her two youngest children were both girls. She told me, when I was about three years old, how deeply she wished that I had been a boy. I think, even at that time, I partly understood; but it did not make me at all sorry for her. I felt, if anything, a bit indignant that she should overlook the advantages of having me (ME) as a daughter. I was, I think, a self-pleased child, perfectly content to be who I was, even if others might wish me to be different, as they often did. (It is perhaps worth remarking how supremely self-centred children are. Having been told by well-meaning adults that my father was in heaven, I did not think it in the least odd that in church everyone should address their prayers to him: 'Our Father, which art in heaven ...')

The nursery, in my childhood, was a separate establishment; our meals were brought upstairs by a maid. Mither (as our mother was later known to me and Stephana and all our friends) visited us from time to time, and sometimes had tea with us, with bread and butter and delicious little triangular sugar cakes. We went down to the drawing room, in clean frocks and coral necklaces, for about an hour every evening, where we had songs, or the gramophone, and played with mosaic bricks. The routine was amazingly old-fashioned, even for the 1920s. Our pleasures and our security were entirely the result of the character of our Nanny, Emily Coleman, who had been nanny to all of us, and who remained in the family, helping us with the next generation of children, until she died in 1976, aged 94, in Stephana's house in Ripon. She was a person of immense energy and imagination. It was impossible for a child to be bored in her company. She had a great fund of songs, an instant memory for which meant that she kept her repertoire up to date. She sang old music-hall songs, First World War songs, Gilbert and Sullivan (for every year the Winchester Operatic Society performed a Gilbert and Sullivan opera in the Guildhall) and numerous hymns, some recollected from the times when the Moody and Sankey services used to be held on the banks of the Test, in her Hampshire childhood.

She was greatly given to 'sayings'. Looking back, I think that these sayings had an almost ritual function; they constituted a use of language to mark recurring situations. They were formalities of a reassuring kind, like the 'good mornings' that villagers exchanged in the street, almost Homeric stock phrases. I believe they contributed to our childhood sense of recurring certainties. She would get up, reluctantly, from her chair and say, 'Work, for the night is coming, When men work no more' (a 'saying' I frequently used to myself as an undergraduate, and even to this day). Or, if we expressed some opinion with which she disagreed, she would say, 'Everyone to his liking, as the old woman said when she kissed her cow'. She did not always need to finish the 'saying'. If we had done something wrong, she used to say 'If it wasn't for taking off my kid glove ...' (and sometimes 'and exposing my lily-white hand to the atmosphere ...'), or 'I'll give you what Paddy gave the drum ...' (It was not until years later that I learned from Geoffrey that what Paddy gave the drum was two big thumps instead of one, and that it is the signal for the march to halt.) The sayings could be drawn from any source. Our older siblings had

had a rhyming story book concerned, I think, with some chickens, a book destroyed long before our day. It contained the lines 'Nothing, they said, could be finer. But just as these words were spoken, the raft ran into a liner'. With these memorable words, Nan used to inject a note of caution, if we seemed to be over-confident. But equally, the sayings could be from the *Book of Common Prayer*.

Nan taught us to knit and to sew and to whistle; she recited our multiplication tables with us when we went on our daily walks. She pointed out all kinds of objects for us to look at or exclaim about, and when we went to school, she was enormously inquisitive about what we had done that day. My sister Stephana was much more open and confiding than I in answering these questions. I think I had learned a lesson of concealment, even deception, from the trouble she sometimes got into with Nan if she naively confessed that she had been sent out of the room in maths, or whatever it might be. Stephana was always Nan's favourite. But I did not mind this; indeed I thought it only right, because Stephana was the person I too most admired and loved. And one thing we knew for certain was that Nan, unlike Mither, preferred girls to boys. She used to say, 'Poor things, men'; and though she had a very soft spot for my husband, Geoffrey, because he did the crossword, was good at changing babies' nappies and enjoyed watching sport on television, on the whole she did not think much of the people her girl-children married.

In later life, Nan did the crossword every day, and retained the keenest interest in sport and current affairs, through the radio and finally through television. When we gave her a colour television in the 1970s, though at first she scorned it, with its help she became deeply interested in racing, and Stephana placed bets for her. Her attitude to our mother was ambiguous. She always spoke of her in slightly derogatory terms, often beginning 'One thing I *will* say for your mother' and then handing out some strictly limited praise. But when Mither died in 1953, she told me that she felt she had nothing left to live for (though she did live, with much pleasure, for more than twenty years).

When I was very young I used to have nightmares about Nan suffering some accident, or deciding to leave us. (If we were exceptionally tiresome, she sometimes said 'I'm going away to be a soldier'; I hated this 'saying'). There was a particular walk we used to take which led us above a steep chalk cliff over a railway cutting, and as I lay in bed I used to envisage Nan falling over this cliff. In the end I refused to allow her to take us on this walk. I never had such fears on behalf of our mother. I suppose that it is true that as long as a child has some rock of strength, it does not matter who it is. Our mother was, to us, a somewhat exotic figure connected with London, rich food, delicious smells. As time went on we grew to like her more and more, and find her more and more interesting, though we never ceased to be partly irritated by her. She was peculiarly tolerant of our crazes, and of our friends, but, compared with Nan, she was remote, in our nursery years. Nan was not a cosy figure, but she represented continuity, the certainties of the recurring seasons, and above all the excitement of each season as it came round. When she began to sing carols, Christmas was in sight.

For me, the other great influence on my life, the source of both security and excitement, was my sister Stephana. We were an inseparable pair as children, bonded together in the nursery in opposition to all grown-ups, and especially to our older siblings, even when they were kindly paying attention to us. Stephana was brave, talkative, never fearing as I always did, that she would make a fool of herself, intensely musical and with a passion for words. We both loved hymns, especially those that contained mysterious words like 'Paraclete' or 'Trisagion'. We loved riding, we loved our holidays at Woolacombe every Easter or at our grandfather's house, Verdley Place, set in damp lush Sussex countryside, with numerous farms to visit on the estate. We had endless private games and rituals, including an ongoing soap opera, which we added to whenever we went for walks, all of whose characters were horses, and which we continued until we were well into our teens. By then it had become unimportant that the protagonists were horses; only their names and some of their virtues and vices bore any trace of their origin. By then, too, the plot was less a succession of terrible disasters, floods, fires, epidemics, escaped lunatics than it had been at first, and was more a matter of putting on new productions of Mozart operas, or fixing the programme for symphony concerts. For these horses had, from the beginning, been keenly interested in music. In the late 1960s, when Stephana was Head of Music at Ripon Cathedral Choir School, where her husband, Duncan Thomson, was headmaster, and I was headmistress of the Oxford High School for Girls, I realised that we were both doing in fact what we had done in fiction for so long (I was a very interventionist head as far as music was concerned, and always had a finger in the pie of who should lead the second fiddles, instead of sitting at the back desk of the firsts; who should audition for the chamber orchestra, and so on). It was always part of our pleasure in riding that we got to know the horses; and when we had our own horses, their characters formed an integral part of our lives.

My mother took it for granted that all her children would go to boarding school; but when it came to my turn, she decided that she had had more than enough of Downe House, where all of my three sisters went, and that I might choose any school in the country as long as it was not Downe. I was bitterly disappointed, because I longed to join Stephana there. I was in love with the school, largely because of the music I heard there when I went over to concerts, and because of Stephana's friends, who seemed to me beautiful, funny and glamorous, beyond any people I had met before. I found the place itself, high up in the woodlands above Newbury, intensely romantic, and the uniform, green djibbahs in the winter, and brilliant-coloured linen tunics in the summer, far to be preferred to the drab brown and dirty flesh-coloured blouses of St Swithun's in Winchester, where I went as a day-girl. But there was no arguing with Mither on this; she was adamant. In the end I decided to stay where I was, but to change to being a boarder.

In those days St Swithun's was an intensely High-Church school, whose aim was to ensure that its pupils were good, rather than clever or well-educated, its ideal being service rather than success, though it had the reputation for 'sound' education, especially in the sciences, an unusual reputation for a girls' school at the time. Nursery life at Kelso House, where we lived, came to an end in 1937, when I started to board.

Life as a boarder at the school was exceptionally dramatic, not because of the unfolding events in Europe from 1938 onwards, but because of the intensity of our failed attempts to live up to the standards of good behaviour in thought, word and deed that were demanded. A burden of guilt hung over us. We knew that the purpose of the school was to make us good and holy, and some of us knew that we could not attain, worse, did not even want to attain, such ideals. All the same, I enjoyed myself there. I thrived on the drama. I felt extraordinarily free to be whatever I liked, to indulge in friendships, passions, secret metaphysical speculations that I would have been ashamed to indulge in at home, now that even Stephana was removed as a potential critic. I greatly enjoyed the work, too, especially when, after School Certificate in 1939, I began to do almost nothing except Latin and Greek and, my favourite lesson, the history of the *Book of Common Prayer*.

Although we were not allowed books in our 'cubicles' (where

we each had a bed and washbasin protected by walls from our neighbours, in a long, windy dormitory) except the Bible, or other holy texts, my mother had given me a marvellous anthology of prose and poetry, edited by Robert Bridges, first published in 1915, and revived in the Second World War, entitled *The Spirit of Man* which, on account I suppose of its title, was allowed past the censors. This was undoubtedly the most educative book I ever possessed. Under the bedclothes with a torch in winter, by the late sunlight in summer, I read and learned Shakespeare's sonnets, poems by Gerard Manley Hopkins, extracts from Spinoza, Tolstoy, Plato, all arranged according to topics, such as 'Mortality', 'Dissatisfaction', 'Salvation'; the extracts were in English or in French; and the authors' names were not placed beneath the extracts, but at the end of the book, so, as Bridges said in his preface, the reader was invited to bathe rather than fish in the waters, reading each piece in its context. For all the years I was at St Swithun's, this book was my bible; and later on, I was amazed by the thought that, also in Winchester, separated by a mile or two of space, and by ignorance of each other's existence, Geoffrey was bathing in the same waters. I doubt if there is any aspect of education so valuable as such solitary reading as this. It may be that the comparative lack of solitude experienced by adolescents these days is genuinely harmful to their education. There is no real evidence to suggest such a thing; but to have been denied it would for me have been a terrible deprivation.

But solitude was by no means the only pleasure. I had several close friends, the most important of whom was another classicist, a year ahead of me, but with whom I shared most of my lessons, our numbers being so small. She was Imogen Wrong, who later married Brian Rose, a Cambridge economist, and who has been my best-loved and most supportive friend for more than sixty years. It was she who opened my eyes to the fact that one need not love, or even like, all of one's family; one could view them as separate people, some liked, some disliked. I remember the shock I felt when, walking round the grounds one day (we always seemed to have endless time to walk round, a great chance for gossip, or for exchanging our literary discoveries; the poetry of Housman, for example, or the outcome of our bathing in the waters of Bridges's anthology), she asked, 'which of your sisters do you dislike most?' I had literally never thought of raising such a question. It was unheard of. So I played for time, asking her to answer it for her own case, and willingly enough she embarked on a long stream of invective against her eldest sister, Rosemary. Imogen's father, Murray Wrong, had died when she was four years old; she was the fourth child of six. We were proud of our fatherless state, and despised our contemporaries who were always prattling about 'Mummy and Daddy'. We used stuffily to say 'My mother'. Imogen, with her two younger siblings, had gone to Canada for part of their early childhood, and when she came back she was conscious that with her Canadian accent and uninhibited conversation, she was prone to seem 'bumptious', a deadly sin at St Swithun's. She was therefore more anxious to be a success at school than I was, to fit in, to be liked, to be in teams, to be a prefect, and this meant that she suffered much more than I did.

I knew I should never be a success in school terms, for, though I was considered quite bright and was the youngest in my form, I never performed very well (I was once told by the headmistress that I 'prostituted my intellect', which baffled me at the age of eleven, and recourse to the dictionary did not much enlighten me). In any case, at St Swithun's, success meant success on the games field, together with piety and a highly developed sense of moral responsibility, none of which fell within my grasp. Yet I somehow seemed to preserve my secret feeling that, deeply as it might be hidden, I was more musical, better read, more philosophical than the other girls. It was not an amiable characteristic, this inner self-assurance, and it may have been a genetic inheritance from my Schuster forebears; but equally, I think it sprang from my love of life at home, in Kelso House, and my feeling that everything truly worthwhile and exciting had its existence there.

Sheltered though we were during term from any knowledge of how the war was progressing, the fall of Paris in the summer of 1940 and the arrival of Churchill on the scene impinged even on us. Our headmistress flew into a panic and, certain that the school would collapse, and that parents would withdraw their children on the grounds that Winchester was too near the coast, closed the school in the middle of that summer term, sending those who had to take public examinations to her old college, St Hilda's in Oxford, promising the main school buildings for use as a hospital, and planning to reopen a much smaller school the next term in some of the scattered boarding-houses. Imogen was at this time, for one reason or another, in deep trouble so when the school scattered she did not know whether she had left or been pushed. At any rate, thankfully for her, she did not return next term. The school was indeed dramatically reduced in numbers, and I stayed only one more miserable term.

Luckily, Mither loved Imogen, her free and open conversation, her wit, her willingness to give her full attention to whatever was said to her and her manifest appreciation of life at Kelso House, when she came to stay. In all her troubles at school, Mither remained her loyal supporter, and this delighted me. All through our undergraduate days, she at Cambridge, I at Oxford, we continued to see a lot of each other in the vacations. We endlessly wrote long letters, both during terms, and after we were married, and she went to live in Washington. Neither of our husbands could quite grasp the nature of our friendship, but regarded it with amused tolerance. (After the sexual revolutions of the 1960s and

'70s, it was assumed by many of Brian's friends in Washington that we were lesbians, and he was sagely advised not to try to prevent our seeing each other.) Especially when Geoffrey was ill, in the last three years of his life, his spirits always rose when Imogen was coming. Though he was astonished by how obsessed we were with our schooldays, and how detailed our memories, he found her unfailingly amusing, as do our children. It is my belief that friendship is an experience too little explored. Especially at school one becomes amazingly familiar with every aspect, every gesture, every tone of voice of one's contemporaries, whether they are friends or not. I have two other surviving schoolfriends who, whenever I see them, I feel are completely familiar, and with whom I immediately 'get on'. The concept of 'getting on' is important, and how it is that one does or does not 'get on' with another person remains mysterious. It is crucial to marriage that in this sense one should 'get on' with one's spouse, always want to talk to him, to do things with him, and never feel bored in his presence. I to this day 'get on' with my sister, Stephana, and certainly with Imogen. It was the greatest good luck, I reflect, that I stayed at St Swithun's after all.

Another lucky chance was that, leaving St Swithun's in December 1940, I still had a year to put in before taking the Oxford Entrance examination, and with another school friend, Anne Wakefield, I went for a year to a small school in Surrey called Prior's Field. This school had been founded by the Huxley family, both Aldous and Julian Huxley having started their education there. It was an entirely different kind of school, comfortable, devoted more to culture and politics than to religion, with evenings given up to reading aloud, or to discussions of what the post-war world should be like. The headmistress, the daughter of the first head of the school, was an extremely emotional woman, interested in Roman archaeology, the history of art and in contemporary poetry. It was here that I first encountered T.S. Eliot, and others whose poems were coming out at the time. It was eye-opening and exciting. It was nice, too, for the first time to be an object of admiration, as I was to the headmistress. As a bonus, I made new friends, and got good music lessons, in both flute and piano (and even learned the viola, at the insistence of Stephana, who was in want of a viola player for the quartet in which she was the cellist; but though I did manage to play in a few quartets, I was never intended by nature to be a string player). So for a year I flourished. I would not have won a scholarship to Lady Margaret Hall, Oxford (LMH) if I had not had these three terms to improve, doubtless over-improve my self-confidence. The whole experience taught me two things: first that confidence makes a huge difference to performance; secondly that when you win some coveted prize it instantly seems not to be worth very much at all.

After leaving school, I spent two terms working in a prep school at the western edge of the Cotswolds, in most beautiful, and to me hitherto unknown, country. There I was befriended by the headmaster's son who, like me, had won an Oxford scholarship, but who was waiting to join the army. We spent hours reading aloud to each other, and each making our own anthology, along the lines of *The Spirit of Man*. We wrote to each other for a few months after he was called up, but quite soon, sadly, he was killed. I felt selfishly thankful that we had not fallen in love with each other, though undoubtedly we 'got on'. I went up to Oxford in the autumn of 1942, where I stayed for five terms, taking Classical Honour Mods. I was doing what I had wanted to do for as long as I can remember, and without having made any difficult or serious choices in the matter. But it was not enjoyable being an undergraduate in the middle of the war. Greats was, in all, a four-year course, but war-time regulations meant I could not do more than a shortened course, and this I did not want. Besides, by the spring of 1944 I was longing to leave Oxford and, as I hoped, do some proper work. I accordingly signed up for the army (the ATS), but discovered that if I joined I would be sent to Bletchley Park to learn Japanese (for this was where anyone who was available and had got a first in Mods was sent) and would have to stay until the end of the Japanese war. At that time it was impossible to predict when that would be; and I was determined to get back to Oxford as soon as I could, to embark on Greats. I wish, in some ways, that I had decided to go to Bletchley. I would now love to have learned Japanese, so totally unfamiliar a language. I may have been partly afraid that I would not be any good at it; but, whatever the reason, I decided to refuse the offer, and go instead into teaching, a 'reserved' activity, from which I could emerge whenever LMH would have me back. There followed two years teaching at Sherborne School for Girls, which, rather to the alarm of my family and friends, I absolutely loved. I felt entirely at home in the school, and discovered a passion for teaching which has never left me. I was at Sherborne when the war ended, but could not go back to Oxford until the beginning of the summer term of 1946, a good time to come back because the Greats course starts in the summer.

The great shock of my time at Sherborne was the uncovering of the horrors of the concentration camps, hitherto totally unknown to most of us, and the reality of the Holocaust. Today I find that I cannot bear the thought of people denying that it happened. Hiroshima, though almost incredible when we first heard of it, did not, I am a bit ashamed to say, cause half such horror. It was difficult not to think simply that the war in Japan was over, and be thankful for that. It was only later that we began to think that if such destruction could be brought about once, it could be brought about again.

By the summer of 1948, when I took Greats, having fallen in love a few times before, I was finally and firmly in love with Geoffrey, determined (for we all thought in those days of marriage as virtually inevitable, that is if we were lucky; and of having children as highly desirable) to marry him or no one. I had had some trouble in deciding what to do after Greats, though I was pretty certain that, if I got a First, I would stay on and aim for an academic career, which I had always hoped for. I was tempted to go on with Greek History, which to my surprise I had enjoyed enormously; but I suspected, rightly, that I was not really a scholar, and in any case, I enjoyed philosophy just as much, and especially enjoyed talking about it with Geoffrey. So it may have been that which made me decide. My philosophy tutor at LMH, Martha Kneale, was kind and encouraging, and urged me to put in for a postgraduate scholarship, the Gilchrist, with the intention of reading for the newly invented examination, the B.Phil. With a good deal of support from Martha, I suspect, winning over her colleagues to elect a philosopher, I got the scholarship. However the B.Phil. was an examination for which one was supposed to prepare over two years, though this was not written into the Statute; and I was torn, because Martha had already offered me all of her teaching for the year after the next, when she wanted to take a year's leave to complete a book she was writing with her husband. I was, of course, flattered by this offer, and also longed to begin to earn. So I rashly decided to do the B.Phil. in one year rather than two, and to start reading for it as soon as I had my Greats results (I was sure that if I did not get a First, I would leave Oxford, and try for the Civil Service). Even so, though I had a lot of work to do, that summer was long and delicious. Mither had moved from Kelso House a year before, to a house near Romsey, where she had a big garden and an orchard, where there were nightingales in the bushes, and a nearby lake where one could swim. The first Long Vacation there, in 1947, was like the summers of our childhood. Stephana was back in Oxford then, reading Music (which is what she had wanted to do all along, but she had been under tremendous pressure from our brother, Duncan, to do a science subject, and leave music as a hobby, which is what it was for him). We spent our days riding, playing our instruments and singing, when we were not doing what work we had to for our degrees. By 1948 she was singing in London with a group of close Oxford friends, and they all came down to stay from time to time. I, relieved from the immediate pressure of exams, divided the vacation between Romsey and Oxford. I had found a flat near LMH which I shared with my schoolfriend Anne Wakefield, who had come back to Oxford out of the WRNS and was going to take her Finals in English in the following year. But my memories of the summer are mostly of sitting in Mither's garden, wondering whether the second post would bring a letter from Leeds where Geoffrey lived; reading Proust, and listening to Verdi opera on the gramophone, a new passion to which Geoffrey had introduced me. It was an absurdly happy and carefree time.

Geoffrey and I got married the following summer, in 1949. He had been elected to a Prize Fellowship at Magdalen in January, and I had been elected to a lectureship at St Hugh's College to start in October (so I had had after all to withdraw from teaching Martha's pupils, about which I felt bad. But, again, she was kind and forgiving). I had managed to scramble through the B.Phil. in a year, Geoffrey having written most of my thesis for me. In exchange I had written his Greek History essays. Since he had read PPE but was a good classical scholar, he had decided to do Greats in a year, in order to increase his job prospects. However, when he became a Prize Fellow of Magdalen College, Gilbert Ryle, the Waynflete Professor of Metaphysical Philosophy and a Fellow of Magdalen, advised him to give it up, on the grounds that it would be embarrassing for a Fellow of a college to be sitting a final examination. So, thankfully, Geoffrey gave up. He continued to teach Plato and Aristotle all his working life, probably the only person ever to do so who had not read them as an undergraduate.

Thus we set out on marriage with two jobs, and absurdly old-fashioned ideas about domestic life. Geoffrey's father, James Warnock, was a very prosperous GP in Leeds, his practice being in the well-heeled end of the city. His brother William was also a GP, also in Leeds, but at the other end of town. They had both qualified in Ireland, being Ulstermen from Cookstown, part of a family of nine brothers and half-brothers. They could hardly have been more different: James stately, slow of speech, very handsome, with blue eyes and extraordinarily white skin; William red-faced, manifestly Irish in speech, and an unstoppable enthusiast. James could not stand the new NHS and retired in 1949, when he and Kathleen his wife came to live near Oxford. They lent us money to buy our first house, in Summertown, North Oxford, and we spent almost every spare moment cleaning it, I taking time off to cook complicated meals (I was not yet a very competent cook). It never struck us for a moment that we need not do all this housework, or have so many proper meals. When Kitty, our first child, was born the next summer, we redoubled our efforts. I seldom went further south than St Hugh's, in the Banbury Road; I took magazines like the then popular *Housewife*, and felt totally submerged.

Because our first two children were born fairly close together, both of them in our little prison house, we had Nan staying with us quite a lot, and, though she was a great help in many ways, she was demanding about what she thought to be the proper upkeep of the house, and about proper meals. However, soon after Felix, our second child, was born, we decided that we could not live like this for ever. We did not talk about it much. I just went off one morning, shortly before I was due to start work again at St Hugh's, after four weeks off, and went to an estate agent to find a house nearer to the centre of Oxford. By the evening I had found one, and the next day we put in an offer for it, which was accepted. It was in Fyfield Road, close to LMH and the University Parks, within walking distance of all the colleges and the Covered Market. It was a tall house, one of those built for the dons newly permitted to get married, in the second half of the nineteenth century. It had recently been used as undergraduate lodgings, and was not in good repair; it was extremely inconvenient, and, as we soon discovered, was infested with mice. No midwife would contemplate a home birth in such a place, so our next two children were born in hospital. Nevertheless we loved it. The rooms were enormous; and, best of all, we knew we could not possibly keep it spotlessly clean. Our life really began when we moved.

This was in 1952. Philosophy in Oxford was then at a high pitch of success. Partly because of the new B.Phil. examination, which attracted graduates from all over the world, partly because of the immense popularity of PPE as an undergraduate degree there was a great number of practising philosophers in the university at the time (while Cambridge had about six or eight members of the philosophy faculty, Oxford had more than thirty). The dominant figures were Gilbert Ryle and J.L. Austin, who held an informal meeting every Saturday morning for invited members of the faculty, all of them younger than he, and all of them full-time teaching fellows. It was some time before women were admitted to this meeting; I remember my delight and amazement when Austin called at Fyfield Road, Felix being in his pram outside the front door, and asked me to join. Then, casting his very bright eye on Felix, Austin said, 'He seems a jolly little fellow'. (So he was.)

Austin's theory of philosophy, in so far as he had one, was that it was a job to be done collaboratively. He believed not in grand theories, nor in confrontations, but in conversation about detailed points, all related to the connections between what we say and what is the case, between language and the world. The exciting thing about this form of philosophy was that, while it was the self-same issue which had engaged the great philosophers of the past, Plato for example, and Kant, it was now being pursued at a much more down-to-earth level, where theories gave place to detailed investigations of language in use, not necessarily only 'ordinary' language, but the language of law, or of moral precepts. This was the time when all the cleverest undergraduates, whether they read PPE or Greats, or the newly conceived PPP (Philosophy, Psychology and Physiology), were eager to go on with philosophy. Oxford philosophers were invited to the great universities in America, to carry this excitement across the Atlantic. For a shortish time, in the 1950s and '60s, Oxford was the philosophical centre of the world.

So, when we emerged from our domestic prison, we found ourselves in the centre of an extraordinarily lively world. We made friends. We had people other than Nan to stay, no longer expecting that everything would be impeccable. (I remember Kingsley and Hilly Amis and their sons and dog coming to stay, and Hilly's tremendous inventiveness and energy in putting together great meals of pasta and tomatoes, among seas of squalor, children and noise. They came as friends of a great friend of mine from Prior's Field days, who was by no means orderly in her way of life.) We began to give dinner parties. We caught up with people we had known as undergraduates. We got to know Peter and Ann Strawson, who have remained lifelong friends. Peter Strawson had just published his *Introduction to Logical Theory*, in which he dared to disagree with Russell, and he was delivering the lectures in Oxford which were later published as *Individuals*: *An Essay in Descriptive Metaphysics* which had a tremendous influence on us all, especially in its treatment of personal identity and the insepa-rability of the mental from the physical aspects of a person. Other new friends were David Pears, and Marcus and Cecilia Dick who introduced us into a rather grander circle than we had known before, including Maurice Bowra, Isaiah Berlin (though he had been Geoffrey's tutor at New College), and David Cecil.

It was the time when the BBC Third Programme was eagerly seeking academics to give talks or hold discussions. I remember sitting next to a Third Programme producer at lunch one day in St Hugh's, who had come to seek a contract with one of the English Fellows; and she said, 'What about philosophy? Is there something we could do about that?' At the time Geoffrey had just written a book about Bishop Berkeley, and I said tentatively that I thought there might be a broadcast in Berkeley. This was taken up, and Geoffrey did a conspicuously clear and lively talk about the Bishop's theory that the world was nothing but God's ideas. He was a natural broadcaster and, before we had quite become accustomed to the idea, another Third Programme producer appeared on our doorstep, T.S. Gregory, who told us that he thought philosophy was a matter not for talks but for debates, and he wanted us to bring together a group of people to debate on air the great issues of philosophy. So it was that Peter Strawson, David Pears, Geoffrey and I formed a philosophical quartet, preparing and delivering so-called debates on the Third Programme over a period of several years. There seemed to be endless things to talk and write about. David Pears, still unmarried at this time, and full of projects and pleasurable plans, both philosophical and domestic (he loved, for example, decorating his rooms, and going on expeditions to buy antique furniture), was a constant source of gossip and amusement, as well as of the most ingenious and sometimes absurd philosophical arguments. It was impossible to tire of his company, though to us married pairs, with our young children, he seemed almost disgracefully insouciant. At any rate these years were philosophically rich, varied and amusing.

The early 1950s were not conspicuous for feminism, but it is reasonable to ask how I felt about my role as the only woman in this quartet, and, more generally, about my role as wife and mother and professional philosopher. The first answer is that I loved it. I loved being the 'only woman', the successful one, whether on these programmes or on committees and boards of examiners. I did not want all women to be in competition with me. I realised how lucky I was to be able to combine professional life with domestic life, though it had been a struggle at first to get things in the right proportion. There is no doubt, however, that an academic career is the easiest to combine with family life, because of the flexibility of the hours. I had never been, and have never been a theoretical feminist. I have always wanted women to be treated as the equals of men if they could show the same ability; I do not believe in the kind of feminism that would separate women from men, as having their own exclusive ways of thinking. I believe that subjects such as mathematics, physics and philosophy are strictly gender-neutral, and that there is not a 'woman's truth' and a 'man's truth'. Therefore, inevitably, women must compete with men as equals in search of equal truth. I do not deny that women have had, and perhaps still have, both a struggle against prejudice in some fields, and also a continuous and undoubtedly everlasting battle to combine all the aspects of their lives. But I do not feel that this is unjust, only inevitable, and also enriching. I could never tolerate the kind of feminism that blamed men, or wished to have nothing more to do with them. Thus I was fascinated by some of the details of Simone de Beauvoir's *The Second Sex*, published in England in the early 1950s, but I had little sympathy with the general message that women felt, and resented, their universal subordination to men. Perhaps I was, and am, too fond of men; perhaps I took too much delight in the give and take of sex, the taking turns between dominance and submission, to be able to envisage a world in which women could do without men, or must regard themselves as always inferior.

Of course I recognise that exploitation exists and, as I have said, prejudice as well. One has only to look at the history of the University of Cambridge, which took so disgracefully long to allow women to take degrees, even if they had taken all the examinations that would qualify them for a degree. But these are battles that will gradually be won, if women really want them to be won. (Sometimes they do not even want them. Years ago I allowed my name to go forward, as a test case, for membership of the Athenaeum, because a friend of mine, Roger Nathan, wanted to see if it would work. Of course it did not, and the rules were not altered. But I have to say that if I had been admitted, I would have been in a difficulty. I simply have no desire ever to pay a large annual subscription to be a member of a club which I would never go to, and have never felt the need of.)

I daresay we would have broken out of our early domestic slavery eventually whatever had happened. But I connect the emancipation with the rash purchase of our lovely and dishevelled house in Fyfield Road. We were, then and later, lucky with the buying and selling of property. We had to move, after three and a half years, because, Geoffrey's father having died, his mother could not face living alone (his sister was by then living in South Africa). So we had to look for a house we could share. Once again we were lucky, though we took more time to decide on this occasion. We bought a large, well-built, sunny Edwardian house in Chadlington Road, almost next door to the Dragon School where both our sons were to go, and within a few minutes' walk from the Oxford High School for Girls which was to be the school of our three daughters, and, for a time, my place of work. It was a quiet and peaceful road, full of children, ideal for bicycling and other games; and the house itself was perfectly suited to our needs. Here we lived from the autumn of 1956 until Geoffrey became Principal of Hertford, in January 1971, and here our fifth child was born.

Meanwhile I had decided or, perhaps better, discovered that I wanted not to be a tutor in philosophy for the rest of my life, or not only that. I loved teaching philosophy, but was not much good at the subject. I felt that my natural habitat was school, not university. I gradually worked my way back into the world of school by becoming a university member of the Oxfordshire Local Education Authority, then separate from the City, and far less political. I took over management of music in the county, by inventing a music subcommittee and chairing it, and enjoyed a period of wonderful freedom, optimism and excitement. This was characteristic of education at the beginning of the 1960s. Just as there seemed few limits to the founding of new universities, so there seemed none to the provision of free instrumental lessons, orchestras and choirs for the children of Oxfordshire.

In 1966, I was invited to apply for the vacant headship of Oxford High School, and urged on by Kitty and Fanny, the two of our children then at the school, and motivated too by the delight I felt at the thought of getting back to a school, I went to be interviewed by the then Girls' Public Day School Trust (now Girls' Day School Trust) at Queen Anne's Gate (having been warned in advance not to wear a hat). I was asked questions such as 'How will your husband manage?' and 'If you were appointed, how long would you stay?' I was never more surprised than when, a few minutes after the interview, I was told that I had been appointed. It was extremely rash of the Trust to give me the job, and such an appointment could never be made now. I had no qualifications for running a school. Nevertheless, I was thankful to get away from St Hugh's. I had inadvertently, as a result of having written some purely commercially motivated books about existentialism, become almost the only person in Oxford prepared to supervise graduate students who wanted to work on Sartre or other continental philosophers. Besides my undergraduate pupils, I had to supervise a number of graduate students, who added considerably to my teaching burden because they wanted supervision in vacations as well as terms. It is questionable whether most of these people should have been doing graduate work at all; two of them were clinically insane, and numerous others were incapable of working alone. (Nonetheless, all but one of my graduate students got jobs in philosophy departments in the then burgeoning new universities, where, of course, they stayed, year after year). It was a very good scene to leave. Once I had, without difficulty, decided to quit, I remember sitting in my room in St Hugh's (which was beautiful and which I was sorry to leave), and singing to myself 'Never weather-beaten sail more willing bent to shore'. I think I have always taken decisions, when they came my way, quickly, rashly and usually without regrets. Geoffrey's view was simply that I would say 'yes' to anything. It filled him with alarm.

It felt odd at first not being a member of the University any more, and being an ordinary citizen of Oxford, but I soon got used to it, and liked it. In a school with numerous academic parents, prepared to dictate what their children should be taught if they were to get into Oxford or Cambridge, it was a great advantage that I was not intimidated by them, knowing as well as they did what would be academically best. I had the advantage, too, of myself having teenage children, at risk, so we all feared, from the new sexual freedom of the 1960s, and the newly available drugs. I got to know some of the parents very well, and enjoyed that aspect of school enormously. Undergraduates, after all, do not have parents (to all intents and purposes).

I could happily have gone on for years at school, but at the end of 1970, Geoffrey was elected Principal of Hertford, and we moved into the Lodgings in January 1971. It soon became clear that I wanted to give more time to the college than being head of a school allowed. And I had thought of a book I wanted to write (indeed a book I had wanted to write since I was still myself at school) about imagination, and the power to see things as symbolic, as speaking of more than their mere appearance would suggest. I had gradually come to realise how this connected with the whole Romantic movement, not only with Wordsworth and Coleridge, but with Kant, and his insistence on the role of imagination in the construction of the world as we experience it, a role hinted at by Wittgenstein, and more systematically explored by Peter Strawson. The book I ultimately wrote was much too short; it was also doomed to failure because it attempted to cross the boundaries between philosophy and literature. Nevertheless, it was the first book I had ever chosen to write, rather than being asked to, and I do not at all regret the few years I spent researching for it; and I still feel an affection for it. For all this I needed more time; and so I left, with many regrets, in the summer of 1972, the term before our youngest daughter entered the school.

Hertford Lodgings in Catte Street had been built in the 1820s. The rooms were large and impressive, but there were very few of them. Only our youngest two children had proper rooms for themselves; but the older children had all left school, and were students, or starting to work, so they did not suffer unduly, and in the Christmas vacation we could take over the top floor of the Lodgings, which had been turned into undergraduate rooms. Christmases were on a splendid scale, with a huge Christmas tree in front of one of the dining-room windows whose lights could be seen as one approached Radcliffe Square from Brasenose Lane.

Geoffrey was Principal for seventeen years, with four years, towards the end, when he was Vice-Chancellor of the University, and a Vice-Principal looked after the college. It was a job that suited him perfectly, and he, like me, had changed jobs at a good time. For one thing, his sister, her two children and entirely penniless husband were coming back from South Africa, and could take over the house in North Oxford, and Geoffrey's mother into the bargain. Secondly, he had become slightly bored with teaching, and being Senior Tutor at Magdalen, and was ready for a change. Like his father, he was a fundamentally melancholy and fatalistic person. He had disliked boarding school very much, including Winchester, when he was young, never thinking to complain, because he simply assumed that this is what things had to be like. After winning a classical scholarship to Oxford, he did not take it up, but went straight into the Irish Guards. He did not dislike the army; indeed he felt a great loyalty to his battalion, and to the whole Brigade of Guards. He loved the drill, and felt secure in the choiceless, often pointless routines of the army, which I, too, began to feel I understood later, from Geoffrey, and from both Evelyn Waugh and Anthony Powell. One of the first things I loved was that this quiet academic figure had actually seen action in so grand a context. He once caught sight of a report on himself, after he had been on a course, which said 'Personality: NONE'. He was always glad to have been in the army. After his death I asked permission of the Officer in Charge to have the motto of the Irish Guards inscribed on his gravestone, 'Quis Separabit?'

Geoffrey hated it when I moaned and complained about things for which there was no remedy. He thought that one should either take some action, or stop talking about the issue. I felt quite differently (as did Imogen, whose husband was inclined to swing into action to change things, often with bad results, if she complained). I was told that my father used to say, 'If I can't grumble at home, where can I grumble?', and with this I agreed. I also used to irritate Geoffrey greatly by sometimes complaining about his apparently black moods. He was pleased, at such moments, by something we found in one of the novels of Ivy Compton-Burnett (which he used to read aloud to me, if I had children's dresses to sew, or curtains to construct): 'Nurse: "Master Henry is in one of his moods". Henry: "Seeing the truth about things is not a mood".' He was stoical and realistic about most aspects of his life, including what he thought of as my chronic and incurable untidiness and rashness, in sharp contrast to his own calm rationality. But he was a romantic, in that he saw through the real world to a kind of ideal of how things might be, and in that his inner world was, on the whole, his preferred place. The poetry he wrote, first during the war, but again afterwards until the 1960s, and which was published here and there over a long time, was sharply observed, economical and sad. In what was probably his best book, *The Object of Morality*, published in the year after we moved to Hertford College, he set out his theory that morality is a necessary device for making the human predicament less awful than it would be without it ... a highly characteristic view.

At any rate when he got to Hertford, he recognised that there were things wrong with the college that could be remedied, and he set about, unruffled, to make things better in so far as it lay in his power. He succeeded, with the help of his colleagues, to an astonishing degree. Symptomatically, the college rose in the league tables from near the bottom to second in the list, and it rose equally spectacularly in the unofficial list of preferred colleges, put out by undergraduates.

While he was there, he had two recurrent worries; one was that our two daughters living at home would behave outrageously and disgrace us all. He could not, he thought, get them to understand that as part of the household of the Lodgings they must be reasonably decorous, and that the fact that we had big rooms (and a huge cellar) did not entail that they could give vast rackety parties. There were some fearsome rows.

His second worry was more irrational, and I did not know of it until after he had retired: it was that he would pass out when reading the lesson in the college Chapel on Sundays in term. He did once, early on, nearly pass out, which I realised, but I thought he had got over it. It was not so. He started to worry on about

Thursday each week, and the end of term was a moment of relief. No one would ever have thought this; his renderings of the more obscure bits of St Paul were impeccable; he always made the 'wherefore' and the 'thus' sound as if they were connectives in a real intelligible argument. He was very much attached to the Chapel and its services, though at first he was afraid that he was being hypocritical in taking part, since he had no religious beliefs of any kind. He consulted Isaiah Berlin about this, knowing that he always attended Synagogue with his aged parents on Saturdays, though not himself a believer. Isaiah's advice was that before he started to read, or to sing hymns (which he loved doing), he should say to himself 'Our Religion Teaches ...' I thought this very good advice.

It gave us both enormous pleasure that we had a bedroom looking out over Radcliffe Square, opposite the end of Brasenose Lane, and with the Bodleian just across the road. Almost for the first time, I felt that I really loved and belonged to Oxford, having hitherto simply lived and worked there. There were drawbacks, of course. In the summer, both tourists and undergraduates swarmed like flies most of the night, sometimes playing guitars, or kicking empty coke cans down the road under our window. Car doors banged, and people took long farewells in the small hours of the morning. Once we were woken by an undergraduate who had climbed up a drainpipe into our bedroom, looking, he said, for a friend. He was not a member of Hertford. Geoffrey, by threats of the police, got him to give his name and college, and escorted him out of the front door. The next day he sent a large cheque for the college appeal, and an apology. But he was a bright chap, and he also sold his story to one of the tabloids, claiming that he had surprised us in bed, discussing the philosopher Kant.

Hertford is the institution of the many I have known that I feel most warmly towards. I still love it, and I am very kindly treated there. I had the best possible role to play. I had no responsibility; I was not annoyed, as Geoffrey was in our first two terms, by the recurrent resignations of John Patten, then a highly volatile Fellow in Geography, and in need of constant soothing and calming. It must in fairness be said that when John settled down (he had arrived from Cambridge only a term before we came), he was an invaluable help to Geoffrey. When we arrived, the college was almost unbelievably scruffy, both inside and out. It smelled strongly of Jeyes fluid, and not a single room, public or private, was decently decorated. John had an infallible eye for interior decoration, and he and Geoffrey set to work, ensuring not only a proper programme of redecoration and restoration, but a serious concern for the period of the building and the suitability of the furnishings. John, in poking through the basements, found a most exquisite set of Edwardian chandeliers, all in rust and ruins, but capable of restoration. He handed them over to Geoffrey, and we got them restored, and hung them in the drawing room of the Lodgings, where they hang still, perfect for the high, splendid room. When John was Steward of Common Room, he set a new standard for the variety of drinks kept in the cupboard, for the number of newspapers available, and for the general care of the Fellows. He became at this time increasingly politically ambitious, was elected onto the Oxford City Council as a Conservative member, and when he found college too tedious, he could turn his attention to political matters. He married the most beautiful wife, Louise, a lawyer, and when he was elected to represent West Oxford as an MP, we had a splendid celebratory party for them both. Sadly, in the end he fell out with the college. After his curiously inept performance as Minister in the Department for Education and Employment, the college refused to elect him to an Honorary Fellowship, as is the normal practice for Ministers. Instead, they rather foolishly offered him membership of Common

Room, which he refused with fury, demanding that his name be removed from all college records. Now, being an Honorary Fellow myself, I skulk round hoping to avoid him. But he does not come much to the House of Lords.

I taught some undergraduate members of the college among my other pupils, but not too many; I helped reconstitute the Music Society. I had the task, quite new to me, of entertaining with the back-up of the college kitchen, and scouts to wait and wash up (though we always enjoyed letting them go at the pudding stage of a dinner party, and finishing the washing up ourselves after the party, so that we could go over it in detail); the college scouts cleaned at least the public, downstairs rooms, which I never had to think about. And if something went wrong with the central heating, or the plumbing, if one wanted a chair mended or a shelf put up, there were college plumbers and carpenters on call.

We had some memorable parties. One of the best was known as the Portrait Party. A very amiable and clever physicist who was a Fellow of the college inherited a farm in Australia, and left to go and work it. Before he left he persuaded the college to get David Hockney to do a drawing of Geoffrey (and I think, but do not know, that he paid for it). Geoffrey spent an extremely enjoyable day in Hockney's studio, where they got on admirably, talking about Leeds United. The studio was full of the new sets for *The Magic Flute*, on which numerous apprentices were working, in a wonderfully old-fashioned way. The outcome was a drawing which both I and the children loved, because it portrayed what they knew as 'Dad's Reading Face', extremely forbidding, with markedly down-turned mouth. I think some of the Fellows may have thought it too severe, but it hangs to great effect in the Senior Common Room. We put it on display in our drawing room and invited everyone we could think of to come to see it. The kitchen did a wonderfully lavish buffet, and for once I really enjoyed talking to people at one of my own parties. Because we had invited, as well as our friends, some people whom we did not know particularly well (I was by now a member of the Independent Broadcasting Authority, and had become acquainted with people of a kind I had never met before, programme makers, advertisers, chairmen of television companies, journalists) I had the delight of observing some of those, to whom he was a legend, falling under the spell of Isaiah Berlin. He was a frequent visitor, and both Geoffrey and I adored him. It is fashionable now to raise questions about his supposed genius, and it is inevitable that that should be so. His writings, in his early days original and arresting, became more repetitive and careless as he started to dictate rather than to compose them properly. After his famously successful radio lectures, he gave up lecturing, so by the 1980s few people under the age of fifty had heard his marvellously illuminating and funny analyses of nineteenth-century political ideas. It was in conversation, by this time, that he was irresistible. He talked at lightning speed, displaying a huge range of knowledge, and illustrating his points with often ludicrous anecdotes, from the historical past or from his own experience. But, sadly, great talkers cannot really be made to live after their death. The very thought of *Table Talk* with Coleridge is enough to induce yawns. And so it may be with Isaiah. Nevertheless, he was central to Oxford life at this time.

Geoffrey saw much more of Isaiah than I did, partly because they were both members of a dining club simply called the Club. I never quite understood the criteria for membership of the Club, and perhaps the members did not either, for they certainly spent much time discussing who should become a member, if a vacancy occurred. Outstanding intelligence was certainly one criterion; being amusing and easily amused was another. It would be easy to suppose that a certain social smartness was considered essential, but Peter Strawson and Geoffrey were members, neither of whom was particularly smart, in the sense in which other members, the historian Raymond Carr or the economist Ian Little, were. Why was the exceptionally clever and amusing Professor of Jurisprudence, later Principal of Brasenose College (BNC), Herbert Hart, who was a close friend of many of the members, including Isaiah, Peter and Geoffrey, never elected? Why not Stuart Hampshire? No one could better fulfil the criterion of smartness, and no one could have been a more constant and life-long friend and admirer of Isaiah. Stuart Hampshire was a fascinating figure, and everyone loved talking about him, analysing his character, counting the women who loved him; and I sometimes suspected that he was never elected because that would have put an end to the delightful discussion of him that must have gone on every time the possibility of his joining was raised.

The Club met twice a term in the college of one of the members (though David Pears, when he was elected, at least once entertained in his own house; and Geoffrey gave dinners, when it was his turn, in the Lodgings at Hertford, because the college had no other dining room so suitable, so I had to keep out of the way on those occasions). The only rule of the Club, which was an eighteenth-century foundation, was that the members addressed and greeted each other as 'brother' ... 'Brother Warnock', 'Brother Berlin', and so on. Roy Jenkins used often to come as a guest, and was the only regular guest. When he was elected Chancellor of the university, he became a full member, and was a regular attender (for all I know he still is). But, at least at first, he found the 'brother' part of the ritual embarrassing, and could apparently hardly bring himself to utter the proper greeting. Nobody else seemed to find it at all odd; but the thought that someone might do so could, I suppose, have been another obstacle to membership in some cases. The Club was generally referred to as The Brothers, by those who were members. Those who were not probably hardly knew of its existence, but in my eyes it was one of the institutions which epitomised Oxford. It stood for gossip, intelligence and friendship, without any pomposity. I never even thought of wishing that I could be a member. Its long history was enough to make it properly and exclusively masculine.

Many of our parties were given after concerts, and at these Geoffrey's belief that musicians eat and drink whatever they see and stay up all night was regularly confirmed. Most of the concerts were Hertford Music Society occasions, the society becoming quite well-known for its orchestra, which included players from other colleges and from outside the university as our daughter Fanny, a music student from 1974, had many instrumentalist friends. It was once most memorably conducted by Simon Rattle, then a student at the Royal College of Music. I enjoyed all this immensely. I also enjoyed the duty that fell on us when Geoffrey was Vice-Chancellor to entertain the Chancellor, Harold Macmillan, though having him as a house guest was nerve-racking in some ways. Not only did he drink a tremendous lot of whisky (he had to have a decanter in his bedroom), but he liked a proper breakfast, and I found myself cooking kedgeree, or kippers, but never knowing when he would come down for breakfast, or indeed whether I ought to send a scout up to see if he was still alive. Once I got so anxious that I did send up the head scout (who loved Macmillan, and liked looking after him), who found that he had shut his trousers in the wardrobe and could not open it, which was why he had not come down.

It was against this varied and never boring background that I began to get involved in more London-based activities, fitting in all my teaching in the first two days of the week, and then usually gadding off for the succeeding days. I became, as I have said, a member of the Independent Broadcasting Authority, in 1973. My appointment was another matter of luck; I had been for some years a governor of Prior's Field, where the headmaster of Charterhouse was an *ex officio* governor, the schools being close neighbours. So I got to know the then Head Master, Brian Young, before he left to become, first, Director of the Nuffield Foundation, and then Director General of the Independent Broadcasting Authority, and I think it was he who suggested me as a member. It was an absurd appointment, because I hardly ever watched television, and had not listened to commercial radio since the days of Radio Luxemburg in the nursery. But I never thought of turning it down. It was by far the most enjoyable job I ever did on the side, and I found for the first time what fun it is to learn new things in an environment of work, with knowledgeable people to teach one. At about the same time I became a member of the Royal Commission on Environmental Pollution, and here had to learn some chemistry and economics. Again, I was working with extraordinarily interesting, knowledgeable people, who I think themselves enjoyed having their arguments scrutinised by a professional philosopher. There followed the Chairmanship of the Committee of Enquiry into Special Educational Needs (it was not called that when it was established: in those days, 1974, it was still respectable to talk about 'handicapped' children). This committee had been set up by Margaret Thatcher when she was Secretary of State for Education and Science, but had been taken on by the Labour government when they won the election that year. The committee sat for four years, and it involved a good deal of work. I met some people who were members who became friends, but on the whole I found the world of special education rather dispiriting, with too many people fighting their own corners. Nevertheless, it was interesting to put the report together, and gratifying to see it enshrined in the 1981 Education Act, although, with hindsight, I think we made some radical mistakes.

There followed chairmanship of a Home Office committee on

the use of animals in laboratories, which again led straight to legislation. My worst moment on that committee was when we went to visit a laboratory where beagles were being used to test the effects of nicotine, and when we got to their laboratory-kennels I thought I was going to faint, not because they were being badly treated, which they were not, but because of the overpowering smell of dog, a smell I have never liked. I managed to hold out, sustained by the thought of what terrible publicity it would be, if the chairman had passed out on entering the lab. While working on that committee, I formed the highest opinion of the people, scientists or technicians, who worked with animals, and of the inspectorate. I was also given great support by the vice-chairman, Richard Adrian, Master of Pembroke College, Cambridge, who became a great friend until, sadly, he died of cancer. I also learned there the use of regulation and inspection, rather than abolition, a concept I made use of on the next committee I chaired, that on human fertilisation and embryology, set up by government in 1982.

That committee was given until 1984 to report our findings; and I was determined to finish on time. I knew from the start that if we had sat for six or eight years instead of two we should never have agreed, so we might as well get on with it, instead of prolonging the endless disputes. The disputes were on the whole civilised: we did not have any rampaging pro-lifers on the committee (and were criticised for that, but if we had had members who would not even listen to arguments on the other side, the work of the committee would never have got on). The first year was relatively peaceful, being spent in reading the 'evidence', or rather the opinions of the general public and of scientific bodies, and, mostly, of learning the facts, as then known, about the development of the embryo, the techniques of *in vitro* fertilisation, and possible future interventions aimed at replacing faulty genes, or at producing clones. This was, for me, the steepest, but also the most enjoyable learning curve of all. I now, looking back, feel immensely grateful that, having had a virtually science-free education, I had these opportunities to extend my understanding of various different aspects of science. On this committee, especially, we were fortunate that one of the members, Anne McLaren, then head of the Mammalian Development Unit of the Medical Research Council, was a brilliant natural teacher. There were several other members of the committee who were as blankly ignorant as I, and we sat at her feet, all this year, thinking that if we had our life again we would be zoologists. We were also lucky in that one of the scientists from the Department of Health, Jeremy Metters, was allocated to the committee and was tireless in keeping us up to date with what was now possible, what might be possible in future, what was going on in other countries, in Europe, America and Australia.

The second year, when we had to start to put the report together, was not so enjoyable. It was then that our different moral views inevitably surfaced. I think I was a fairly ruthless chairman, having by now had some experience. I could not bear it when people kept saying that they 'were not happy' about this or that. I tried to get them to state clearly what their objections were, but they used to repeat that they did not know, but that all the same they were not happy. I was reduced to telling a bishop's wife that we were not brought into this world to be happy. Most fortunately, the statutory Roman Catholic member of the committee, who was doctrinally opposed to the use of live embryos for research, was also a very clever, very rational professor of neurology, and a most excellent draftsman, always ready with a better-turned sentence than I had managed to think up; and though he wrote a minority report, it was in fact an excellent exposition of the arguments on both sides, and a positive addition to the final published report.

But I think that by the summer of 1984, tempers were a bit frayed, and we were glad to be through with our meetings in the then Department of Health at Elephant and Castle, where we met in a room that was a kind of box in the middle of a landing, with no windows, no natural light and very little air.

The year after that, I spent a lot of time, sometimes with Anne McLaren, talking to MPs, women's groups, and various scientific bodies about our report, I became a member of the House of Lords, and also became Mistress of Girton College, Cambridge. Geoffrey was still Vice-Chancellor at Oxford, and I felt very bad about leaving him to it, though I postponed going to Girton until January 1985, having been elected for October 1984, so he had only two more terms to run. All the same, I spent my first two terms at Girton dashing up and down between Oxford and Cambridge, when there was urgent entertaining to do in Oxford. I suppose I accepted Girton because I had not got anything particularly urgent on hand in either Oxford or London, and because it felt agreeable to be offered a new job at the age of sixty, when if I had still been a headmistress I would have had to retire.

Geoffrey retired from Hertford in 1988, I from Girton in 1991. By then we had bought a house in Wiltshire, close to Marlborough, in a village on the Kennet called Axford. It was a modern house, built on the side of a hill, with a steeply sloping garden, whose soil was the purest white chalk. Geoffrey loved it there; and so did I, but by the time I retired and he had been there alone in term time, he had made it very much his own house. He loved retirement. Our great friend Nicko Henderson once asked him what he was doing, now that he had retired, to which Geoffrey replied 'Nothing'. Nicko looked surprised, but then said, 'How very original'. The fact was that Geoffrey loved reading, loved watching sport and current affairs on television, loved gardening and what he referred to as 'footling about'. For the first time ever he was beginning to enjoy cooking and even shopping, especially in the Marlborough Waitrose.

However, by 1992, it was plain that he was ill, and he was diagnosed that year as suffering from fibrosing alveolitis, a lung disease for which there is so far no cure (it was also said to be 'cryptogenic', which rather pleased him). He died in October 1995, ten days after he had managed to get, by ambulance, to the opening of the new hall of residence for Hertford undergraduates, called Warnock House. There, though breathless, he made an unrehearsed, extremely fierce speech about the current state of university finances, and said goodbye to the Fellows, the scouts and the friends who were there. And since then, apart from my moving house, to a cottage which I guiltily know Geoffrey would have hated because of its small windows and low ceilings (but it has an extremely fertile garden, and is in a proper village with shops), really nothing has occurred, except for the gradual encroachment of age, and the attempt to put some of my recollections in order.

Some Women Philosophers (1): Philippa Foot and Elizabeth Anscombe

In this chapter and the next I shall describe three remarkable and original women, all philosophers, and all of whom I met first when I was an undergraduate. To demonstrate their originality, I shall try to set them in the context of Oxford philosophy immediately after the war. If nothing else, this will serve to emphasise the fact that there was not just one kind of philosophy practised in Oxford at this time, but several. As far as I can, I shall try to describe the impression that each of them made on first encounter; but then I shall go on to say something about how their achievements seem now, when it is easy to look back and see them more clearly and more historically. On whether their originality had anything to do with their gender, I cannot make a final judgement, but I suspect that women are less prone to jump on to bandwagons than at least some of their male colleagues, and are also more reluctant to abandon common sense; and these observations seem to fit most conspicuously the first of my subjects, Philippa Foot.

However, with a view to carrying out my purpose of presenting these women in their philosophical context, I must go back quite a long way. One cannot understand post-war Oxford philosophy without understanding where it came from.

Oxford was pretty gloomy when I came up in October 1942, and nowhere more so than Lady Margaret Hall. I had two friends in college and none outside. Oxford was empty, it seemed. I could, with better management, or if I had been more grown-up, have had more friends in college. For example, Rachel Trickett, who later became one of my dearest friends, came up at the same time as I did. But I alienated almost the whole of my year because, by a barbarous custom, the senior scholar of each year had to produce an 'entertainment' halfway through the first term. I had toiled away at a supposed musical comedy before I came up, and my sister Stephana had written an elaborate score for it. Of course it was impossibly boring and led to nothing but bad temper. It was performed, and as it happened, Rachel had a leading part, but it was an undoubted flop and reeked, as they say, of the lamp. A number of people rebelled and performed a second entertainment on the same occasion, much more suitably light-hearted. It was a bad start.

At any rate, one of my two friends was a fellow-classicist called Nancy Pym, who remained a friend until she died in 1998. She and I shared the misery of having been badly taught at school, and feeling unable to live up to what was expected of us. She was, though apparently quite tough, even hearty, in fact rather vulnerable, and her father, Canon Pym, who had been Chaplain of Balliol, was slowly dying of MS. My other friend was the elder daughter of General de Gaulle, Elisabeth, and she, as an exile, had her own troubles and was frequently in tears, when some disaster fell on the French navy, or when her father believed he had been insulted by Churchill. She had spent a year at a convent school in Shropshire before coming up to read History at LMH. We became very fond of each other, and the nuns from the convent, where she often spent her university vacations, prayed for me when I was doing my exams and, even better, sent me pots of the most extravagant lemon curd (lemons and eggs and sugar being all unattainable luxuries at the time). Elisabeth was very pious and quite often took me to Mass with her, a lovely, simple Dominican mass at Blackfriars. But we used to have the most violent quarrels over such matters as whether the London Underground ought to divide its trains into first and second class so that she could travel first, leaving more room, she said, for other people to use the second class. These quarrels always produced more floods of tears. It was a taxing friendship and, sadly, I lost touch with her. But I think of her often, clever, witty, elegant and melancholy.

Most of the Classics dons in the university had left, either to join the army or to go to Bletchley Park to crack codes. One retired Fellow of Balliol College, Cyril Bailey, who had strong LMH connections, had been recalled to teach us and others. He was a very nice man but unfortunately he had been the tutor of my brother, Duncan, eleven years before, and could not but be deeply disappointed in me. It was not just my ignorance that upset him; he had classical daughters himself, and knew what a struggle it was for girls to keep their heads above water in Mods, an examination based on the assumption that boys had been learning Latin and Greek almost as soon as their education had started. He could forgive ignorance; and he and Nancy, whose father he had known at Balliol, got on extremely well. 'Nancy and I speak the same language', he once told me sadly. What he increasingly objected to in me was my over-serious attitude to classical scholarship, ludicrously and inappropriately combined with a deplorable proneness to make terrible mistakes, 'howlers', in my proses and unseens which formed, for old-fashioned Mods dons, by far the most important part of the syllabus. Cyril Bailey was a good scholar himself, his edition of Lucretius being greatly respected, but scholarship to him was a diversion with which to occupy the vacations, or retirement, when there was leisure from the true business of classical studies, to teach people to translate, both from English into Latin and Greek, and the other way round. I was becoming, he said, thoroughly Germanic in my approach. Duncan, by contrast, had been the ideal Balliol scholar, not only effortlessly turning out impeccable and elegant 'versions', as translations were called, but singing madrigals, acting in Aristophanes with the Balliol Players and playing tennis for the college.

It was not surprising that I was accused of being Germanic. Apart from Cyril Bailey himself, all the other people who taught us were refugee scholars, mostly Jews, who had come to Oxford by invitation from the mid-thirties onwards. These great men, Fraenkel, Maas, Jacobi, Brink, Pfeiffer and others, had a profound effect on classical studies in Oxford, not only on literary studies, but on ancient history as well (though before the war there had grown up an indigenous school of young Greek archaeologists, influenced but not dominated by foreign scholars). I believe they had an effect on philosophy as well, not simply because so many Oxford philosophers came to the subject from the rigours of Classical Honour Mods. The effect was more general. We learned from them the uselessness of wild interpretations without evidential support; we learned always to ask what a particular word could have meant at the time that it was used; we learned to treat classical authors, as far as we could, as coming from a culture vastly different from our own, a culture we had to study in all its aspects if we were to understand the texts. Nancy and I used to go to a class on Greek lyric poetry (we may have been the only members) given by Rudi Pfeiffer, an enchanting man, always deeply grateful to his host country. The text we had to study for Mods was a part of the *Oxford Book of Greek Verse* which had been put together in a fashion more bold than scholarly by Maurice Bowra, just before the war. It was a source of constant amusement to us to witness Pfeiffer, besides struggling with his own imperfect English, struggling too with his internal battle between politeness and outrage, as he explained to us how the text as printed could not possibly be what the poet had written. This deep desire to get things right, even quite small things, undoubtedly reappeared in post-war philosophy, leading hostile critics to think of Oxford philosophy as a kind of pedantic lexicography.

Cyril Bailey was therefore quite fair in accusing me of getting caught up in a culture different from the amateurish, brilliant style that had characterised people like my brother. Though we knew we were very lucky to be taught by these great men, they opened our eyes to the depths of our ignorance, and it seemed to me that hard work was the only way to get by. And this was not the mark of the perfect Oxford classicist for the people of Cyril's generation.

When I was not working, or mopping up Elisabeth's tears, there was compulsory work in the college gardens, preparing vegetables in the college kitchen, sweeping the corridors and training to be an air-raid warden, a farcical process which Nancy and Elisabeth and I all undertook under the watchful eye of an Incident Officer called Mr Dab who, unlike Cyril Bailey, suspected me of not being wholly serious. There was nearly an international incident when he caught me helping Elisabeth with her warden's written test. She had difficulty, excellent though her English was, with the specialised vocabulary of poison gas. One way or another I was glad to leave Oxford in the spring of 1944.

The Oxford I came back to in 1946 could not have been more different. For one thing it was crowded. Undergraduates were coming up straight from school, but they were joined by people like me, who were coming up for the second time, and others who had gone into the forces straight from school and were taking up their places only now, or as soon as they could get demobilised. The government gave a grant (a Further Education and Training Grant) to all those whose education had been interrupted, and colleges were generous in accepting a huge influx of undergraduates, some, like New College, putting up special huts in the grounds to accommodate them. Optimism was in the air. It was not only that we and those who taught us were glad to be back, but we had become politicised. The 1945 General Election, the first we had voted in, was widely seen to be the beginning of a new era. The social changes that were promised in the Beveridge Report on the social services, the Butler Education Act, the National Health Service, widely publicised almost throughout the war, were now all coming about, and added to the academic sense of new beginnings. It was too early to worry, except occasionally, about the Iron Curtain, the Cold War, even the threat of nuclear disaster. Most of the rather elderly undergraduates were looking forward to the future, to making up for lost time, getting jobs, marrying and settling in this new order; but for the interlude, before they could embark on that, they were content to work hard at their academic subjects and enjoy the social life and the intellectual buzz that characterised the university at this time. The hunger and cold that had depressed those of us who had been up during the war, though now in fact more severe than ever before (with the terrible winter of 1947, and the rationing of bread), seemed now not a signal of doom but a competitive challenge. We were good at sharing our food and our fires (at LMH we had one scuttle of coal a week, and our rooms had no central heating. People with gas fires became instant friends). We cheerfully queued for cakes and cigarettes and bottles of sherry for the parties we all gave. I read a substantial part of Kant's *Critique of Pure Reason* in the Oliver and Gurden cake factory queue in North Oxford where, if you were lucky, you could buy tarts filled with a heavy mixture of dates and chocolate, and other nasty but filling confections. Food was, by present standards, disgusting but to get enough was a triumph.

Senior members of the university had come back from the war with their heads full of new books which, before they were written, could be tried out in lectures and tutorials. They too were glad to be back and worked for exceedingly long hours teaching the influx of undergraduates, as well as writing their books. Greats, in those days, consisted of philosophy and ancient history, both Greek and Roman. There were virtually no choices. As I have said, the study of ancient history had been transformed and there remained no vestiges of the Glory that was Greece or the Grandeur that was Rome which we had been taught about at school. The returning dons had, many of them, had dashing war careers, not only decoding at Bletchley, but also fighting in Greece and Italy. I was fortunate enough to have as my Greek History teacher Tom Dunbabin, one of the group of young archaeologists who had started work before the war, and who, having been in Greece for quite a lot of the war, was enormously excited by getting back to work. I was much attracted by the idea of becoming a Greek historian myself, and indeed did not finally abandon the idea until just before I took Schools.

Nevertheless, at this time, it was philosophy which especially began to blossom in Oxford and it continued to flourish for at least fifteen years, though not admired, still less understood, by everyone in the university. Before the war, Cambridge had been the centre of philosophy in this country, with Russell, Moore, Ramsey and, on and off, Wittgenstein. Now things had changed. The foundations of the change had been laid before the war, when A.J. Ayer, then a newly elected Research Student at Christ Church, went off to Vienna, encouraged by his supervisor, Gilbert Ryle, to find out about the doctrines of the Vienna Circle, otherwise known as the Logical Positivists. When he came back, he had swallowed these doctrines whole, and had introduced them to the British public in his explosive and exuberant book *Language, Truth and Logic*, published in 1936. Logical Positivism, in the interests of the advance of science, held that there were two, and only two, possible kinds of meaningful propositions: those that were necessarily true ('tautologies' as they were called in the jargon of logic), including the propositions of mathematics; and those that stated facts which could be verified by observation. The meaning of these latter propositions consisted in the method you would use to verify or falsify them. Thus, if I asserted that there was a wasps' nest outside my window, this meant that if you went outside you could see and hear it. The plain evidence of your senses would tell you that either what I said was true or that it was false, and this was the meaning of what I had said. But a sentence such as 'wasps' nests are terrifying' was not concerned with a fact, but a value. It could not be verified. (If I had said '70% of the population reacts with fear to wasps' nests', this would have stated a fact, and of course it could be verified by conducting a poll.) This distinction carried two important entailments. First, it followed that all metaphysical statements, claiming, that is to say, not to give information, but rather to share some sort of insight, such as that God is Love, or that Time is Unreal, could have no meaning assigned to them at all. The second entailment, even more striking in its impact, was that none of the propositions containing moral or aesthetic judgement were meaningful either. To say that some course of action was right or wrong was to say no more than you felt favourably or unfavourably towards it; indeed it did not say anything, but only pretended to. In uttering such a proposition, all you were doing was expressing pleasure or displeasure in the contemplation of the act. You need not have spoken at all; you could just as well have smiled or frowned, clapped or booed or stamped your foot. In speaking, you had uttered a 'pseudo-proposition'. It was not only professional philosophers who were outraged by this doctrine, but the old guard in every subject, and those who were outside the academic field altogether, the readers of the Sunday papers and the weeklies. Theology, metaphysics, morality and aesthetics all seemed to have been thrown out of the window. The distinction between reality, the facts of science, and subjective emoting, was to be regarded as absolute. Only the scientific was to be respected as true.

There was not much time before the war to examine these doctrines in detail. However, from the mid-thirties there had been a group of philosophers in Oxford who used to meet at All Souls College to discuss, among other things, Ayer's book and, in particular, the idea of perceptual evidence and its role in establishing claims to knowledge. This group consisted of Ayer himself, J.L. Austin, Isaiah Berlin, Stuart Hampshire and one or two others. The group was informal and lively, the most notable battles being those between Ayer and Austin on the nature of perceptual evidence. Berlin, in his essay 'Austin and the Early Beginnings of Oxford Philosophy' (*Essays on J.L. Austin*, 1973, p.12) writes: 'All I can recollect is that there was no crystallisation into permanent factions; views changed from week to week, save that Ayer and Austin were seldom, if ever, in agreement about anything'. Austin's approach in these encounters was, on the whole, entirely negative. He wanted to puncture any overarching theories about perception which would necessitate the introduction of such terms as 'sense-datum' to stand between the perceiving, language-using person, and the 'external' world. Berlin records that once, in exasperation, Ayer said to him, 'You are like a greyhound who doesn't want to run himself and bites the other greyhounds so that they cannot run either'.

Just before the war, Ayer wrote another book, *The Foundations of Empirical Knowledge*, published in 1940, presumably in order to defend himself against some of Austin's attacks in these All Souls meetings, and to set out the position he then adopted. But the disputes were put into cold storage until after the war.

The original group, along with Gilbert Ryle who had come back to take up the Wayneflete Chair in Metaphysical Philosophy when he left the army, formed the nucleus of the Philosophy Sub-faculty in post-war Oxford, though Ayer, never at ease in Oxford, left for London quite soon. But there was a large increase in the size of the Philosophy Sub-faculty at this time because of the popularity of the subject among undergraduates, almost all colleges having to make new appointments; and so it was that my three women philosophers came to be appointed.

The Vienna Circle, as such, was no more; its members scattered to the USA or England, or, in one case, the victim of a murder. All of its living members had modified their views and no one would any longer describe himself as a Logical Positivist, though many were so described by the general public. But there was a legacy we all inherited with the mood of post-war Britain in general. We were all wary of pretentious claims. Theoretical or rhetorical edifices were out of fashion. Anything that was said was scrutinised to see whether, at a common-sense level, it could be believed or made sense of. We had become extremely sceptical about assertions for which no evidence could be adduced. On the whole, we wanted to get a few things right rather than mess around with vast and vague concepts. We preferred to burst balloons rather than inflate them. After six years of propaganda, no one was about to pull the wool over our eyes.

In 1948 Ryle persuaded the university to institute a new postgraduate degree in Philosophy, the B.Phil. (and later other subjects instituted similar degrees). His reason was that in Oxford no one could read Philosophy except in conjunction with one or more other subjects, Ancient History or Politics and Economics, whereas in Cambridge and some other universities Philosophy could form the subject of a whole undergraduate degree. Ryle thought that therefore Oxford undergraduates seeking to become professional philosophers were at a disadvantage. He also thought that to take a further degree of the usual kind, consisting of a thesis on one particular topic, would not be suitable, partly because undergraduates simply did not know enough to choose a topic, but, more importantly, because sitting by oneself in a library was not, in his view, a proper way to learn Philosophy (and with this Austin agreed). Philosophy must be a collaborative effort, carried out by discussion and dialogue. So the new examination, uniquely among postgraduate degrees, consisted in a short thesis, a viva and a choice of three papers to be written in three hours, like Finals papers. The teaching was to be through seminars and lectures. The new examination became a huge success, attracting people not only from Oxford but from abroad, especially from America and Australia. It filled Oxford with bright foreigners, it necessitated even more new appointments, and it made Oxford, for fifteen years or so, the philosophical centre of the world.

Numerous and various as were the philosophers in Oxford, there was one characteristic they nearly all shared, and that was a lack of interest in moral or political philosophy. Moral philosophy was a despised subject, though it had to be taught because 'Morals and Politics' was a compulsory subject in both Greats and PPE. But it was here that the dead hand of Logical Positivism seemed most difficult to shake off. For Logical Positivists, moral philosophy, as a subject, was over and done with. There was, however, one exception to the lack of interest in moral philosophy, and that was R.M. Hare. He came back from the war, where he had been in a Japanese prison camp, to complete his undergraduate degree, but was made a Fellow of Balliol before he had even taken his final examinations, so brilliant and dedicated was he. He accepted the 'positivist' view that moral judgements, and indeed value judgements in general, were quite different from judgements of fact, but he elaborated this thought in a new way. He held that such judgements, that some things were good (or of course bad), were, despite appearances, in reality commands, of the form of Choose It (or do not). For he believed that while factual judgements answer requests for information, moral judgements (and even, he thought, aesthetic judgements), since they were related to conduct and sought to influence it, were answers to the question 'What shall I do?' Moral judgements thus had two characteristics which marked them off from others. One was that they were crypto-commands (in other words, that they were prescriptive); the other was that they were capable of being made universal in their application. In the case of an ordinary command, if I tell you to shut the door, this carries no implication about what I shall tell you to do another time, nor about what I shall tell someone else to do. There would be nothing contradictory in my telling you to leave the door open another time, nor in my telling someone else to break the door down. But in the case of morality, there must be consistency if the command is truly to be moral. That is to say, if you ask me why I should do the thing that I am morally commanded to do, I shall cite a principle of a universal nature. Thus a properly moral dialogue might, if analysed, go as follows:

You: What ought I to do with this purse I have picked up off the floor of the bus?
Hare: You ought to take it to the police station.
You: Why should I? I found it, after all.
Hare: Because taking what does not belong to you is stealing, and Stealing is Wrong.

This dialogue was taken by Hare to exemplify the form of all specifically moral arguments. Any argument which fitted this pattern could be said to be a moral argument, and no other could. In three books, very widely read by undergraduates and other philosophers, Hare reiterated and refined this formal description of 'The Language of Morals' (the title of his first book). However, he never satisfactorily answered the question (which in fact was never put to him with any seriousness) of where the principles which stood as the major premise of the arguments came from (principles such as Stealing is Wrong). Indeed he stated categorically that we choose our own principles and our freedom consists in our ability to choose any principle whatever from which to derive our moral imperatives (though often we choose those which, as he innocently said, 'we have learned at our mother's knee'). But there was, in his view, absolutely no limit to what principles we might choose. Morality would exist all the same, provided that the forms were maintained, that the arguments used were prescriptive and universalisable. It was still the case, as it had been for the Positivists, that moral philosophers could be concerned only with the forms, and not with the substance of morality. The pattern of *Language, Truth and Logic* remained unchanged. It speaks much for Hare's persistence and ingenuity that he more or less dominated the field of moral philosophy not only in Oxford but in the United States for nearly ten years.

It was against this general background that I first came across the three very different women who form the subject matter of this chapter and the next. The first was Philippa Foot. Philippa was born in 1920 and was already a Fellow of Somerville when I came back to Oxford in 1946. My first contact with her was indirect, through a distant cousin of mine, Jenny Turner, who had left Sherborne the term before I went to teach there, and had come up to LMH straight from school. Though we were only distant cousins (my mother being a cousin of her grandfather, who was a Chancery lawyer called Claud Schuster) we had always seen quite a lot of each other. Claud and his only daughter, Betty (Jenny's mother), used to come and stay with us in Winchester from the time when Jenny was quite small, Jenny being much disapproved of by our Nanny ('That Jenny' Nan frequently exclaimed when Jenny was thought to have taken more than her share of the nursery sausages). Cousin Jenny was reading PPE, and doing equally well in Philosophy, Politics and Economics. One of her optional special papers was to be the Philosophy of Kant, a paper our LMH philosophy tutor did not enjoy teaching and for which she sent her pupils out to be taught. Jenny had been sent to Philippa, and so it was through her that I first encountered Philippa's meticulous, imaginative and graphic philosophical mind. Jenny was, while undoubtedly very clever, also undoubtedly 'smart'. She led a full and, to me, impossibly glamorous social life and was involved as an actress in OUDS. The production of essays for her tutorials was therefore usually a matter of 'crisis'. We lived next door to each other after my first term back and we shared our fires, our coffee and our cigarettes, and frequently worked in each other's rooms. And so we fell into the way of jointly writing essays on Kant for Philippa. This was a wonderful way for me to get to know *The Critique of Pure Reason*, on which I would not have tutorials for two more terms, and I read it all, unknown to Philippa, entirely under her guidance and through her eyes. The complexities were, of course, enormous. If I failed to understand something, I would pack Jenny off to her tutorial to ask my questions as well as her own, if they differed, and when it came to the essay evening, we would together construct an answer to the question Philippa had set. It was fun collaborating in this way, and I learned a great deal, not only about Kant, but about how a really inspiring tutor taught her pupils. Jenny used to take notes in her tutorials, so I was often fed with Philippa's exact words; and, actress as she was, Jenny also, without meaning to, reproduced her actual tones of voice, so that when I came to meet Philippa, I felt I knew her already, but I did not tell her of my former connection with her. I met her a few times, usually at meetings of the undergraduate philosophical society, the Jowett, including at the memorable meeting in May 1947 when Wittgenstein came over from Cambridge; but even after I had graduated, I never got to know her well.

However, I vividly remember an occasion when, in the early 1950s, she read a paper entitled 'Moral Arguments' at the dons' philosophical society. This paper, or a version of it, was published in the periodical *Mind* (of which Ryle was then editor) in 1958 and it turned out to be a paper of enormous influence, opening the door to what amounted to a revolution in moral philosophy. The paper was specifically directed against R.M. Hare's contention that what made an argument a moral argument was that its conclusion ('so you ought to do x') was both prescriptive and universalisable, and that any argument could be shown to be 'moral' if it took this form. Values were to be freely chosen and no consideration of facts could compel you to choose one value rather than another. It was in this that moral freedom consisted. Philippa's paper put forward two linked propositions: first, that the form of an argument could not determine whether it was a moral argument or not; secondly, that for it to be 'moral' it had to be concerned with something that mattered to people, in the sense that acting against the conclusion ('you ought to do x') could be shown to be harmful or offensive. She was, in effect, challenging the belief, weakly held by empiricists since Hume, and turned into unchallenged dogma since the days of the Vienna Circle, that Fact and Value are two completely separate things, the one not deducible from the other. She illustrated her thesis by the concept of 'rudeness', an indisputably evaluative idea. You could not call some behaviour rude, unless it could be shown to be offensive. If that criterion is dropped, the term 'rude' has no use, and becomes meaningless. (Of course, as she conceded, what gives offence in one society may not do so in another; bad manners in the dining room may not be so seen in the hospital ward. Nevertheless the idea of 'bad manners' itself cannot be separated, in a given context, from the idea of actual or potential offence.) In her paper, she sought to show that there can exist factual evidence for a moral judgement, and that a man 'can no more decide for himself what is evidence of rightness or wrongness than he can decide what is evidence for monetary inflation or a tumour on the brain'.

At the time when Philippa read this paper, most of us, I suspect, saw it simply as an elegant and enjoyable bit of Hare-bashing. We were becoming tired of the arid orthodoxy of *The Language of Morals*. There may have been those who were clear-sighted enough to see what a revolutionary suggestion she was making. By 1958, when 'Moral Arguments' was published, and another article in the *Proceedings of the Aristotelian Society* for the same year, entitled 'Moral Beliefs', it was clear that morality was concerned, in her view, with what is beneficial or harmful to humans, and that what is beneficial or harmful is not, and cannot be, a matter of choice. To non-philosophers, such conclusions seem a matter of plain common sense, but to philosophers, to be freed from the absurd restrictions of the so-called Naturalistic Fallacy (you cannot deduce an Ought from an Is) was freedom indeed. At last, the absolute barrier erected by Logical Positivism between Fact and Value had been breached, and moral realism began to be sniffed in the air.

There were doubtless other factors influencing this new movement, which had the effect of permitting moral philosophers to interest themselves in real moral problems, rather than the words or forms in which these problems were discussed, and certainly by 1960 I noted in the conclusion to my Home University Library *Ethics since 1900* that I thought there were 'signs that the most boring days were over'. In writing thus, I was undoubtedly thinking in part of Philippa Foot. The impressive thing about her original intervention against Hare was that it was done with the help of detailed though invented examples, meticulously, stage by stage. Hers was no voice of impatience, nor was it a broad brush appeal to the deadliness of moral philosophy, or the exciting new world ahead. It was a modest, accurate instantiation of the ideal of getting small things right. But in this case the outcome was far from small. I hope very much that the perhaps ladylike non-aggression of Philippa's style will not in the end rob her of the proper recognition of her originality and intellectual courage.

As I have said, I never knew Philippa at all well. I was always intimidated by her. This was perhaps reinforced by her choice of the concept of rudeness as the central example in her seminal 1958 paper. I regarded her as someone infinitely above me, as one might regard a much older member of a great family. And indeed it was well known that she had grand origins. Her maternal grandfather was a President of the USA, and her mother was born in the White House. Her mother married into the Bosanquet family, much admired by my mother (as well as having philosophical resonances). While the rest of us were inelegantly dressed in skirts home-made out of blackout material, without stockings (and with the consequent unlovely mauve legs), Philippa, tall and aristocratically long-faced, seemed always to be dressed in 'good' clothes, conspicuously not home-made. She was a great friend of Iris Murdoch, from undergraduate days, and in the Trinity Term 1999 number of *Oxford Today*, a magazine distributed to all alumni, she wrote in her obituary piece: 'We lived together for two years in the war, and she and I were the closest of friends to the end. Yet I never felt I altogether knew her, perhaps because she was a private person, frank but unwilling to volunteer much about herself'. I wonder whether Iris, and many other people, felt that the same was true of Philippa. But it has to be said that most of the people whom I have tried to write about in this book have been described to me at least once as 'private people'. It is perhaps the case that everyone wishes to retain an area with boundaries round it, with notices informing the world that Trespassers will be Prosecuted. I would certainly never venture to trespass in the case of Philippa, but my admiration for her, and her genuine philosophical nonconformity, is very deep.

My second subject, linked to Philippa Foot only by the bridge that both were Fellows of Somerville College when I returned to Oxford, is Elizabeth Anscombe. Having been an undergraduate at St Hugh's College, reading Classical Mods and Greats, and taking

Schools in 1941, she later went to Newnham College, Cambridge, with a research award. There she became friendly with a younger Research Student in Classics, my close friend, Imogen Wrong. Imogen, who appears more than once in these pages, was a member of one of the great Oxford dynasties (not as powerful or numerous as the Cambridge dynasties, but important nonetheless), the Smiths of Balliol. A.L. Smith had seven daughters of whom one, Rosalind, was Imogen's mother. Rosalind Wrong lived in Oxford, her husband, Murray Wrong, having died many years earlier. Imogen spent her vacations in Oxford, and it was she who introduced me to Elizabeth. Imogen hated Philosophy and at school had always wanted to go to Cambridge where, reading the Classical Tripos, she would not have to tangle with it. On first introducing me to Elizabeth, she did not tell her I was reading Greats, but inevitably this fact soon came out. From then Elizabeth took me on as a protégée, believing that she had a duty to rescue me from what she regarded as the evils of Oxford philosophy, and open my eyes to the truth. In order to explain this, and my unhappy connections with Elizabeth at the time, I must say something about the extraordinary relationship between the later philosophy of Wittgenstein and philosophy as practised in Oxford, though I have to confess to being far from clear, even now, about the exact nature of the relationship.

Wittgenstein, who had held the Chair in Philosophy in Cambridge from early in 1939, left it for war work in 1941, the year before Elizabeth went up to Newnham as a Research Student. But he came back from London, where he worked first as a porter at Guy's Hospital, then from Newcastle, where he worked as a laboratory technician, to lecture in Cambridge every weekend. Elizabeth started attending these weekly lectures; and then when he was called back to Cambridge in 1944, she became an enthusiastic disciple and friend. Even when she took up her Research

Fellowship at Somerville in the academic year 1945/6, she went to Cambridge every week for his classes. Wittgenstein had then been working for some time on what would become the *Philosophical Investigations*, a descriptive analysis of psychological concepts and those concerned with perception and knowledge, through the investigation of words like 'think', 'expect' and 'imagine', in numerous different contexts, real or imagined. Having once, in the early days, when the *Tractatus Logico-Philosophicus* was written, been possessed of a great metaphysical vision, namely that insight into the nature of a simple basic proposition could teach not only the structure of logic, but the structure of the world, he had now come to see philosophy quite differently.

Instead of seeking one great solution to the problem of the nature of things, he now held that philosophy was a series of different, discrete problems or perplexities caused by the ambiguities of language. One could be cured of these perplexities if only one took seriously what language is ordinarily used to do. Grammar can seriously mislead. Nouns may be thought all to stand for the same sort of things; adjectives for the same sort of properties. This is a gross over-simplification, obscuring the relation between language and its users. He no longer believed that there was one form of 'basic' proposition. Instead there were numerous different kinds of propositions and linguistic utterances, questions, commands, exclamations and so on, all of which we must describe if we are to escape from our philosophical contortions and conundrums. Equally, there is no such thing as 'the meaning of a word', only numerous different ways in which a word may be used and understood, in different contexts, and with different intents. He said of himself (*Philosophical Investigations* para. 116) 'What *we* do is to bring back words from their metaphysical to their everyday use', and again (para. 118) 'Where does our investigation get its importance from, since it seems only to destroy everything interesting, that is all that is great and important? … What we are destroying is nothing but houses of cards, and we are clearing up the ground of language on which they stand'. The philosophical houses of cards to be destroyed are theories that set out to explain things that in fact need no explanation. So if we puzzle, as all philosophers have puzzled, about the relation between Mind and Body, this is because we have been deceived by language itself. We think that the nouns 'mind' and 'body' must be the names of two things, and two things that can be compared with one another and stand in some relation to one another. This leads us also to suppose that the kinds of questions we can ask about minds are like the questions we can ask about bodies. The purpose of the later Wittgenstein's philosophy was to lay bare by description the differences between linguistic uses in different contexts, such as, for example, the difference between what we might mean by saying that a dog 'hoped' to be taken for a walk, and what we might mean when we said of a man that he hoped to have recovered the use of his broken ankle in a few weeks' time. This, he claimed, would bring philosophical problems to an end, and with the end of problems would come relief to philosophers.

When Elizabeth first took me on, she used to try to get me to say which particular philosophical problems worried me. To encourage me, she used to recall how, as an undergraduate, she had felt hopelessly trapped by problems about perception: what do we actually see, for example, when we claim to see a matchbox? Is it an oblong, yellowish 'sense-datum'? Is it a set of complex 'data'? Is it an impression or an idea in our own mind? If such answers are correct, then how do we reconstruct it into a matchbox which we can converse about, and agree with other people in whose mind it also exists as an impression or 'datum'? She used to sit in the Cadena Café, or in her own room in college, she told me, agonising about such questions.

The problems were familiar enough to me. The problems of perception, as I have said, occupied an enormous amount of our time in Oxford in those days, stemming as they did from Descartes' separation of mind from body, and the subsequent exploration of perceptions and knowledge carried out by the British Empiricists, Locke, Berkeley and Hume (our staple diet), and continued by Russell and Ayer. Both of these claimed that the language in which the 'plain man' talks about what he perceives is actually wrong. We do not see the planet Mars, as the plain man supposes, if we look into the sky at night. What we see is something within ourselves, a sense-datum or percept of the planet. For the planet itself, because it is so far away, might have ceased to exist by the time we claim to 'see' it. So how can it be the planet itself that we see? And if this is true of distant things like planets, it must also be true of near things like the screen in front of which I am sitting at this moment. I do not see the screen itself, but 'have' a sense-datum (rather as I might 'have' an itch) which I somehow construct into something I call a screen. All these empirical philosophers were concerned to explain how the 'internal' ideas or impressions or data of perception were related to the 'external world' and what therefore we could claim to know of that world.

These problems very much interested me. They were closely related to questions that I, like nearly all children I have ever met, had asked for years, namely how can I be sure that when I see something green I see the same green as you see when you claim to see green? In those days, as an undergraduate, I was very much enjoying reading the texts which set out and discussed such things, especially Hume's great sceptical *Treatise of Human Nature*, and indeed Kant's heroic attempt to deal with this scepticism once and for all in the *Critique of Pure Reason*. But I could not honestly say that the problems kept me awake at night. I was intrigued by them, absorbed in them even, while I was in my philosophy rather than history part of the week, and while I was not engaged in playing or listening to music or talking to my friends. But I no more worried about them than I worried about how to establish the date of the Battle of Marathon, a problem that also, as a matter of fact, engaged quite a lot of my attention.

Pressed by Elizabeth, I could never come up with a genuine problem of my own, except possibly a problem in the interpretation of one of the texts. Oxford philosophy, from the point of view of an undergraduate, was very much a matter of reading and understanding philosophers of the past, distant or recent, in this markedly differing from philosophy in Cambridge. It was assumed that one could understand what a problem was only if one understood how it had arisen, and how proposed solutions differed from one another, perhaps inching towards a final solution, perhaps not. Because of the central importance, at least for those studying Greats, of Plato and Aristotle, philosophy in Oxford was inextricably linked with the history of ideas, and it was this, though I hardly realised it, that had really attracted me. But though Elizabeth had had her philosophical education first in Oxford, and though she could, if she chose, show herself a learned and perceptive interpreter of Plato, Aristotle or Hume, she had at this time so entirely identified herself with Wittgenstein (she had, for example, adopted all his agonised head in hands, furrowed brow gestures and had even begun to speak with a hint of an Austrian accent) that she despised the reading of other philosophers almost as much as he did.

There was one occasion, as I have said, when Wittgenstein came to a meeting of the Jowett Society. The President of the Society, an undergraduate from Corpus Christi College called Oscar Wood, who later became a great friend, read a paper on Descartes, and the interpretation of the *cogito, ergo sum* argument, by which Descartes sought to prove that among all the things he could doubt, his own existence was something he could not doubt, as long as he was capable of conscious thought. Wittgenstein started his reply (uttered in tones of disgust and disbelief) with the words, 'Mr Wood seems to me to have made two points'. He then abandoned Mr Wood and Descartes altogether and started to talk in his own style about what 'the cogito' could possibly be thought to mean. At one point he said, 'If a man says to me, looking at the sky, "I think it will rain therefore I exist" I do not understand him' upon which a very old philosopher, H.A. Prichard, who had been Austin's tutor at Balliol, and had greatly influenced him, interrupted with 'That's all very fine; but what I want to know is, is the *cogito* a valid argument or not?' Prichard was very deaf, his voice was ancient and querulous, and he had a terrible cough, but he interrupted three or four times. Wittgenstein never once mentioned Descartes, and at one point was provoked into saying that Descartes was of no importance. Prichard's last contribution was, 'What Descartes was interested in was far more important than any problem you have addressed this evening', and with that he tottered out. There was considerable embarrassment, as I recorded in my diary, at Prichard's rudeness. It proved to be his last outing. He was dead within a week. The exchange, however fruitless, indicated the vast difference between Wittgenstein's methods and those which had been generally prevalent in Oxford. Like New Labour, the New Philosophy abandoned history.

Indeed, Wittgenstein gloried in a probably exaggerated ignorance of earlier philosophy. According to Gilbert Ryle, he not only 'properly distinguished philosophical from exegetic problems, but also, less properly, gave the impression that he himself was proud not to have studied other philosophers – which he had done, though not much – and that he thought that people who did study them were academics and therefore unauthentic philosophers'.

Elizabeth had by now adopted the same attitude. I remember a seminar she gave in 1949 where a young man from Christ Church, not very bright, raised a naive question about perception (I believe it was the child's question referred to above: how do I know that 'my' green is the same as 'your' green) which Elizabeth fastened on with delight. For two further weeks we discussed 'Mr Topham's problem' but then, alas, Mr Topham's fame went to his head and he began to read Hume, or perhaps Berkeley. The next week he mentioned one of these philosophers and immediately he fell from grace. I found myself in the opposite situation from Mr Topham. I had read too many philosophers and could not think of any problems of my own. My futile efforts to think up problems that worried me left Elizabeth aghast and completely convinced that I would never be a philosopher.

We used to meet, I suppose, about once every ten days, always at her suggestion. We met either in my room in LMH or in her house in St John Street. Elizabeth was married to a logician, Peter Geach, but he had a job in Birmingham and was seldom to be seen. But there were at least three, possibly four, children, and I dreaded my visits to St John Street, not only because of the exposure of my philosophical inadequacies, but because of the intense smelliness of the ambience. In Elizabeth's upstairs study there was a huge hollow column, used as an ashtray, which was seldom, if ever, emptied, there were toys scattered on the floor and sometimes even dirty nappies in the room. On one occasion I had a baby thrust into my arms when I arrived, with instructions to give it its bottle while Elizabeth finished something she was writing. I knew absolutely nothing of babies. All I knew was that this damp and malodorous object was something the like of which I never wanted to see again.

However, the philosophical content of our meetings gradually improved. Elizabeth had embarked on her translation of Wittgenstein's *Philosophical Investigations* and, despairing, I suppose, of getting me to contribute in any way to proper philosophical discussion, she fell into the habit of reading some of her translation aloud, and discussing linguistic or grammatical points or, sometimes, substantial points about the text. I enjoyed this, not least because I found the whole inconclusive style, the approach by hints and suggestions and unanswered questions, more reminiscent of Coleridge (selections from whose notebooks I had just been introduced to by my brother) than of any philosopher I had ever read. On one occasion she lent me a few sheets of her translation to take back with me to LMH, to copy out if I liked. So it happened that before many people in Oxford had seen any of the later work of Wittgenstein, I saw some of it directly. I was deeply grateful to Elizabeth for this. Later some typewritten sheets, transcripts of students' notes from his lectures, known as the *Blue Book* and the *Brown Book*, passed from hand to hand in Oxford, causing enormous excitement. But I never saw these as an undergraduate and I did not know they were about until a year or so later. This shows how strangely clandestine connections with Wittgenstein were.

Meanwhile, I was, as I thought, beginning to be genuinely interested in some aspects of philosophy, and to feel as if I might understand them. There were two sets of classes that I attended which were especially enjoyable. The first used to take place in a small, dark room on the ground floor of the New Bodleian and was given by a speaker of very imperfect English called Georg Katkov. Quite often there were only one or two other people present. Katkov had in his possession a number of papers, notes for lectures, unfinished articles and so on, by the German philosopher Franz Brentano, who had died in 1917. Some of these papers were later translated into English and published in America. Brentano is generally thought of as the founder of the philosophical movement known as Phenomenology, whose more famous exponent was his pupil and one-time follower Edmund Husserl. Husserl had a profound influence on the Existentialism of Jean-Paul Sartre (though I knew nothing of that at the time). Brentano held the apparently simple view that the difference between the physical and the mental could be expressed in the formula that the mental was always directed towards an object, the physical not.

This distinction, put forward to replace the Cartesian view that mind and body were two totally different substances, mysteriously conjoined, represented the beginning of a revolution in philosophy. Descartes held that the existence of mind, his own mind at least, was something that could not be doubted. The material world, however, was always subject to possible doubt, since all one could ever know of it was the idea of it that was part of one's own mental experience, whether this was called an idea, image or sense-datum. I may claim to see a tree, but all I really know is my own idea, image or sense-datum of the tree, existing in my own mind. This separation of the mental from the 'external' world dominated philosophy from the time of Descartes until Kant's heroic attempt to bring the two worlds together through the concept of the imagination, constructing the external world according to fixed laws. The great question was always how my idea of the world could be shown to relate to any genuine world beyond my ideas. There were always three items to be accommodated: myself, the perceiver; my ideas or images; and the things in the world to which my ideas or images were supposed to relate. For Brentano, however, there were just two things: myself (a being capable of psychological or mental activity) and the outside world. Thus, thinking, loving, hating, imagining or any other psychological activity was always the thinking *of* something. All such activities were Intentional, that is defined by being directed to something. This was, in Brentano's view, a great simplification. No third intermediate internal entity, idea, image or sense-datum, an object in the mind, existed. If you saw something, heard it, longed for it, hated it, there was just the object and you, related in different psychological ways. The relation between the inner and the outer world was explained just by the complex notion of Intentionality.

In the second term of his class, Katkov went on to discuss Husserl, and the obscurities became more and more dense. I was not at all certain that I understood what he was saying, and the conduct of these classes became more and more chaotic, the language less intelligible, the shuffling round of papers more frenetic. But, all the same, I was conscious of a feeling of excitement. Descartes had held that we have ideas of other people in the same way as we have ideas of tables and chairs. We acquire ideas of them as we acquire ideas of other physical objects but we can only infer, by analogy, that they have minds like our own. We look down from our window onto a rainy street below, and we see hats and umbrellas passing by and think 'That's how I would look if I were out in the rain, so perhaps inside those objects there is something else, a mind which feels cold and wet as I would, and wishes, as I would, that the rain would stop'.

Husserl, on the other hand, held that perception, if one examines it properly, is not like this. We do not, for example, make up the notion that what we are looking at is a garden fork by having data of handle, shaft and prongs and somehow adding them together to make a fork. On the contrary there are, he argued, two elements intrinsic to perception. One is a sense of time, of the thing we are looking at having duration even if we take our eyes off it. If we hear a long note held on a flute, it is intrinsically held, not made up of discrete sounds put together. The other element is that other people exist, and that the garden fork can be perceived and used as a tool by people other than ourselves. A tool is a tool for anyone. Even if one were the last person in the universe still using language to identify things, though, as it happened, for one's self alone, the implication of potential other people would still be there.

These ideas, whether properly ascribed to Husserl or not, seemed to me wonderfully to release one from the prison of 'sense-data', the internal objects in the mind which had, with so much difficulty, to be related to the external world, and to open up the thought that a common world shared by all human beings could actually be heard, seen or smelled by everyone in more or less the same way. The external world is what there is, there for us all, and this in turn makes sense of language, that is, makes it possible to understand how language can exist and function.

At the same time as I was finding out about Husserl, Elizabeth was showing me her translation of a central part of the *Investigations*, to become paragraphs 243-315, containing what came to be known as the Private Language Argument. Wittgenstein maintained that the idea of a language whose terms primarily referred only to a speaker's own sensations, experienced by himself alone, was strictly nonsensical. And yet such a language seemed to be presupposed by all those philosophers who thought that perception gave one only 'private' ideas or impressions or sense-data, and that it was upon such experiences that all empirical knowledge was founded. It had always been a problem for such philosophers to explain how, if our language had, fundamentally, a private reference, we could ever come to understand one another.

Wittgenstein's argument was designed to show that the problem did not really exist because the idea of such a language was a contradiction. For if one seriously tries to imagine a language in which, let us say, one used the word 'plonk' to describe a sensation one had, and no one else had, then it becomes clear that one could in fact use the word only once, at the time when one decided to call the sensation 'plonk'. For the next time one had a similar sensation, one could never be absolutely sure that it was sufficiently similar to justify the re-use of the word consistently. There would be no way of checking. One might have to fall back on calling the second sensation 'plink'. There could be no criterion by which one could identify a wholly private and momentary sensation as the same as another. Yet it is the very essence of language to enable us to identify and re-identify objects. Any language whatever, if it is truly a language, must be able to be general, that is, to refer to kinds of things, cats, let us say, or trees. Even if I want to be able to refer to a particular cat, Simpkin, I have to be able to say 'There is Simpkin again', and show you, this afternoon, that it is indeed the same cat as we saw this morning. And this itself is possible only against the background of our being able to identify and refer to a cat as a cat.

It is further essential to a language which is to work that when two people use the same word they are referring to the same thing; and words for sensations are no exception. When I say I am cold, I am using the word 'cold' to mean exactly the same as it means when you say you are cold. In this way it can be argued that when I say I am cold, I am not naming an entirely private and non-recoverable sensation. There are public rules for the use of the word; and, if so, there are ways of establishing between people what these rules are, in other words what the word means. This was more or less how, at the time, I understood the part of the *Investigations* that Elizabeth showed me, and I was fascinated.

These were the sheets I took back to college, copied out and more or less committed to memory before I sat my examinations. I thought I began to see how one might do away altogether with Descartes' difference between the inner and the outer world. We could think of ourselves as all members of the 'external world', in it and parts of it together, though each perceiving it for ourselves. But the fact that we each perceive it need not entail that we could talk only about our own perceptions. However, when I tentatively suggested that this was like what Husserl had argued, Elizabeth dismissed the idea out of hand. She thought it yet another example of my refusal to engage with philosophy, only with texts. No one, she said, had ever thought of anything like this before. It was Wittgenstein, and he alone, who had invented the Private Language Argument. (Of course this was undeniable; all that I was suggesting was that it led in the same direction as Husserl's thoughts.) Elizabeth was annoyed with me on this occasion, but not really angry. I had, predictably, simply misunderstood the argument, if I did not see that it was brand new.

But I made a far worse blunder. Apart from Katkov's classes, the other aspect of philosophy I was beginning to enjoy (in fact had enjoyed since the first term I came back to Oxford) was attending the lectures and classes of J.L. Austin. Perhaps the best of them was a small class on Aristotle's *Nicomachaean Ethics*, a set text for Greats. These were exactly to my taste. Held in his rooms in Magdalen, attended by only four or five people, they were funny, precise, learned and enormously illuminating. But there was another class which he gave jointly with Isaiah Berlin, and which probably covered a good deal of the ground they had covered together in All Souls in their conversations before the war. The class appeared on the lecture list under the title 'Things' and Elizabeth used to go (as did Geoffrey: I first saw him there, sitting, smiling and pleased, his gown rather widely spread around him and apparently surrounded by admirers). Predictably enough, we discussed all the propositions often uttered by Russell and Ayer that ordinary people, 'plain men', held the mistaken belief that what they saw were 'material objects' or 'material things'; whereas in fact what they saw was a collection of sense-data. The class covered many different aspects of perception, such as, for example, what one saw when one was seeing double; was it one thing, a candle flame, say, or was it two? Such questions always involved trying to find out what you would actually say in certain specific circumstances, and trying to avoid, as far as possible, the introduction of any technical term such as 'sense-data'. It was enormously enjoyable, both to discover how many perceptual distinctions one could draw, using words in their ordinary senses, and how little justice the 'sense-datum' philosophers did to the actual complicated facts of perception.

Elizabeth attended these classes, I suppose, in part, to observe Austin in action (though she had been to classes of his while an undergraduate at the very beginning of the war) but also as the champion, or even the spy, of Wittgenstein. In any case she was a troublesome presence and frequently intervened to pour scorn on what was being said. On one particular evening, when she had behaved with notable rudeness, I tried to evade her afterwards by scuttling very fast out of the Magdalen back gates, but she caught up with me as I was struggling with my bicycle lock in Longwall, and hissed 'To think that Wittgenstein fathered that bastard'. A good deal later, I plucked up my courage and tried to say that, from what I was learning about Wittgenstein's present stance, I thought that he would agree with much of what had gone on in the Things class. After all, had he not spoken himself of bringing back words from their metaphysical to their everyday use? Had he not said that he was concerned to destroy houses of cards? Elizabeth was absolutely furious. She turned white with rage. She said that if I thought there was anything whatever in common between Austin and Wittgenstein, then I had totally misunderstood everything she had taught me about Wittgenstein.

I now found myself hopelessly confused. I thought then, and still think, that their determination to examine the language that is really used for communication about the world was something they shared, and that it showed the way out of the difficulty of understanding how language ever came about. Language was not, in the view of either of them, a matter of fixed, hidden meanings, but of use specifically to communicate, even in difficult or non-standard circumstances, like that of seeing double. This seemed to me an important, indeed crucial, element in common. And so I came to feel that since I must be wrong, and seriously wrong, if Elizabeth was so angry, I had completely failed to understand what either Wittgenstein or Austin were up to. I must have missed some absolutely central point.

It is true of course, as I later learned, that their views about what philosophy was, what it should do, were very different. But Austin never talked about that kind of thing, and it has been plausibly argued that he did not hold any very strong views on the matter. Philosophy was a collection of traditional philosophical problems which had not been sorted out by any of the sciences, and his motive for tackling them was partly negative. His criticism was mostly of faults apparently endemic to philosophers: carelessness, haste, not actually examining what they meant by invoking the great dichotomies (the real and the apparent, for example, or the factual and the evaluative) which he so much distrusted; and often not believing what they said. (For instance he claimed, doubtless rightly, never to have met anyone who was, in practice, a determinist, though many philosophers argued that determinism was true.) But because he did not talk much about the purpose of philosophy, but simply engaged in it as his profession, it was difficult, at least for an undergraduate, to piece together any general views, even if he held them. Indeed I, and most others, I think, did not begin to do so until after his death, when those who had benefited from his presence, and missed it deeply, began to try to sum up what he had achieved. However there was one view that I suppose even undergraduates knew that he held, which was that philosophy was a matter not of disputation, point-scoring or competition, but of conversation, a cooperative rather than a solitary occupation, in which, if you were not too hasty, you might end up saying something which, on however small a scale, was true.

Wittgenstein, on the other hand, was quite certain what his 'aim in philosophy' was. It was therapy, the curing of disease. The fly was trapped in the bottle, buzzing miserably about, and must be let out. Philosophical problems, arising as they did out of the misleading nature of language, could be dissolved for ever if we looked properly at language; and there would be an end of it. No one need ever again go through the mental agony that he had gone through. I did not understand this either, with my extremely limited knowledge of his new work, but anyway I thought I could see a connection between Austin's arguments against 'sense-data' and Wittgenstein's arguments against a 'private language'; and I thought I could see at least a common interest between both of them and phenomenology, with its rejection of a tripartite account of our engagement with the world, the observer, the 'idea', and the external object, all separate. But, as I have said, I concluded that I must be wrong, that my ideas were too broad and vague. How could I possibly hope to understand philosophy when I was so manifestly adrift in it?

I thought a lot then, and have since, about Elizabeth's deep hostility against Austin. On what was it based? I never heard her express such loathing of Gilbert Ryle, who had been a friend of Wittgenstein at one time and whose current lectures (which were turned into his book *The Concept of Mind* a few years later) could more plausibly, though certainly falsely, have been taken for plagiarism. For I understood, I thought, that plagiarism was the charge contained in Elizabeth's 'bastard' remark. Yet if she was really accusing Austin of plagiarism, how could she also claim that there was nothing whatever in common between Austin and Wittgenstein? It was well known at the time that Wittgenstein's pupils, or disciples rather, were excommunicated from time to time for publishing extracts from his lectures, or simply for getting things wrong, or failing to understand the teachings of the Master.

But this could not be true of Austin, who had never been a pupil or even a friend.

In any case, as I have suggested, Austin must have been thinking along the lines of the Things class ever since the publication of Ayer's *Language, Truth and Logic*, and *The Foundations of Empirical Knowledge*, before anything much could have been known of the direction in which Wittgenstein's later philosophy was developing. It may be that Elizabeth could not bear the alternative to plagiarism, namely that Austin had independently been working in the same, or nearly the same, field, and had come up with some rather similar conclusions. Certainly her hostility to him was implacable, and dated from before the time when she could have become Wittgenstein's disciple, for she attended a class given by Austin on the subject of perception in 1940/41, her last year as an undergraduate, and it was plain even then that she could not stand him. Another member of the class had been Jean Coutts, who became Austin's wife the following year, and Elizabeth reproached her bitterly for marrying someone so awful (rather as she later reproached me for marrying the person she disobligingly referred to as 'that shit, Warnock').

I suppose in the end it may have been a matter of style; but matters of style can go very deep. Though Austin took his profession seriously, and the duties he believed to go with it, he was neither solemn nor agonised. The very aspects of his lectures and classes that I increasingly loved, his wit, his attention to detail, his proneness to make really quite silly jokes, though the least silly of men, his habit of embroidering his examples with somewhat outdated Edwardian slang (for example, in his paper on pretending, there was the case of someone's pretending to be a hyena, and actually taking a fair size bite of Austin's calf, upon which he says 'Not much pretence about that, is there? There are limits, old sport', a passage which a bewildered French translator once concluded with the words 'vieux plaisanterie'). All this enraged Elizabeth. She longed to wipe the grin off his face. Perhaps she felt that she, or Wittgenstein, was being made a fool of, though he was not mentioned by Austin in any class or lecture that I went to, and only later (after the publication of the *Philosophical Investigations*) was he discussed at 'Saturday Mornings', Austin's informal meetings of practising philosophers. Whatever the reason, Elizabeth detested him, and he represented the kind of philosophy from which she had first felt it necessary to rescue me.

At last, in my final term, I really had to make up my mind what I was going to do next. I had already written off, and had even paid my fee, to take the Civil Service entry examination, on the advice of my brother, and my brother-in-law, Michael Balfour, an academic historian by nature but still, since the war, in the Civil Service. Jenny, too, was by now in the Foreign Office. But I hankered for an academic career. Being at Somerville, Elizabeth had heard from my Roman History tutor, also a member of that college, that she and Tom Dunbabin were urging me to put in for the Craven Fellowship, a university award which, if I had won it, would have taken me to the British School at Athens. Elizabeth pressed me most urgently to put in for it (as, for different reasons, did my mother. She hated philosophy, believing it to lead to cynicism, and a nasty habit of arguing with her). But, in the end, as I have said already, I very hesitantly applied to stay in Oxford for a year, to see if I could do the new B.Phil. examination in that time, so that I could see whether this was really what I wanted to go on with. And by the end of the year, as it turned out, events had overtaken me.

In the last of my long conversations with Elizabeth, she told me that I had made a most dreadful mistake. In the first place I was no good at the subject and, secondly, even if I had been, I would soon be corrupted and sucked even further into the mire of Oxford philosophy. On that uncheering note, I went off to start my final examinations the next week. One of the things that drew me towards Geoffrey Warnock (the shit), whom I had now got to know, was that when I reported that conversation to him the next day, he stated his intention of buying a horsewhip for use on Elizabeth.

In the Logic paper of my final examination, being ever a good examinee, I made quite ingenious use of the bits of Wittgenstein's *Investigations* that I had managed to commit to memory. It happened that Austin was one of the examiners that year, and he congratulated me on my Logic paper, so I felt quite pleased, and marginally vindicated in my view that he and Wittgenstein had something in common.

Although Elizabeth continued for many years to work on Wittgenstein's papers, after his death in 1951 she had to become reconciled to people other than herself discussing his work and writing about it as if he was an ordinary philosopher in the public domain, and not a Christ-figure, access to whose thoughts were confined to those who had been privileged to know him. She gradually, at least in part, dropped his mannerisms and her own writings became more and more distinctive. Her book, *Intention*, published in 1957, was manifestly original and highly illuminating. She was elected to the Chair of Philosophy in Cambridge in 1970 and her collected philosophical papers, published in 1981, showed her true stature as an independent philosopher. She mellowed, too, and we had an agreeable correspondence about the inclusion of her Inaugural Lecture (on Causation) in my book of pieces by women philosophers, published in 1996. But I still feel confused about Wittgenstein and I still sometimes, in reminiscent mood, raise Trollope's question, *Can You Forgive Her*? The answer, I hope, is Yes.

Some Women Philosophers (2): Iris Murdoch

When I first met Elizabeth Anscombe, I was immediately struck by her appearance. Though dressed in shapeless black trousers and a nondescript baggy sweater, though her hair was longish, greasy and of no particular colour, held back in some kind of 'bun' behind her head, her face was of astonishing serenity and beauty despite her having a noticeable cast in one eye. She had the look of an angel in a depiction of the Nativity. One instantly wanted, even expected, her sympathy, her blessing and her care, as a believer might hope for the favour of the Holy Virgin. And what was even more striking was the beauty of her voice, when she spoke. This, later, made the frequent coarseness of her language even more devastating in its effect.

My first impressions of Iris Murdoch, the subject of this chapter, were almost equally striking but quite different. I met her first, as I met Elizabeth, when I was still an undergraduate, and she had returned to Oxford after a time as a Research Student at Newnham College, Cambridge (or indeed she may still have been at Newnham, and only visiting on this first occasion). I was introduced to her at some philosophical meeting held in Somerville College, by a man with whom at the time I was in love, called Charles Salter. He was older than me, and had known Iris when he was taking Mods, before the war. He had joined the army at the outbreak of war, and had returned with the rank of Major, which seemed rather grand. Most of the ex-army people I knew had barely made it to Captain. He was an extremely good-looking man, in a melancholy way, his almost shaven short hair, brown eyes and bony face, with its remarkably short upper lip, merging into a kind of spiky unity. He treated me with unbending scorn, mixed with a kind of mocking affection, as if I were a slightly tiresome dog. (Later, though I could not at this time have imagined it, I moved on and our roles were reversed; he became the dog, his brown eyes fitting him well for the part.)

Because of his age, though like me an undergraduate, and like me reading Greats, he knew a lot of people who had already embarked on teaching or research. He saw Iris across the room with manifest pleasure, and said to me that I must meet her, because she was both extremely clever, and, unlike me, a proper person with real experience. He repeated some of the stories that were then current about her (her fame in Oxford was considerable, even before she came back); that she had been much admired by, and had fallen in love with a Wykehamist Communist called Frank Thompson who had been killed; that she had spent the end of the war in Europe (in itself a matter for remark); that she had been in Belgium and Paris and had met Sartre in person. I had no way of knowing how much of this story was true, but it made her a figure of enormous glamour and romance in my eyes. It was certainly true that she had worked for UNRRA (the United Nations Relief and Rehabilitation Agency) in the last part of the war, though she had been in London for most of the time, and had not got to Europe until after the war, in the autumn of 1945. It was certainly true that she had met Sartre. None of us knew anything about Sartre's philosophy, but we knew that he had been deeply involved with the underground press in Paris, and some of his plays were beginning to be admired. For example, a translation of *Huis Clos* was chosen as part of the opening night of the BBC Third Programme in the autumn of 1947, *Les Mouches* being performed a few days later.

All this made me look on Iris with nervous awe, as someone from a different world. When Charles introduced me, I noticed that he was experiencing much the same nervousness. Iris herself was cheerful ... jolly, even. She had thick tawny hair, which looked as if she had chopped it off herself, and this, combined with her rather stocky figure (in equine terms she was a cob, or perhaps a moorland pony) and her glow of health, gave her the air of one who was full of energy, for whom nothing would be too difficult or adventurous. Her voice, unlike Elizabeth's, was curiously monotonous, and all her vowels came out sounding much the same, a kind of ubiquitous 'u' sound, vaguely Celtic. This, despite her apparent amiability, gave her utterances a kind of solemnity. We talked for a bit before she was swept away by someone else, but as she left, she turned and said, with a memorably enchanting smile, 'We must meet again SOON.' But whether this was addressed to Charles or to me or (which was what I hoped) to us as a pair, it was impossible to tell. Later on, when we sometimes had occasion to write notes to one another, she always ended with the words 'à bientôt, Iris'. But we did not meet often, and I never knew her well.

Yet it was inevitable that one should know about her. She was a subject of endless gossip and speculation, not of a malicious kind but because she was, as I had immediately perceived, an exotic, and a romantic figure. She was widely thought to be adored by numbers of the Fellows of St Anne's (at that time all women) where she had become a Fellow, and by numbers of men as well; and one of my friends at St Hugh's, Rachel Trickett (about whom I write in the next chapter), herself a member of the English Faculty, seemed to follow, blow by blow, the prospects of John Bayley's managing to marry her.

I think I had only one real conversation with Iris. This I cannot exactly date, but it was at a party given by Rachel Trickett in honour of Virgil Thompson, the American composer who was staying briefly in Oxford, and whom Rachel had got to know on one of her academic visits to the USA. She had invited a number of the Oxford Music Faculty, with whom she was on friendly terms, having been working on a libretto for a new opera to be staged by the Operatic Society, a flourishing and ambitious group in Oxford. There were also, naturally, some members of the English Faculty, of which she herself, as I have said, and John Bayley, by now long married to Iris, were part. The party was held in her spacious rooms in the new building at St Hugh's, rooms which had excited the envious longing of our eldest daughter Kitty who, when we first took her to meet Rachel, had decided there and then that this was how she wanted to live. (She became a pupil of Rachel's, reading English at St Hugh's, but never in the end aspired to a seriously academic career.)

Usually, at parties like this, one tends to drift about, being introduced to the guest of honour, but thereafter talking mostly, and less than satisfactorily, to people one already knows well, and would prefer to be talking to at home, in peace and quiet. But this time, for some reason that I cannot now remember Iris and I fell to talking about what it had been like for both of us reading Classical Honour Mods, and this soon led us to discover that we had both been Fraenkel's girls in our own days.

Eduard Fraenkel had come to England as a refugee in 1935. He was an eminent scholar, both in Latin and Greek, and in spite of a certain amount of criticism and opposition from some of the 'old guard' of English Mods dons had been elected at the beginning of the war to the Corpus Chair of Latin. As a professor he should not normally have taught undergraduate pupils, except in lectures and classes. Iris had been taught by him, however, before his elevation, and, according to John Bayley, had been warned by her Somerville tutor Isobel Henderson (a notably 'worldly' don, who was my Roman History tutor, and was famous for having married an archaeologist who died on their honeymoon) that Fraenkel would probably 'paw her about a bit', but who sent her for tutorials none the less. I, on the other hand, was picked up by Fraenkel from the small number of those who attended his lectures on Aeschylus's *Oresteia*, which he gave three times week in a dark, poky lecture room in Corpus Christi College. He invited me up to his room, and thence up onto the roof of Corpus, which had a splendid view out over Christ Church Meadows. Another time we went into the Fellows' Gardens and sat on a wall overlooking the Meadows while he talked to me about music. This developed into an invitation to come to be taught by him after dinner in the evenings once a week on Mondays. (I soon had to change the day from Monday, because that was the day the Bach Choir used to meet; I had joined the choir in order to appease my real tutor, the aged Cyril Bailey, who, without knowing that I was being taught by Fraenkel, nevertheless thought I was becoming too earnest about the classics. This led to further trouble, because Cyril had gone back to singing in the choir himself, which he adored; and we used to have to start our tutorials by practising our parts together. He was a bass, I an alto so there was a good deal of counting of bars to be got through until our entrances came; and there was, of course, paralysing embarrassment.)

Fraenkel was appalled by my ignorance of Latin and Greek, my limited reading and poor vocabulary. He also deplored my love for the music of Brahms who he told me was a fraud, and had corrupted music from its final and high point in Beethoven's middle period. He also and increasingly, as he opened my eyes to the nature of scholarship, indulged in 'pawing about'. I was sexually innocent to a degree that is nowadays almost impossible to imagine, and at first I was disconcerted and embarrassed, even disgusted by his attentions. Then I devised a plan, though I knew it could provide only temporary relief. My school friend Imogen lived in Oxford, as I have said, and spent her vacations there. Cambridge and Oxford terms did not exactly coincide, and I had the idea that I would introduce Imogen to Fraenkel, and that he should teach us together. I did not, I fear, at first reveal to her why I thought this such a good idea.

I planned that I would stay in Oxford for much of the vacations, getting free accommodation in college in exchange for fire-watching at night, for by now I was entirely given up to the excitement of learning, not only much more about Aeschylus's *Agamemnon*, of which Fraenkel was preparing a edition of extraordinary learning and originality, but about numerous other authors, Latin and Greek, whom Fraenkel could link together in an intricate web of references and cross-references, drawing connections of which I had had no real grasp before. From schoolgirl classics teaching one had learned a little, of course, about the relation between Greek and Latin authors, Homer and Virgil for example, but now, in place of that superficiality, the details and intricacies of the connections began to become visible. I learned, too, about Greek lyric metres, and how they were translated into Latin, and, best of all, how in the early Latin playwright, Plautus, of whom I had never hitherto read a word, there were to be found not only obvious borrowings from the Greek comedians, but also relics of a much earlier kind of Latin, a Latin which used a simple stress metre, as opposed to the complex arrangement of feet in the line, dependent on the length of the vowels, which was characteristic of Greek prosody. At school (my enlightened second school, Prior's Field) I had been introduced to Helen Waddell's book, *The Wandering Scholars*, and to numbers of late Latin hymns and secular lyrics which used these same simple and strictly non-classical metres. I found it incredibly moving to discover that these hymns went back in form to the pre-Christian era of Latin that had continued in a mostly unwritten tradition, in playground songs and rhyming proverbs, for countless years, bypassing the Latin of the classics. For learning about all this, for having it presented to me, not just as a set of facts, but by means of hundreds of examples, I was prepared to sacrifice even the pleasures of going home to Winchester and riding my horse. I felt a unique excitement in these discoveries of continuity. I remember being moved to tears a few years later, when I read about some shepherds, discovered in the south of Italy, who did not speak Italian, but a kind of Latin, introducing themselves to their anthropological visitors with the words, 'Nos sumus pastores'.

Fraenkel was a great Italian scholar, and had a profound love of Italy. He could trace elements in the plays of Plautus down to the very earliest beginnings of Italian opera, and even to Mozart. It was this continuity that I loved; it made me feel that scholarship was infinite. There would always be more. Of course my plan involving Imogen did not work. Fraenkel was delighted to accept her as a pupil, but quickly discovered that we were interested in different things, and that she needed, for the sake of her Tripos examinations, to read Pindar, while I would be better employed following my new passion for early Latin, and learning more about the *Agamemnon*, one of my set books. So he continued to teach us both but on separate evenings, referring to us as his black sheep and his white (Imogen having corn-coloured hair, while mine was dark). We spent many hours over the next year discussing 'the situation' and comparing notes. There was undoubtedly an extremely comic side to the difficulties we found ourselves in. But it never struck us for a moment that there was anything we could possibly make a public fuss about; nor that Fraenkel wanted more than kisses and increasingly constant fumblings with our underclothes. In any case, we were both in the grip of a feeling that war threatened classical studies, or at least ours, and that we must get as much as we could, at whatever cost.

However, in the end it all unhappily came to light. Fraenkel picked up another girl from Lady Margaret Hall, who was extremely pretty, and wore a scholar's gown (a necessary condition for his interest), but who was neither particularly interested in classical studies, nor anything like as naive as I was. She briskly said 'no thanks' to his advances, and that anyway her fiancé would not like it; and then revealed what had happened to her tutor. I, as may be imagined, came out of it in a very bad light, when directly asked what had been going on over the last year or so. Imogen in any case took her Tripos examination (with a First) and went back to Newnham to embark on research. I, made to feel inexpressibly wicked by my Bach-singing Balliol tutor, saw no more of Fraenkel. I learned much later that he was only briefly deprived of his girls. In talking, in the 1980s, to a famous and remarkably beautiful soprano, who had got a First in Greats at Somerville before becoming a singer, and who had come to Girton to give a lecture-recital, I discovered over dinner that she had been one of Fraenkel's girls, and she was at least twenty years my junior.

I deeply missed Fraenkel's teaching (though I had only a term to go, before I was to take Mods), but what appalled me was that I had never, after the beginning, seriously minded his advances. They came to seem part of the extraordinary excitement of the world into which he was introducing me. One was always on tenterhooks, one way or another, in Fraenkel's presence. For example, I used to go to a class he gave on Aristophanes's *Birds*, attended by only one or two other undergraduates, and otherwise by senior Classics Fellows of the University, and one very old modern historian from Corpus, R.C.K. Ensor, who, being a Wykehamist, was revered by Fraenkel. (He had been deeply moved, he told me, to have been taken to visit Winchester College once in the summer term, soon after he came to England, where he found boys sitting out in their gowns in Meads, composing Greek verses.) Ensor was properly thought of as an honorary classicist, and on the last day of the class he recited from memory a major part of Euripides's *Hippolytus*, a trick he had learned at school.

This class was an agony to me because, though I marvelled, as usual, at the scholarship Fraenkel displayed, I was embarrassed when he sometimes quite sharply ticked off some of the elderly dons present for their crass ignorance, and, worse, I lived in terror of his making me read choruses aloud to show off my newly acquired understanding of Greek lyric metres. My performances never came up to his expectations, and I was sure that everyone must know, or guess, how I had come to know anything about the matter. There was also the constant terror of making mistakes in translation. Iris had been to a similar class, this time on the *Agamemnon*, where Fraenkel had tried out his interpretations on those present, before incorporating them in his great edition. After our Fraenkel conversation, she sent me a copy of a poem she had written and dedicated to the memory of Frank Thompson. It had been published in the *Boston University Journal*, and was entitled 'Agamemnon Class, 1939'. It contained the lines

> In that pellucid unforgiving air
> The aftermath experienced before,
> Focused by dread into a lurid flicker,
> A most uncanny composite of sun and rain,
> Did we expect the war? What did we fear,
> First love's incinerating crippling flame,
> Or that it would appear
> In public that we could not name
> The aorist of some familiar verb.

When I read these lines, the whole sinister atmosphere, the flickers of dark and light, both real and metaphorical, the different dreads merging into each other came over me again, and I gratefully wrote to tell her so.

Imogen, I knew, did not altogether share my feelings about Fraenkel. She found his behaviour, though comic, genuinely disgusting, and she told me recently that she thought it had had a lasting and bad effect on her attitude to sex, which I deeply hope was not true. At any rate, when Iris and I started talking about him at Rachel's party, nearly thirty years later, we discovered that we both felt exactly the same. In one way, the impropriety of his sexual behaviour seemed utterly trivial compared with the riches he offered us, and the vast horizons he opened up. In another way, the conjunction of the physical with the intellectual seemed the most natural thing in the world, a conjunction of mind and body which it would have been silly and ungrateful to attempt to disjoin, and which indeed may have shown a glimpse, however faint and indeed absurd, of some sort of ideal for both of us. In his *Iris*: *A Memoir of Iris Murdoch* (Duckworth, 1998, p. 49), John Bayley explains how this was: 'She had already told me how fond she had been of Fraenkel, both fond and reverential. In those day there had seemed to her nothing odd or alarming when he caressed her affectionately as they sat side by side over a text, sometimes half an hour over the exact interpretation of a word, sounding its associations in the Greek world as he explored them, as lovingly keen on them as he seemed to be on her. That there was anything dangerous or degrading in his behaviour, which would nowadays constitute a shocking example of sexual harassment, never occurred to her.'

I was less totally accepting than Iris, that is to say more conventional, no doubt, at least at the beginning. I also had a confidante with whom to compare experiences. But fundamentally our attitudes were not different; and it was, even so long a time later, a relief and a pleasure to talk about it. Geoffrey, of course, knew all about Fraenkel, but as a joke, a kind of comic saga from an era of my life of which he knew little, and in which perhaps he was not particularly interested, like my life at school. Iris and I doubtless behaved badly at Rachel's party. I certainly did not talk to anyone else, and I never talked to her so analytically and so seriously again. John Bayley was not quite right, incidentally, when he suggested, after the passage I have just quoted, that Fraenkel's family did not suffer from his predilections. Much later I was asked to write a short piece for a Sunday paper about the best teacher I ever had, and I chose to write about Fraenkel, emphasising especially the great power he had to excite one's imagination with the feeling I have mentioned (and about which Iris agreed), of the infinite horizons of the world of scholarship. But I thought I would be less than honest if I did not refer, briefly, to the price that had to be paid. I had a letter from his elder son, a medical professor in Australia, who had been shown the piece by his younger brother, also a professor but in England: he said that he was glad I had mentioned it, and how his mother did not at all like his father's predilections, even though she knew he was never 'unfaithful in the vulgar sense'. She had had to put up with a good deal of Oxford gossip about his father. Fraenkel, I learned, had not been kind to them as children, unable to bear it if they made mistakes in Latin and Greek, and meting out what seemed to them terrible punishments if they did not come top in both subjects at school. He knew, he said, that his father had been an inspirational teacher, and was proud of that, and pleased that I had written about him. But it seemed that he could not altogether forgive him. Even if Fraenkel did wrong by us, and indeed by his wife, I cannot think that anything would have been improved if Iris or I or any other of Fraenkel's numerous girls had indulged in displays of self-important feminism, or otherwise brought our education with him to an end.

Other conversations I had with Iris on social occasions, though friendly, were not memorable, John on the whole making more impression on me than Iris, who was often silent. John, on the other hand, has the great gift, a gift that his tutor and great friend David Cecil also had in generous measure, of making one feel not only interesting, but the person he found most interesting in the whole of the assembled company. Therefore it could not be anything but a pleasure to talk to him. There was one somewhat bizarre example of this charm that I remember. It must have been in the mid-1970s. We had some American academics to stay, perhaps for one or other of them to get some kind of honour from the university. We asked them, before they arrived, who they would like to meet in Oxford. They named various people, to whom they were introduced over lunch, but they had put Iris and John at the top of their list, and so we decided to have them to supper, so that they, the Americans, could talk to them properly. We had just settled to our drinks before dinner when our middle daughter, Fanny (whom Geoffrey used, perhaps unkindly, to call 'Goosey', after a village near which we at that time owned a cottage), came in unexpectedly. She was then a student at the Guildhall School of Music, and had come down to play in a concert the next day. I asked her how she planned to spend her weekend, and she said, 'Well first, of course, I must catch up on *The Archers*. (There was a kind of weekly round-up of the daily programmes of this radio saga every Sunday morning.)

At this both John and Iris looked keenly interested, and John immediately started to talk to Fanny about what had been happening in the story in the last few weeks. Iris struggled for a short time to talk to the Americans, but Fanny had by now settled at John's feet with her drink, eagerly discussing the various char-

1. Mary Warnock.

2. Stephana and Mary, Winchester 1926.

3. Lady Margaret Hall, Oxford, Freshmen 1942. Mary Warnock in the centre, Rachel Trickett centre first left, Elizabeth de Gaulle second row far right, Nancy Pym seventh row middle.

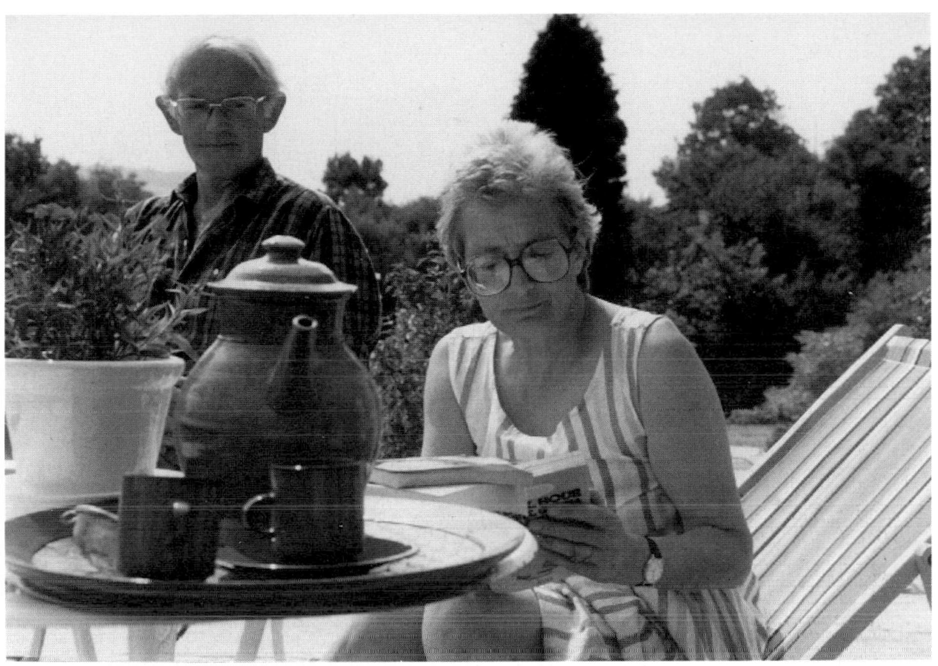

4. Geoffrey and Mary Warnock in the garden in Wiltshire, 1993.

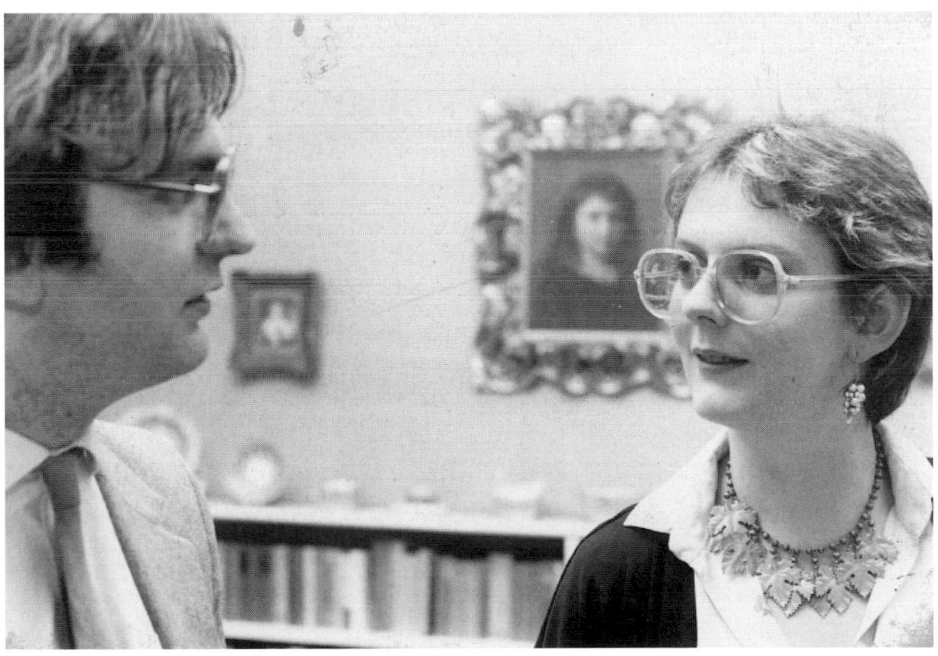

5. James Warnock, Fanny Warnock (Branson) in the drawing room at Hertford Lodgings, with a portrait of Mither as a child in the background.

6. Imogen Rose (Wrong).

7. Dick Southern and Geoffrey Warnock.

8. 'The Club', Oxford. From the top: Lord Jenkins, Lord Blake, Angus McIntyre, Bill Williams (former Warden of Rhodes House), John Sparrow (former Warden of All Souls), Geoffrey Warnock, David Pears, Patrick Gardiner, Raymond Carr, Peter Strawson.

9. Geoffrey Warnock as drawn by David Hockney. Described by G.J.W. himself as 'Looking like Faldo when he has just missed a putt'.

10. Geoffrey Warnock, Isaiah Berlin and Peter Strawson at the 'portrait party' of the drawing of Geoffrey Warnock by David Hockney.

11. Harold Macmillan, Visitor of Hertford and Chancellor of Oxford University, at the opening of the new quadrangle (1985).

12. Elizabeth Anscombe, Professor of Philosophy in the University of Cambridge, by John O'Connor

13. Philippa Foot, Fellow of Somerville College, Oxford

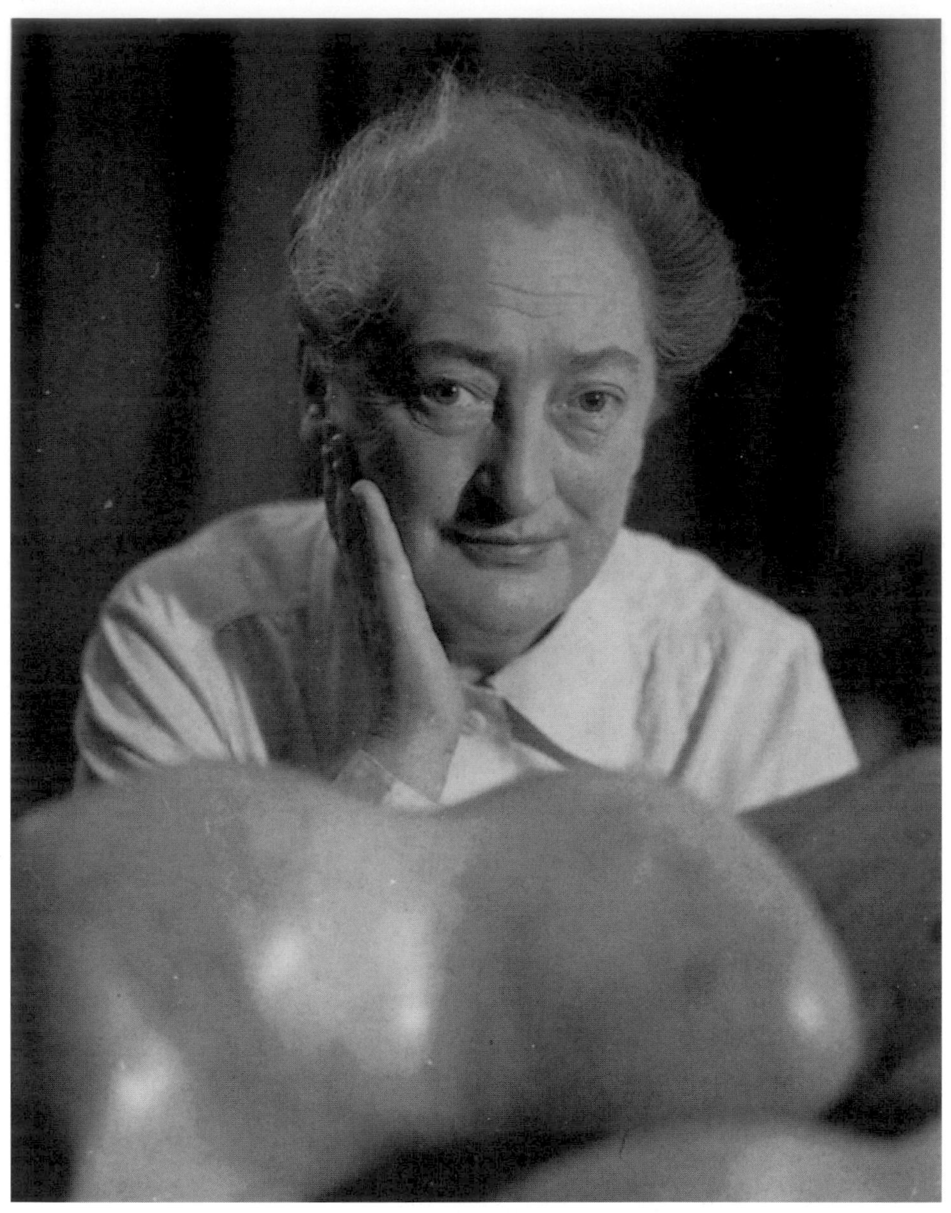

14. Rachel Trickett, Principal of St Hugh's College, Oxford.

15. Rachel Trickett and Peter Strawson at Hertford Lodgings, 1979.

16. Iris Murdoch at Cedar Lodge, 1959.

17. Margaret Thatcher.

18. Mary Warnock photographed by her daughter. The portrait now hangs in the Oxford High School.

19. Peter Shore, MP, canvassing in his constituency.

20. Sir Duncan Wilson (brother), at home in Islay.

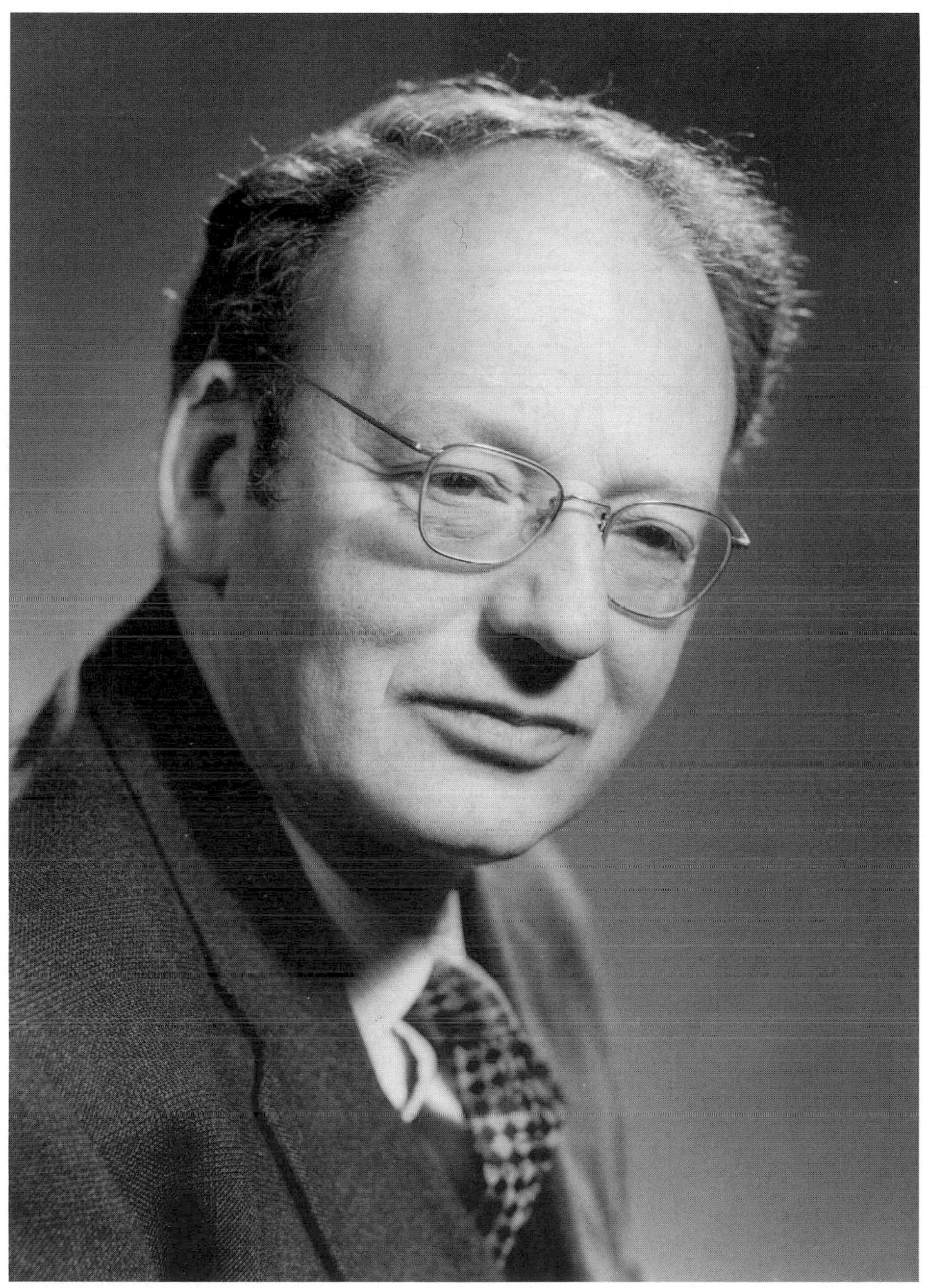

21. Sir Duncan Wilson, Master of Corpus Christi College, Cambridge.

22. Mary Warnock in the garden in Wiltshire.

acters, which one had had her baby, which was suffering from infertility problems, whether another would be able to hold down his job. Iris fell silent. The Americans were astonished. They had no idea that what was being discussed was a soap opera. At last I got Fanny away to get herself some supper and ring up her friends, and we went next door to have dinner. The conversation at dinner was all right, but not sparkling. It certainly contained no memorable aperçus on the English novel, as the Americans might have hoped. After dinner Fanny was back, having made coffee for us, and immediately she and John started again. Finally, catching my despairing looks, and realising that Geoffrey had a real problem on his hands, Iris being far more interested in *The Archers* than in our American guests, Fanny took herself off. Iris was not, I think, an easy, or a particularly energetic conversationalist, unless something or someone caught her fancy. John had mischievously little sense of duty in such matters, it seemed to me, though Fanny was, of course, enraptured.

Iris's knowledge and love of Greek, her willingness to try to understand what Aeschylus's words actually meant, and had meant at the time they were written, all of which she had learned from Fraenkel, led later to a deep love of Plato. This was a more than accidental connection. Those of us who had been taught by some of the most brilliant refugee scholars during the war had learned, among other things, a respect for Greek authors, poets, historians and philosophers, as they existed on their own, separate, alien and original, not merely as precursors of the European enlightenment, their words having connotations perhaps different from the English words traditionally used to translate them. Coleridge divided all philosophers into two natural categories, Platonists and Aristotelians. (Gilbert Ryle later divided them all into dogs and cats.) The division, though doubtless simplistic like all dichotomies, was nowhere more manifest than in the sphere of moral philosophy. Aristotle, as much a scientist as a philosopher, treating human life as a part of all animal life, sought to find what was the best form of life for human animals, producing the best specimens of the species. Plato, on the contrary, interested in science only in so far as cosmology and mathematics were sciences, had no vision of biological species as a whole, but concentrated, instead, on where the human concept of good came from, and how it was to influence human life.

Iris was a thoroughgoing Platonist. In *The Sovereignty of Good* (1970), *The Fire and the Sun* (1977) and finally in *Metaphysics as a Guide to Morals* (1992) she showed a sympathy with, even a hankering for, an Idea of the Good, which should be the goal of human aspiration, and a substitute for the no longer credible concept of a personal God. This Idea was to be, as it was in some of Plato's dialogues, the object both of intellectual contemplation and of ineffable love. It was the intellectual purity of the search for a vision of this idea, and the desire to protect this purity, that led Plato to attempt to exclude artists, as seducers and false comforters, both from the ideal state in the *Republic* and from the yet more dictatorial and closely regulated state envisaged in the *Laws*. Iris took this attempt seriously, and understood its motive. She longed to be able to found moral philosophy on some infallible intuition of the good. In her virtually unreadable final philosophical work, *Metaphysics as a Guide to Morals* (Chatto and Windus, 1992) she writes at the end, with sympathy, about Paul Tillich. Almost her last sentence is: 'We need a theology which can continue without God. Why not call such a reflection a form of moral philosophy? All right, so long as it treats of those matters of "ultimate concern" [Tillich's expression], our experience of the unconditioned and our continued sense of what is holy.' Such a moral philosophy was what she hoped to find in Plato, but she realised the dangers. Earlier in the same book (p. 512) she wrote:

'In my own case I am aware of the danger of inventing my own Plato and extracting a particular pattern from his many-patterned text to reassure myself that, as I see it, good is really good, and real is real. I have been wanting to use Plato's images as a sort of Ontological Proof of the necessity of Good, or rather ... to put his argument into a modern context, as a background to moral philosophy, as a bridge between morals and religion, and as relevant to our new disturbed understanding of religious truth.' There was no doubt that this was, by then, what she deeply wanted.

This book was a version of the Gifford Lectures, a series she had delivered ten years earlier. I know from the same experience how exceedingly difficult it is to turn what was acceptable, even reasonably impressive, as a series of lectures into something that will do as a book. Neither she in her case, nor I in mine, managed this very well. (See Warnock, *Imagination and Time*, 1994). In an interview with Bryan Appleyard, published in *The Times Saturday Review*, October 3rd 1992, she said 'It's very chaotic, I'm afraid. It's difficult to write a long book based on lectures ... bits and pieces, jumping from one bit to another. I'd hoped to weave everything together, but I haven't succeeded.' Appleyard makes a valiant attempt to understand, and ends by praising her for 'trying to make the whole culture stop in its tracks and think again, to pick up the still unbroken thread of truth that runs from Plato to now, to rise up from the rubble.' Iris must have liked this.

In the same year, Bernard Williams, then White's Professor of Moral Philosophy in Oxford, and I, recently returned from Cambridge, were invited by the BBC to present separate reviews of Iris's book, which would then be replied to by Iris. We consulted anxiously about what on earth we were going to say about the book, which seemed little but an end-on string of quotations, and we finally worked out how to carve up the material between us. We were to record our pieces separately. When I delivered my broadcast, there was some kind of crisis at the BBC. I was seated in a passageway rather than a studio, and there were constant interruptions as people tramped to and fro. Although I had more or less prepared a script, I have never been left with such a feeling of disastrous confusion as when I came away. A date was fixed for the whole programme to be broadcast, about ten days ahead; but after a few days, I had a letter saying that it had been cancelled as 'Iris had not been at her best' in replying to Bernard and me. I felt enormous relief. I assumed that she had been drunk, such an ominous phrase seeming to suggest such a disaster, but I have since wondered whether this was an early sign of her approaching confusion, or whether, equally likely, she simply found our contributions hopelessly inadequate. Whichever explanation was true, I have been left with a permanent sense of guilt with regard to this book.

For, as a topic, the relation between metaphysics and morals has always fascinated me. I have loved Plato (though being, if anything, more of an Aristotelian by temperament, and having become more deeply admiring of Aristotle, the more I have learned about his biological theories and his moral philosophy); I love both Spinoza and Kant, for both of whom morality is firmly grounded in a theory of the nature of the universe as a whole and man's place in it and understanding of it. And I became interested in the early philosophy of Jean-Paul Sartre, in which the same connection is central. But I did not find that Iris's book lived up to its title, though the fault was certainly at least partly mine.

Sartre, or rather his early work, was to have and retain a central influence not only on Iris's philosophical interests, but on her whole outlook on the world, or so it seems to me. It is difficult to describe accurately the early introduction of Existentialism, and particularly of the philosophy of Sartre, to the English-speaking world in its historical context, but it is perhaps worth recalling it, at least as it affected myself, and as I believe it affected Iris (though she knew of Sartre's philosophy much earlier than I did and at first hand).

There was deep hostility to the very idea of 'continental philosophy' in Oxford and Cambridge in the 1950s. It was regarded as an uneasy mixture of philosophy and belles-lettres, wordy, vague, deliberately obscure, and far from properly academic. Existentialists were not thought of as a philosophical school but as a social or political group, meeting in cafés, wearing black polo-necked sweaters, drinking wine and smoking Gauloises, a kind of hangover from the Paris resistance movement of the war years. Freddy Ayer was the only person (apart from Iris) who was credited with any knowledge of their philosophy; and I remember a peculiarly dismissive talk he gave in the Oxford Playhouse, to introduce a translated version of *Huis Clos* that was being staged there. (Freddy, with his French mother, was held to have rights in the matter of French intellectual life; but his style of philosophy could hardly have been more remote from that of Sartre.) There was one university in the USA, Yale, where there was expertise on continental philosophy, both French and German, but otherwise it simply did not translate into English, and most Americans were busy educating themselves in the kind of philosophy that was being pursued in Oxford.

It was thus an act of genuine imagination and originality for Iris to have published, as her first book, a slim volume in tiny print (almost wartime 'austerity' in format), entitled *Sartre: Romantic Rationalist* (Bowes and Bowes, 1953). The book was mostly concerned with Sartre as a playwright and novelist, but in order to make his literary work intelligible, Iris had to include a dense chapter of exposition of the philosophical position adopted in *L'Être et le Néant*, which she, probably uniquely among Oxford philosophers, had read soon after it was published in France, in 1943. It did not appear in English until more than ten years later (*Being and Nothingness* translated by Hazel Barnes, 1957).

I had reason to be very grateful to Iris and this book in the year 1959. I had been commissioned by the Oxford University Press to write a short book on the history of ethics since 1900, as part of the Home University Library series. When I had written quite a lot of the book, J.L. Austin, of whom I stood in great awe, and who was a Delegate of the Press, rang me up to say that he thought I ought to include in it a chapter on Existentialism, and in particular on J-P Sartre, since this would distinguish the book from other contemporary books on ethics. I had not read a word of Sartre, but recognised that I must get down to *Being and Nothingness* during the Long Vacation, just about to begin. Iris's philosophical chapter was eye-opening for me, and it served as an indispensable and saving thread to guide me through the labyrinth of what seemed at first the impenetrable prose that I had to make sense of, in a busy Long Vacation. I should not have managed without it.

In any case, apart from the use I ruthlessly put it to, this first of Iris's books is both an extremely good book, and illuminating in a far more general way, throwing light not only on Existentialist thinking but on Iris herself, as I believe. It was, for one thing, an attempt to bring together literature and philosophy, a marriage which was often held, later, to be her own hallmark, and which Sartre had managed to make fruitful. What is often thought to be the central concept of Existentialism is its insistence on the freedom of human beings to decide for themselves whatever they choose. And in acting on these decisions, they build up their own nature. There is no such thing as a generalised human nature. Nor are people's choices determined by their history (Sartre was especially hostile to the Freudian theory that what has happened to us in the past dictates the rest of our lives at a deep and often unfathomable level). Nor did he believe that people are determined even by their circumstances, in that how one responds to and understands those circumstances is itself a matter of choice.

It is easy to see that such a theory of human life is, intrinsically, theatrical. In a lecture given in America in 1946, Sartre defended Anouilh's *Antigone* against charges of lack of a deep representation of character in the figure of Antigone herself. He agreed that, in the ordinary sense, she was not a character. 'She represents a naked will, a pure free choice; in her there is no distinguishing between passion and action ... Man is a free being entirely indeterminate, who must choose his own being when confronted with certain necessities' (see David Bradby, 'Sartre as Dramatist' in *Sartre: a collection of critical essays* edited Warnock, Doubleday, 1971). All his plays illustrate such choices. As for morality, this too is a matter of choice. People are afraid of the infinity of their freedom to do whatever they like with their lives, and so they pretend to themselves that they are bound by unavoidable duties, or by the moral law, to choose one thing rather than another. But this is 'bad faith', or 'the spirit of seriousness'. There is no such binding moral law. A human being stands completely alone, and is by himself responsible for his actions. In this way, each one of us is a romantic hero. Recognising this essential isolation is a proof of 'authentic existence'; and if there is any room for virtue, in Sartre's theory, authenticity or sincerity, the absence of bad faith is the only one.

Now Iris rejected such a moral philosophy entirely. In *The Sovereignty of Good* she classed together as Existentialist all moral philosophy that concentrated exclusively on the will, on freedom, and on decision-making, including the moral philosophy of Kant, and in our own time of Hare, Hampshire and Sartre. She regarded them as narrowing the world of morality to actions, stemming from the 'needle-thin' will, forgetting the inner life of the individual, his private thoughts, emotions and powers of attending to the world and other people in the world, in a moral (or indeed an aesthetic) mode; that is of seeking the good, by means of an inner concept of perfection. In this, she was a follower of Plato rather than of Sartre. But, unlike Plato, she held that by attending to particular things or people in the world, and concentrating on them, 'really seeing' them (a favourite expression of hers, which I fear Geoffrey and I used to ridicule), we could discover their true nature, and refine and improve both our understanding and our love of them. Her memorable example in *The Sovereignty of Good* is of a mother-in-law who attends to the characteristics of her daughter-in-law, whom she has been inclined to write off as vulgar, noisy and impertinent, so that she begins to be able to see her as spontaneous, good-natured and friendly. Such a development of sentiment by properly attending to an object has little to do with decisive action, and may indeed have no perceptible effect on what the mother-in-law actually does; but it is, nevertheless, a moral development, both of understanding and of love.

But though Iris rejected the Existentialist philosophy of pure choice, at a different level she understood and, I think, was profoundly affected by the view of the world within which Sartre placed his bleak moral theory. The world, according to Sartre, consists of two kinds of entity, Beings-in-themselves and Beings-for-themselves, or things endowed with consciousness (there is also another mode of being, Being-for-others; but this does not constitute another natural kind). Conscious beings are also essentially physical objects in the world, but with the added characteristic that they are conscious both of other things in the world, and also and always of their own physical existence. Consciousness consists in the ability to raise questions about the world; to be, that is to say, at a sufficient distance from the world to be prepared for an answer to a question that is either affirmative or negative. If I am asked what colour something is, I may say 'yellow', but I could also say 'not pink', 'not blue' and so on. This is the same as to say that conscious beings are capable of imagining possibilities and of imagining things as they are not, as well as seeing them as they are. This, in turn, implies that conscious beings are able to conceive both of past and future; things which are not present at the moment. It is out of this ability that the freedom of such beings arises. They can envisage, imagine and create, by deliberate 'projection' or choice, a future which is their own.

It was part of Sartre's inheritance from the German phenomenologists, and especially from Husserl, that he thought the task of philosophy to be a description of what it is like for a conscious being to perceive and exist among those objects in the world from which he is perpetually separated by the space and distance created by his own imaginative consciousness. The existence in the world of a particular thing, in particular circumstances, whether as a conscious or an unconscious thing, is referred to by Sartre as 'facticity'. Things without consciousness are capable of being wholly known, their behaviour in principle predictable, since, having no consciousness, they have no freedom. For a conscious being, the contemplation of these predictable objects is a matter not merely of awareness or knowledge, but of certain inevitable attitudes or emotions. For one thing, conscious beings are afraid of their own limitless freedom, and therefore, through bad faith, prone to pretend, as I have said, that they too are determined, compelled by, for example, the nature of their past, or by the moral law, to act in one and only one way. They therefore, in one sense, envy the 'massif', the undivided, the solidly predictable objects around them, nothing except what they are, bound to behave as they do; and they show their envy by pretending to be one of them. An artefact, made for a specific purpose, will inevitably fulfil that purpose which is its destiny.

Sartre supposes that to understand this, and to understand the nature of a conscious being's attitude to things in the world, it is necessary to concentrate attention on the particular, to see how each particular object is nothing but the thing it is. Simone de Beauvoir records how Sartre, when quite a young man, met someone at a café, who, looking at a bottle on the table between them, said that what he wanted was a philosophy of things. Sartre felt immediate sympathy with this desire. To understand the truth about the world we must keep our eyes on one concrete object at a time. And we must not be seduced into thinking that objects enter into our minds through the medium of ideas or impressions, swallowed up in our own inner world. When Sartre came back from a visit to Germany in 1939, where he had encountered for the first time the philosophy of the phenomenologist, Husserl, he wrote an article proclaiming with high excitement the revolution in philosophy that he had discovered. (The original article was translated by Joseph P. Fell and printed in the *Journal of the British Society of Phenomenology* vol. no. 2, May 1970.) He wrote: 'Husserl persistently affirms that one cannot dissolve things into consciousness. You see this tree to be sure. But you see it just where it is; at the side of the road in the midst of dust, alone and writhing in the heat, eight miles from the Mediterranean coast. It could not enter your consciousness'. And he went on to explain that our contact with the world, according to Husserl, was allowed to be more than bare consciousness. 'Our consciousness of things is by no means limited to knowledge of them. Knowledge or "pure representation" is only one of the possible forms of my consciousness of this tree. I can also love it, hate it, fear it … so it is that all at once hatred, love, fear – all these famous "subjective" reactions which were floating in the malodorous brine of the mind – are pulled out. They are merely ways of discovering the world. It is things which abruptly reveal themselves to us as hateful, sympathetic, horrible, loveable. Husserl has restored things to their horror and their charm. He has restored to us the world of artists and prophets; frightening, hostile, dangerous, with its havens of mercy and love.' If this is not the origin of Iris's 'attention', then it is certainly very close to it.

Sartre also held that, though we may sometimes feel a kind of longing to be ourselves, nothing but things, absolved from the responsibility of freedom, there are also features of the world of things that we necessarily and instinctively fear and loathe, by which we are terrified of being swallowed up. Besides being hard-edged and predictable, the subject matter of the exact sciences, things may have at their centre a kind of sticky viscosity which threatens us, because we cannot control it. His image for this in *Being and Nothingness* is that of the honey which slides off my spoon into the honey pot, and slowly sculpts itself onto the surface of the honey in the pot and then fuses into it. The horror of the viscous is that it is soft, 'The viscous is docile. Only at the very moment when I believe that I possess it, behold, by a curious reversal, it possesses me'.

The most explicit account of such a discovery of the nature of things, a discovery that arises out of 'really looking' at them, is contained towards the end of one of Sartre's novels, *Nausea*, published in 1938. Here the hero, Roquentin, keeps a diary, and in it records how, sitting in a park, gazing at the roots of a horse chestnut tree, he discovered what existence was. Existence had lost 'the inoffensive look of an empty category; it was the very stuff of things'. And there was too much of it. It was pointless and superfluous. It was absurd. What made him see this was the black twisted impenetrable convolutions of the roots of the tree. Looking at them reduced everything else in his field of vision to the status of 'stage-scenery'. For Iris, this vision would show how close the aesthetic is to the moral. A painter could have produced a picture of these roots which could convey their blackness and their superfluity, the sinister nature of existence itself. The roots were more than a symbol; they spoke directly of the nature of things.

In a conversation with Bryan Magee, shown on television in 1978, and later published in *Men of Ideas* (BBC, 1978), Iris distinguished between philosophical novels and novels of ideas, and said that Sartre's *Nausea* was the only good philosophical novel she knew. And she went on to say that Sartre's early philosophy made him into a special case, in the sense that there was something novelistic about *Being and Nothingness* itself. It was full of 'pictures and conversations'. She said that for herself she had a horror of putting 'theories or philosophical ideas as such' into her own novels. Nevertheless, on rereading some of her novels recently, I was struck by her deep awareness of, almost obsession with, the recalcitrant 'thinginess' of things, things in themselves, solid, massif and accurately described only by one who really attends to them. There is the Riley slowly sinking into the river, the extreme heavy angularity of the filing cabinet that, it is wrongly thought, has to be carried downstairs, and of course there is the bell. When I first read the novels, these descriptions bothered me. I wondered in each case (and there are numerous such descriptions, as every reader of the novels will know) whether I was supposed to understand them as somehow symbolic, as meaning something other than themselves. But now I do not think so. I think they are what they seem, the results of intense imaginative attention; and what emerges, if it is in any way especially significant, is, like Sartre's honey sliding off the spoon, significant only of how the physical world, the world of things, actually is. There is, as Sartre well understood, a number of natural symbols in the world; things that are of their very nature understood in a particular way; things that are, therefore, naturally and immediately felt as significant, such as, for example, water. To this extent, I suppose my first reaction to the scenes in the novels was not altogether surprising; but, more important, I think they tell us something about Iris herself, that is about the way she engaged with the world through what one might call the concrete imagination.

In the conversation with Magee from which I have already quoted, and indeed in *The Sovereignty of Good*, Iris distinguished between what she referred to as fantasy and imagination. The former was the pursuit of personal fantasies, of power or of sexual prowess, or of worldly success, which, when written in the form of a story, were nothing but self-indulgence. Imagination, on the other hand, whatever its medium, was the pursuit of truth. This distinction was different from the famous distinction that Coleridge drew between imagination and fancy: what he was contrasting was the genuine originality and creative force of imagination with the putting together of ready-made images, material out of the stock, as it were, in however elaborate or elegant a form, which constituted fancy. Yet in other ways there seem to me to be strong analogies between Iris and Coleridge. I am not here talking about influence, but simply about similarity. This is different from the comparison with Sartre who, I have suggested, probably was an influence, however much they disagreed about the nature of the moral.

Iris constantly said (for example in the conversation with Magee) that philosophy was very difficult, and that therefore the aim of a philosopher must be to write in a plain style and make things absolutely clear, one by one. This is not, in fact, how her philosophical style most strikes the reader. I once discussed *The Sovereignty of Good* with Frances Partridge, who read Moral Sciences at Cambridge, and who, then aged ninety eight, took a keen interest in philosophy. I said I liked and enjoyed the book but she would have none of it. There were too few arguments, too much 'yearning' for her taste. (After that conversation, I lent her J.L. Austin's *Sense and Sensibilia*, because she said she wanted a funny philosophy book to take with her on her holiday to Italy. That was much more of a success; she said it had made her laugh aloud. I might have given her *The Concept of Mind*.) It is true, I think, that there are not many more arguments in Iris's philosophy than there are jokes. What there is is passion. Nor would she have claimed, I think, to be an original thinker. Her tremendous gift was for interpreting a philosopher with whom she had sympathy, whose way of doing the subject she loved.

In some ways she was a magpie, flying over a wide field, picking up what caught her eye and making it her own. The same was true of Coleridge; he was subject to crazes, more so than Iris, who was faithful to Plato for all her philosophical career. Yet she too was overwhelmed with enthusiasm for Sartre when she first encountered him and his philosophy in Paris before the end of the war, and was doubtless, as we all were, bowled over by Wittgenstein's later work, when we all first came to set eyes on it. Coleridge, too, like Sartre and Iris, combined serious, if largely interpretative, philosophy with literature. But far more important than these shared characteristics was the common nature of their imagination, this concrete imagination to which I have referred. For Coleridge, more than for any writer, things in the world were to be seen, 'really looked at', for what they revealed of the nature of the world itself. In his detailed observations of things, his imagination, the faculty, if I may put it in such old-fashioned terms, which enables one to see more than at first meets the casual eye, was at its highest level. His notebooks and his letters show this again and again. On his travels he used to make the most minute observations of what he saw, including man-made objects, clocks, ships, anything that intrigued him so greatly that he wanted to be able to understand how it worked.

Iris, in her desire to find a concept of good that would replace God, wanted a way of perceiving a platonic universal in a particular. This, precisely, was what Coleridge wanted. In a notebook entry dated December 1804 he wrote '"O" said I, as I looked on the blue, yellow, green and purple-green sea with all its hollows and swells and cut-glass surfaces "O what an ocean of lovely forms" – and I was vexed, teased, that the sentence sounded like a play of words. But it was not; the mind within me was struggling to express the marvellous distinctness and unconfounded personality of each of the million million of forms, and yet the undivided unity in which they subsisted.' Iris said of herself that she was a natural seeker after unity. For Coleridge the function of imagination was to enable us to see individual forms of things as universally significant, to enable us to see objects in the world as of more than particular significance, and by the same process, to feel love for them. This was, I believe, the significance of the story in *The Sovereignty of Good* of the virtuous mother-in-law, looking again and more intently at her easily despised daughter-in-law. You can see the universal Good, and aspire to it by means of 'really seeing' the particular.

As a philosopher, this was the nature of Iris's imagination. And this is the reason for my likening her to Coleridge, different as they were in almost every other way. In her novels there is certainly a concentration, among other things, on the exact description of material particular things in the world, and a sense, as I have said, of the impenetrability and dense ineluctable nature of things in the external world. But I have not yet managed, as I never managed when I knew her, to bridge the gap, or rather make the connections between her philosophical imagination and that peculiar to her novels, such of them as I have read. Someone may one day enlighten me. But I think it was the presence of this mysterious gap which I could not fill that made me incapable of knowing Iris well. I found her an amiable but totally mysterious object in the world. One of Sartre's proofs that other people really exist was the experience he recounted of seeing a man sitting on a bench in a park, reading his book. There he was, a physical object among others. But you could not see him as that alone: the fact that he was reading, and you neither knew what he was reading, nor how he was reacting to whatever was on the page compelled you to recognise that here was a sentient, intelligent being with a view of his own, who saw the park itself from a different point of view from yours, and who was at this moment experiencing an inner life that was unavailable to you. He had a form that you could see; but beyond that, you could see nothing. It was perhaps the idea of Iris as a physical object, very much in the world, among the tables and chairs and mountains and rivers, among the *Archers* on the radio and the amazing clutter in the kitchen, but with a life of the imagination that was entirely her own that made her a mysterious and somewhat daunting figure, to me at least.

Rachel Trickett
Novelist, Teacher, Principal of St Hugh's College, Oxford

I learned of Rachel Trickett's death only a day or two after I had written to arrange a time to visit her to talk about the chapter which, as she knew, I was planning to write about her. We were, I think, both looking forward to talking about it. I had known that she was ill, but thought her better, and I was quite unprepared for her death. I bitterly regretted that I had seen so little of her in the previous few years. As I write this, I have just come away from the British Library, where I have been listening to the tapes of some broadcasts she gave in 1990, entitled *A Life Dense with Promise*, about her parents, and her own childhood. Sadly, only the first two (of six) are preserved in the National Sound Archive, but listening to them was an astonishingly moving experience. They are not just chat, but elaborately and carefully composed, read aloud quite slowly in her full and subtly expressive voice, which had made her a powerful speaker, commanding attention whether she was delivering a sermon in Chapel, making an after-dinner speech (at which she was masterly), or simply engaging in conversation. My eldest daughter, Kitty, who was Rachel's pupil at St Hugh's, especially remembers her voice, which she describes as 'vibrant'. For me, it is her voice in conversation that is most missed.

Rachel had intended the memoir of her parents for publication. I do not know what became of this project, whether she decided against it herself or whether it was rejected by publishers. As radio, it was extraordinarily successful. At any rate, in the late 1970s, she rented a cottage in Savernake Forest for part of the Long Vacation (she was then Principal of St Hugh's) from a friend of mine. It was a tiny cottage, with two small bedrooms upstairs, a sitting room, bathroom and kitchen downstairs, and a lovely garden mostly taken up by a huge apple tree. There she stayed, for more than two months, with her dog and her faithful maid, Kathleen, contentedly writing about her parents. It was a situation characteristic of her life. She felt no embarrassment, as I should have, in being enclosed in this restricted space with someone with whom in one sense she was intimate, but whom in another sense she did not regard as an equal, and who waited on her in a way unimaginable to most of us, accustomed to shopping, cooking, cleaning and looking after our children ourselves. She had friends not far away, and she visited them, or invited them to visit her, but not too often. She drove round the country, and exercised the dog, though on mild and unadventurous walks. (Isaiah Berlin once said 'The class of country walks with Berlin is the Null Class.' The same could be said of Rachel.) Rachel and I recognised this difference between us. I loved walking and riding, and often felt an absurd urge to lie down on the grass, scale the mountains, climb the trees or the rocks, become physically part of the country and its textures and smells. She did not feel this primitive and often ludicrous impulse. For her the country was landscape, a purely visual pleasure. Yet she loved the country, and on this occasion fell in love with the Forest.

She was enchanted by the thought of the absent family of her landlord. One day, one of his sons, then a schoolboy, called at the cottage to fetch a tennis racket or a pair of shoes he had left there. He charmed her by saying that she must come with him to see the church where he went to pray (he did not remain so godly), a huge Victorian church, built in an opening in the Forest, an extraordinary building, reminiscent of Girton or Keble, suddenly visible only from close quarters, St Katherine's, Savernake. Rachel disliked the building, partly because she was expecting to be led to a little barn-like church, but was pleased by the paradoxical nature of the whole occasion, not least by the tall, fair-haired athletic boy leading her, whom he had never met before, on this pious visit. It was the kind of novelistic scene of which her life was made up. Later, I took her to visit these friends when they had bought two adjoining cottages, and turned the three into a splendid house, now with vast well-landscaped gardens. She could not bear it. In her eyes, all the romance had gone.

For Rachel was a romantic, someone who not only understood, as a professional critic, the romantic imagination, but was possessed of it herself. Yet she was far from sentimental, and this may have been her genetic inheritance from her parents, both northerners. On the other hand, they too were powerfully imaginative; in fact their memories, and the significance they saw in their lives, became part of her own.

At the beginning of the Memoir broadcasts she used the image of the turning tide: an object on the beach is pulled forward out to sea, but then thrown back, almost equally far to the high watermark. So, though life advances gradually, we do not immediately leave the past. The past as much defines our present position as does the present itself, and the future; it is necessary in order to explain how we came to be where we are. Such an explanation was what she constantly sought. It would not be unreasonable to describe Rachel's life as a story, with chapters, each leading from the one before. And this, I believe, was how she saw it, with a certain detachment; with orderliness as an author developing a plot.

Her father, she said, was a most remarkable man. He worked in a post office, near the suburban village of Orrell, outside Wigan, where they lived; and he, like his father and grandfather, was also a minister in the Independent Methodist Church. This gave him status and a taken-for-granted moral and intellectual authority, both within his family and in the community outside. He was a thinker and a reader, and used to read aloud to Rachel, the novels of Jane Austen, Thackeray and Dickens, but never of Scott. This was because he himself, as a boy, had loved Scott so much that he did not want to go back to the novels, in case he found that the charm or the power had gone. He was partly Scottish himself, and Rachel was inclined to put down to this fact his intense feeling for landscape, what she referred to as 'the deep protestant feeling for Nature', exemplified in the Authorised Version of the Bible (especially perhaps the Psalms), in Bunyan's *Pilgrim's Progress*, and in the poetry of Milton. His was a powerful influence, moral, aesthetic and religious, on his family, including Rachel herself; the father, Joseph, in her first novel, *The Return Home*, is manifestly derived from him. Yet he was not intolerant or bigoted; Rachel herself as a child used to attend not his church but the more accessible Congregationalist church in their own village; and her father had a deep feeling for Anglicanism, her mother having been brought up an Anglican. His life displayed a remarkable coherence and continuity. As a minister, he was doing what his father and grandfather had done; the people among whom they had worked still, in a sense, existed as the people among whom he worked. There was no place for nostalgia.

It was very different for her mother. She was the daughter of someone who had been an indoor servant in a great house in Lancashire, and Rachel was born in a cottage, Lord's Cottage, which was part of the estate. Rachel's father had indeed, towards the end of the First World War, fallen in love not just with his future wife, but with the whole ambience of the estate. Rachel was brought up with her maternal grandmother and her mother's sister as well as her parents, and her imagination was fed with stories of life in this vanished world, the hierarchy of the servants' hall, the rituals and ceremonies of squirearchic life. The estate had long been broken up, but the big house itself was still visible from the train that ran between Wigan and Stockport. Her mother's stories were in their very essence nostalgic but they were not fantasy: the places were still real. They told, Rachel said, of a world that both existed and did not exist.

I suppose most children love to hear stories of how their parents lived when they were small. My mother did not like talking about her childhood, which had been unhappy and oppressive, but we children got our shot of nostalgia from our Nanny, who had left school at thirteen or fourteen and gone to be under-nurse at Mottisfont Abbey, near Stockbridge, close to the village of Houghton, where she had been born. She was one of the many children of a gardener and an indoor servant at the big house at Houghton, who had to be allocated two lodges, one each side of the drive, to accommodate their family. To be taken, occasionally, to see the village school at Houghton, or the great rose gardens at Mottisfont Abbey was, for me, what the glimpse of the great house from the railway was for Rachel, a proof that, as Sartre put it, the past is not over and done with. I recognised, in Rachel, the truth that one's childhood is composed of vicarious as well as immediate memories, and this is what gives the recollections of it their depth. Such stories are, after all, one's first encounter with history. They also serve to invest particular places with a kind of meaning that they may retain for ever. Rachel had been told repeatedly the story of her great-grandmother's being driven in a wagonette all the way from Herefordshire to Lancashire to be married, and weeping all the way, for the loss of her home. All her adult life, Rachel regarded Herefordshire as a deeply romantic county, a symbol of a paradise lost.

One summer vacation in 1968, when Rachel was trying to

persuade her mother to move down to Oxford, we lent her our house in Chadlington Road while we were in Italy, so that her mother could see for herself whether she could settle so far south. The experiment was a huge success. Rachel's mother had a great love of antique furniture, and she was delighted by the size of our house, and the number of 'things' it contained. (We were still in the house which we shared with Geoffrey's mother, who was temporarily abroad, and his father had been a great collector.) And yet she found the house home-like and unpretentious, and she had an enjoyable fortnight, which successfully converted her to Oxford. Afterwards, when she had moved, I always felt extremely fond of her, and as if I at least partly understood the things she liked, but her roots remained in the north, as did Rachel's own. When Rachel was at Hull, in her first academic post, and when she first became a Fellow of St Hugh's in Oxford, she used to go home for most of her vacations, and it was there that she wrote all her novels; when she moved her mother down to live in Oxford, she seemed to lose the urge to write novels, or perhaps the ability; and many of her novels have strong connections with the north.

Rachel and I were exact contemporaries as undergraduates at Lady Margaret Hall, but we did not know each other. She had first wanted to become an artist, and to prepare for this by going to art school, but her English teacher at the grammar school to which she had won a scholarship persuaded her, as she said, that she had little talent for art, and great potential talent for literature, and that she must try for Oxford. Oxford was a revelation to her. At first she was scornful. She wrote to her father after a week, saying that from their conversation at meals she had decided that her contemporaries took frivolous things seriously and serious things frivolously. But first her deep awareness of the beauty of Oxford, and then her increasing pleasure in academic work soon reconciled her (and she also had made many friends).

Her tutors in Oxford were totally different from each other, and together suited her perfectly. In LMH her tutor was Kate Lea, a shy, almost reclusive scholar, dedicated to accuracy and clarity, as well as to good works. Rachel's probably over-long, discursive essays were subjected to detailed and salutary analysis. She became a lifelong friend, and they continued to see each other frequently after Kate's retirement. Out of college, her tutor and, again, lifelong friend was David Cecil. He was her model of what a tutor should be, bending his whole attention to her essay, taking her remarks as original and as seriously worth pursuing, endlessly getting up to get books from his shelves, in order to illustrate her points with further confirmation, or a new dimension, or a different angle. Every tutorial was a brilliant conversation, leaving Rachel exhilarated and increasingly confident of her own powers. At the end of her undergraduate life, her First Class degree was never in doubt.

Rachel planned then to take a postgraduate Diploma in Education, for which even in wartime one could get an extra year. She wanted to teach, because she wanted above all to be able to go on thinking and talking about literature. But her plans had to be changed at the last moment, because her father died, and it became urgently necessary that she should get a job, and earn money to contribute to the household at Orrell, the village where her mother and aunt lived. It was at about this time, too, that it became clear that her older sister was not going to recover from the schizophrenia from which she was suffering, would need to live in hospital and could not contribute to the family expenses. Rachel never talked to me much about either of these traumatic events. She remained devoted to her sister, visiting her regularly and, in later years, taking her out for drives into the countryside. But it is certain that the cruel waste of this life affected her deeply, and, I always thought, contributed to her fundamental pessimism, or, if not pessimism, then an ability to make the best of what she had, and not expect too much.

So Rachel went back to the north, leaving Oxford with many regrets, and took a job as an assistant curator in the Manchester City Art Gallery, where she had worked from time to time during her vacations. She enormously enjoyed this work, and was always glad to have done it, but she soon began to find it lonely, and increasingly to miss people with whom she could talk about literature. So, not having a teaching qualification to enable her to make a career in school-teaching, she decided for a university post. It was difficult, especially for women, to get a job in an English Faculty after the war, but after several months of gloomy unemployment, during which she became increasingly disheartened, her mother pointed out to her an advertisement for a post in Hull. Rachel was scornful: 'Who's ever heard of Hull?' she asked. However, she put in an application and was appointed. She spent eight years in the English Faculty, learning quite soon that this was the life she really enjoyed; and indeed she loved Hull. She made many friends, among them Philip Larkin, who was librarian of the University Library, and wrote her first novel, *The Return Home* which was published in 1952, and won the John Llewellyn Rhys Memorial prize. She also, during this time, spent a year in the USA, the first of many visits, as a Commonwealth Fellow at Yale. There she met her first great love, a modern linguist also on a temporary Fellowship. Asked by Alistair Hetherington, one-time editor of the *Guardian*, years later, in a broadcast about her life, whether this was unrequited love, she replied, a bit huffily, 'Well, it was unrequited in the sense that we did not get married'. But it was not at the time unrequited, nor unconsummated. In any case, she said, in the same interview, unrequited love is love in its essence; it forces you to think about the nature of love.

In February 1954 she was elected to a Tutorship at St Hugh's

College, Oxford, and joined the college in September. I remembered her, from our days at LMH, as an alien, remote figure, then called Mabel. Now, as a Fellow of St Hugh's myself, I was one of the electors, and though on paper she was by far the strongest candidate, before she came into the room I would not have put much money on her being elected, as the person I remembered. I was astonished by the transformation. She had written not only a highly acclaimed novel, but the libretto for an opera; she was talkative, confident and wholly at home in Oxford. Her election was assured and we soon became great friends.

From her first term in St Hugh's, we increasingly sought one another's company in college. Our first long, time-wasting conversations were about LMH. We found we could make each other laugh endlessly about the horrors of the food, the vindictiveness of the Bursar, the appalling tedium and discomfort of the compulsory hours of war work we had to put in. It made it all the more fun that we had not known each other at the time, but could come at these experiences from different angles, focusing our sights on the same point. There was a particular occasion of which I reminded Rachel, which she had forgotten, though she was the participant and I a mere observer. For her compulsory gardening, she and a friend of hers, a large beefy girl, were harnessed side by side to an immense roller, meant I suppose to be drawn by a carthorse, and were set to roll a patch of ground to prepare it for the sowing of vegetables. The other girl was much stronger than Rachel, and pulled much harder, with the consequence that the roller would not go straight, but kept turning sideways, and coming to a stop. I happened to witness this scene from an upstairs window. At the side of the patch there stood one of the Fellows, a geographer, appropriately called Miss Gardiner, who was in charge of the College gardens for the duration of the war. She used to dress in Land Army uniform, corduroy breeches, green socks and an army sweater. There she stood, a formidable figure, shouting 'Come on, Trickett. Pull UP, like a man'.

Other members of the St Hugh's Senior Common Room formed the opinion that we were slightly mad. Could anyone have hated their undergraduate life as much as we apparently had? But, though we enjoyed dancing on the table on the subject of LMH, we soon found other things to talk about, particularly the dramas and divisions of St Hugh's itself.

St Hugh's was a strange and not particularly prestigious or happy college at this time. There was a sharp division between the old guard of Fellows and the new, younger women who were being elected after the war. I had another great friend in the common room, Susan Wood, a medieval historian, a Somervillean who, as Susan Chenevix-Trench, had joined the college at the same time I had, in October 1949. I was already married when I arrived (though at my interview I had had to confess that I was going to be married, and I think was elected only because my prospective husband was by then a Prize Fellow of Magdalen, deemed to be respectably academic); but poor Susan had had to go see Miss Procter, the Principal, after she had been in the college for a few weeks, and confess that she had become engaged. This was especially dreadful because the Principal, herself a medievalist, and a most formidable woman, pale and reserved, but capable of deep passions, had plainly set her heart on Susan's following her as a dedicated scholar. Susan came out of the Principal's office, shaken to the core.

Susan and I had been appointed as lecturers, and there was a genuine split in the college about whether we should ever have been made Fellows. There was one married woman among the Fellows, but her husband was either dead or divorced. There had never been a fully paid-up married Fellow before. It was thought impossible that we should give our minds properly to our jobs; and worse, we would not live in college, as all the Fellows did at that time. We would not be available for consultations far into the night; we could not be responsible for our pupils, twenty-four hours a day. By the time Rachel joined the common room, that issue had been settled. Both Susan and I were Fellows. (I had outraged conservative opinion by having three children in quick succession, two conveniently in Long Vacations, the middle one on the first day of a Hilary Term; but even then Geoffrey taught my pupils, and I was back in my place halfway through the term. By another piece of good luck my first two children were called Kitty and Felix, and so the Fellows could politely ask after them as they asked each other about the pets; cats, dogs and tortoises, which they themselves kept, and which formed much of the conversational material in this claustrophobic society.) The issue of our Fellowships was, in any case, a mere symptom of much deeper divisions which remained. The oldest Fellows had been members of St Hugh's at the time of the Row, as it was always known, in 1924. Although it was now thirty years on, one was warned on arrival never to mention the Row.

The Row involved the dismissal by the then Principal, Miss Moberly, of a Fellow of the College, called Cecilia Ady (who was now reinstated as a Research Fellow, a scholar of Italian history, and, as it happened, a friend of my mother's). Miss Moberly and her close friend, Miss Jourdain, who had jointly written a highly suspect and, at the time, immensely popular book about the spooks they had seen at Versailles (*The Adventure*), had become increasingly dictatorial and bizarre in their behaviour towards the Fellows, and when Miss Ady was sacked, most of the Fellows resigned. The university as a whole was outraged by the treatment of Miss Ady, and there was a boycott on teaching St Hugh's undergraduates, temporary tutors for whom had to be found by advertising in the press. This drama did immense damage to the college, whose reputation took many years to recover. It was no wonder that the shadow still hung over us, thirty years later. Miss Gwyer had been the Principal to succeed after the Row; and then Miss Procter, who was one of the first Fellows newly elected in 1925, had been elected to succeed her, both on the grounds of her distinction as a scholar, and because it was felt that she, all those years before, had helped to hold the College together. A highly evocative group portrait, painted in the 1930s by Henry Lamb, of the older Fellows, many of whom were still alive, hung above the High Table in Hall, reminding us of what the College had been through, and of our place in it.

Besides Susan and Rachel and me and some others of our age, there were one or two Fellows older than us by a few years, who played an intermediary role between the old and the young, forming strong attachments to one or other of the older fellows, and causing endless trouble, as it seemed to us, acting as spies and go-betweens. Meetings of the College Governing Body were sometimes fraught, even hysterical, events and tension was never absent when all the Fellows were gathered together; jealousy, spite, passionate suppressed love, suspicion of the new, the generally iconoclastic ethos of the university after the Second World War, were all ingredients in the excitable atmosphere. When Rachel began to visit Geoffrey and me at home, he was amused and incredulous at our conversation. He referred to Rachel as Blue Streak, because of the speed and intensity of her talk (which dates us, of course: Blue Streak, the sole nuclear missile to be manufactured in this country, was abandoned in 1960). He used to imitate our style: 'No! She can't have said that! I don't believe it!', and so on, and he marvelled at how the business of managing St Hugh's differed from the stately conduct of affairs in Magdalen, where he was a Fellow. But, though we became excited by the dramas in College, we never took them wholly seriously, and the enormous pleasure in 'going over' things with Rachel was that everything appeared in a brilliantly ludicrous light. Her conversational voice was one of continuous laughter.

I was disapproved of in St Hugh's in those early days, not only because of being married and having children, but also because of tangling with broadcasting. The very idea of popularising one's academic subject was anathema to Miss Procter and those who thought as she did (A.J.P. Taylor, as a fellow historian, was her demon-figure, left-wing, an immensely popular lecturer and teacher, making himself rich by journalism, all features designed, as she thought, to degrade and trivialise her precious subject). Looking back, and reading the scripts of our Third Programme broadcasts, I can hardly think that they did much to popularise philosophy. Geoffrey, Peter Strawson, David Pears and I, as I have explained already, used jointly to compose scripts in the form of conversations, which we used to rehearse, and read out, with no deviation from the script. They were amazingly stilted and unrealistic. I benefited greatly from these broadcasts, or rather from the preparation of them. I was generally cast as the goofy woman who asked that things be explained again, when we thought that our explanations were a bit quick for the audience, and who used to say things like 'But surely there must be something deeper?' to be firmly and politely put down. I was the only one of the four of us who ever got letters from the general public, who felt that I shared their bewilderment. We spent hours planning how we could explore in a coherent sequence all the issues in such questions as the nature of personal identity, causation, perception … all the central topics that we, all of us, had to pursue with our pupils, week in week out. It was, for me, highly educational and confidence-inspiring. Our radio contact was T.S. Gregory, known to us only as Gregory. He was a surprising man. He had been a Methodist minister, but at some stage had converted to

Catholicism, and had been editor of *The Tablet*. He had been recruited to the BBC in the Talks Department soon after the opening of the Third Programme, which was dominated at first by the brothers Grisewood, who were Catholics. Gregory loved nothing better than to come down to Oxford to find people willing to broadcast. His criterion of good broadcasting was that it would be mildly controversial, and of interest to him. He openly declared that he did not mind if nobody listened, as long as it appeared as a 'debate' in the *Radio Times*, the blurb, which he wrote, ending with the words 'the debate continues'. He used to come and stay with Geoffrey and me, and drink quantities of brandy, eager to entice more philosophers and others into his net (into which, of course, we all happily entered, because we earned £20 a broadcast). Though almost unbelievably muddle-headed, he was a genuine intellectual and had a great gift of getting other people to talk, while he sat on the edge, in a cloud of smoke, beaming. After his retirement, Geoffrey and I used to visit him in a tiny bungalow in the grounds of the convent of the Passionate Sisters, near Daventry. His heart was in very poor shape, and the sisters used to take him up to Mass every day. We brought him books, in which he was still deeply interested. He lived with his wife, still a Methodist, who cooked us the most wonderful scones and cakes when we came. We never learned his Christian names.

I introduced him to Rachel, but he was not so much interested in literature as in philosophy and theology; and it was not until a little later that she was discovered by the Third Programme as an absolute natural broadcaster, with the perfect voice for it, certainly better than any of our philosophical friends, with the exception of Geoffrey, who, he was told, sounded like a bishop, with the very faintest hint, detectable only on the telephone or the radio, of an Ulster accent.

Even before she started broadcasting, Rachel was suspect

because of her novels. She recalled that after her appointment, Miss Procter sent for her, and looking at her total list of publications, a novel and a libretto, she said 'Now Miss Trickett: no more of these lower forms.' Rachel continued to write novels, and composed another libretto. She wrote one, and only one, critical work, *The Honest Muse*, published in 1967, a study of some Augustine poets, setting them in their historical background, and concentrating on the taken-for-granted ethos of the poems, rather than on their style (though her various learned articles were concerned for the most part with style). When asked, in the BBC interview to which I have already referred at the beginning of the chapter, why she had written no more books of criticism, she laughed and said that it took too long. It had taken her fifteen years to write this one. Also, she added, she was not a natural scholar; she was in too much of a hurry. The article or review was her preferred medium. These were invariably thoughtful, original and elegantly composed. Her novels, however, were a different thing. These she wrote for pleasure. It was generally said that her first novel was the best. It was, like most first novels, partly autobiographical, and contained a striking portrait of the heroine's father, Joseph Hallam, who like Rachel's own father was a Methodist minister, and, as I have suggested, was probably closely based on him. David Cecil, in his introduction to the book, wrote 'The heroine and her father ... are intensely civilised spirits, alike in the refinement of their sensibility and of their moral feelings. Further, they are soaked in an ancient and noble tradition which leads them to relate their personal dramas to a spacious and spiritual conception of the universal scheme. Yet they are not too stately to be human'. But stateliness, along with an intense evocation of place, perhaps most characterises the novel. It is certainly extraordinarily unlike other novels published at the same sort of time, by Iris Murdoch, for example, or Kingsley Amis. However, I personally do not think it her best. In my view, her novel-writing became more and more assured. In 1966 she published *The Elders*, of all her novels my favourite. In it two poets, giants in reputation, are in rivalry for the Chair of Poetry in Oxford, though neither had sought this honour. They had once been very close friends, but had fallen out, and had not seen each other for many years. The story is told through the eyes of two Oxford dons, who had been members of the circle of admirers, indeed worshippers of the two poets when they were young, one having been the mistress, the other the devoted friend of the more solemn and respectable of the two. It is a story set in contemporary Oxford, and I know of no more powerful evocation of the atmosphere of the Long Vacation in Oxford, as I knew it. After the frenzy of examining, there followed the long days, perhaps broken by a holiday, a length of time for dramas to unfold, friendships to change, excitement and boredom to succeed each other, so that when the welcome term starts again the doldrums of late July seem years away, an alien country. When I first read the novel, that was how I saw it. I was delighted by the accuracy of the depiction of both environment and atmosphere. It was only when, short of something to read, I reread it in the 1980s that I recognised the great protagonists as Wordsworth and Coleridge. By then I had, as it happened, immersed myself in the lives of both poets. I recognised the solemn, austere, unapproachable nature of the one, and the overwhelmingly talkative, maddening, unreliable, hypochondriac, irresistible nature of the other. And the quarrel had, obviously, been about plagiarism. When I told Rachel about my revelation she said, 'Yes, of course'. But only one of the reviewers had seen the point. Perhaps she might have made the connection explicit but I think, on the whole, she was right not to do so. At any rate, I think this was a good novel at various levels, and I wish that some publisher would bring it back into print.

It was a novel about friendship. And I suppose friendship was Rachel's great genius, whether with people of the same or the opposite sex. Just as, in her novels, she was able to present realistically friends of either sex who took their love for each other wholly seriously, whether or not their relations were sexual, so in real life she took her friends seriously, and was loyal to them, whether or not sexual relations were part of the friendship. In her BBC interview, she said that on the whole she thought she had gained from the fact that, as they say in the obituaries, she 'never married'. In her case this was certainly not a euphemism for homosexuality but it gave her a freedom which she very much valued, to enter into the concerns of her friends, spend time with them, make what social arrangements with them she wanted. She used to go fairly often to the USA, either for whole semesters, or to take part in summer schools at a university outpost, delightfully named Bread Loaf, deep in the country, twelve miles from the nearest town. This was a place ideally suited to sudden friendships and love affairs, and she relished it greatly. She was an excellent correspondent, and we exchanged regular letters when she was away, because she longed to be kept up to date with affairs in Oxford, as well as wanting to tell me about the people she was meeting and living among, in the heightened atmosphere of a six-week term.

Once, when she was on one of her longer trips to America, at the height of the Cuba crisis in 1962, she wrote of her extraordinary feeling of detachment, like the feeling one has on a long flight, when one is in neither one place nor another. And she added that this was a rare experience for her. She was right about herself. Wherever she was, for long periods or short, she became attached to the people and the places about her. This meant that, in America, she could fall in love, experience the intense excitement of some of the countryside she stayed in, fully entering into the life, intellectual, creative and emotional, of the campus. Her letters are full of pleasures and dramas. At home, equally, she was attached to her colleagues, her dog, her family and the social life of Oxford.

She used occasionally to stay with us in the house at Sandsend, on the coast of North Yorkshire, which we acquired in 1958, and which was the base for family holidays until the early 1970s. It was an extraordinary house, a converted bungalow with numbers of small bedrooms fitted into the added upper floor under the eaves; and it was ideal for the accommodation of our five children and their friends, as well as our own friends. It was a minute's walk from the beach, had a large garden and orchard, and, though always cold and damp when we first arrived, got a lot of sun, when the sun shone, and could be easily warmed when it did not, with an old-fashioned Rayburn stove in the kitchen. Rachel loved staying there, though it was not of the standard of comfort that she normally enjoyed. She did not particularly like children or babies, but she took each of our children seriously as separate individuals, entering into their troubles, and regarding them as, on the whole, to be pitied, pathetic creatures, as they often are. She was never censorious. They found her a reassuring figure. She always kept a few vestiges of North Country idiom in her talk; and I remember her asking some child in trouble, 'What's to do?', and being told, through tears, what it was. The first time she stayed she asked our son James, then about four years old, how she could post a letter. He said, 'Well, there is this red box, a kind of pillar, and it has a slit at the top, and you hold the letter by its corner, and put it through the slit'. Such absurdities delighted her. She loved driving round the North Yorkshire moors, and she loved as well the garish, ancient excitement of Whitby, our nearest town. In fact she 'took on' anyone, children or friends to whom she was introduced. Susan Wood recalls how much Rachel enjoyed the company of Brigadier Chenevix-Trench, Susan's distinguished, clever and old-fashioned father, about whom there were many stories. (Geoffrey, for example, spending a night once with Susan and her parents, was told in confidential tones, 'Of course, it makes such a difference if the Vicar is a Gentleman', a quotation often used by us in later years.) Susan was telling a story about her father, which illustrated his perception and his sympathy, and Rachel exclaimed 'Oh Susan, your *dear* father!' I can hear Rachel's voice exactly in this exclamation. In fact, the word 'dear' was a favourite of hers. When she came round to our house we used to embrace, and she would exclaim, '*Dear* Mary!' She sometimes even addressed her friends as 'dear', something that I could never quite get used to, because for Geoffrey and me the expression was a joke. Once, in our early days of marriage, having been asked to supper by my former philosophy tutor, Martha Kneale and her husband, Bill, also a philosopher, we were enchanted to hear their domestic conversation: 'I'll just put the potatoes on, dear' and so forth. For some reason this struck us as funny, and from then on we used to say things like 'I'll just put my slippers on, dear'. We, probably more embarrassingly, were prone to address each other as 'darling', a habit I think we picked up from Marcus and Cecilia Dick whom we saw most of all of our friends. Their 'darlings' became extremely painful to listen to, as they got locked into the rage and disgust that finally led to their divorce.

But to return to friendship: Oxford itself was a place of extraordinary freedom for friendship, and indeed for adultery (though gossip and the grapevine were for most people partially inhibiting factors in this field). Every Fellow of every college had a private room and a telephone. It was the custom to invite one's friends to sherry before lunch, or to spend afternoons going for walks, or simply talking in each other's rooms. (The afternoons were not open to me. One of the ways in which I shocked my colleagues was by teaching between the hours of 2 and 5 o'clock, or 4 o'clock if I was lucky, so that I could get home in time to put the children to bed.) It was generally thought that the afternoons must be left free so that undergraduates could play games at this time. There were fixed days, Wednesday afternoons mostly, for college meetings and committees (I much missed this aid to forward planning, when I was in Cambridge; there every committee meeting had to be arranged *ad hoc*, a cause of endless wasted time). Otherwise one was free to fix one's own schedule. And of course in the vacations one could entertain in one's own room whenever one wanted. It is not that we did not work hard. For the whole of my time at St Hugh's, for example, I never taught fewer than eighteen hours a week, as well as lecturing; and all this took preparation. But it was the flexibility of the work that was so delightful. And there was absolutely no presumption that husbands and wives must do everything together, nor were they expected to know the details of each other's movements. There can be no other profession so well suited to friendship or, as I have said, for extra-marital flings, which were not only relatively easy, but also conveniently cheap. There was no need for the hiring of expensive hotel rooms. The life was also exceptionally well-suited to the obstacle race of combining children with a job. And in the case of Geoffrey and me, since we taught the same subjects, in an emergency we could always take over each other's pupils.

Rachel's greatest friend was a Fellow of Somerville, also in the English Faculty, called Rosemary (always pronounced by Rachel as Rose Mary) Woolf, who came from a large Jewish family who had suffered terribly under the Nazis. She died of cancer in early middle age; and Rachel missed her sadly. Rosemary's stories of the sufferings of her relatives affected Rachel, and contributed to what I have referred to as pessimism, but which was really a kind of deep, but not unhappy, melancholy, a conviction that human beings were capable of immense evil, as well being liable to suffer appalling blows of fate, which made her view of the world in some ways Shakespearian. Despite her ready attachments, she highly valued her own company; one of her favourite quotations was from the Bishop and hymnist, Edward Henry Bickersteth, 'Peace, perfect peace, With loved ones far away'. She also set great store by the retention of a perceptive and observing eye.

Because of her widespread sympathy, Rachel was a wonderful tutor, having learned from David Cecil to take her pupils' work seriously, and to try always to build on what they had written in order to widen their horizons. She was a strong believer in what she called the 'grand element and principle of pleasure' in the study of literature, which, as she realised, too easily gets overlooked in the teaching of English as an academic subject, and more easily still in the writing of critical books. She took enormous pleasure in the success of her pupils, and especially liked to see them become themselves members of the Oxford English Faculty, appointments in which she took a great, some thought unduly great, interest. She was a member of the Board of the Faculty from 1964 until 1970, becoming chairman in 1967, and this occupied a good deal of her time when she was in Oxford.

To my sorrow, she was a fierce opponent of a joint school of English and Philosophy, for the establishing of which there were some enthusiasts, including Geoffrey and me. Indeed, she generally had a poor view of philosophy, and those who practised it, though she made an exception of friends, myself and Geoffrey and Susan's husband, Oscar Wood. She had an amused and fond feeling for both Geoffrey and Oscar, especially the latter, who did not find her conversational style as exhausting as Geoffrey did, and who was often prepared to sit up until all hours talking, after Susan had gone off to bed. She shared with Oscar a romantic passion for landscape gardens, and other aspects of eighteenth-century taste; and she enjoyed his considerable collection of books on such topics. But, on the whole, she thought philosophy a deadening subject, within which there was no room for imagination or indeed for pleasure.

I sometimes tried to talk to her about this, especially when I was myself writing a book about imagination, and, later, one about memory. But she thought that if philosophers were allowed to get their hands on the imagination the poor thing would be pulled apart, analysed and stripped of its enlivening power. I tried to explain that to be a philosopher meant above all else to try to look through what people said to the unexamined presuppositions that lay behind them, and that this was exactly what she had tried to do in her book about the Augustan poets. But I could not persuade her; she was still dismissive.

I was sorry about this, because numbers of joint-subject schools were beginning to grow up in Oxford. For example, I often taught undergraduates who were reading the joint school of Philosophy and Modern Languages, and I found them great fun to teach, their knowledge of either German or French literature being capable of throwing light on the history of ideas. However I think Rachel held that my essentially historical view of philosophy was not widely shared (though in Oxford, unlike Cambridge, this was not altogether true) and that proper philosophers would despise and ruin literature. I suppose in the end it was her insistence that the study of literature was to do with the pleasure that the text gave, the pleasure of words and thoughts together that made her suspicious of philosophy. One certainly should not read a philosophical text simply as literature; yet I still believe that the two ways of reading can be fruitfully conjoined.

Whatever she thought about philosophy, by the end of her life, Rachel certainly hated the new tendency to make the teaching of English in universities in some way 'scientific' and theory-based, deconstructing texts regardless of their literary worth; and she, surely rightly, deplored the barbarous and jargon-laden prose in which criticism increasingly came to be written. The pleasure-principle seemed to have been generally abandoned. She had little sympathy, either, for the radical feminism that had taken root in many English Faculties, especially that of Cambridge. In this she and I were in complete agreement. Without in the least wishing to deny that women's writing might be expected to show some kinds of sensibility that would be particularly feminine, she nevertheless believed that the pursuit of literary pleasure and of truth was gender-indifferent, whether this truth was of the imagination or the intellect.

Miss Procter had retired as Principal of St Hugh's in the summer of 1963, and her successor was the archaeologist, Kathleen Kenyon, who, by way of contrast, was jovial, energetic and uninhibited. She was far from being an intellectual, and her fame as an archaeologist, digging round about the walls of Jericho, was based not on scholarship so much as on force of personality, and her discovery of new techniques for extracting fragile items unharmed from piles of rubble. She did the college good, on the whole; was considered a bit of a joke by the outside world, and was inclined to treat the Fellows like a team of subordinates in the field. She used to drink a mixture of gin and sherry every night before dinner, and this meant that her rendering of the Latin grace we used, especially the phrase 'quae ex liberalitate tua sumpturi sumus' was at best sketchy. But the tensions in the college were eased, the lines of division less fixed and predictable. She shared the Lodgings with someone universally known to the Fellows as 'My Friend from the Red Cross'; and I suppose that this was good for us all. If Kathleen felt frustrated by the recalcitrance of the Fellows, or by what she sometimes saw as their lack of loyalty to their leader, she had someone at hand who would listen to her with unvarying admiration and calm. She retired in 1973 and

Rachel succeeded her, and remained Principal until her retirement in 1991.

Speaking for myself, the only part of my life that I would not choose to live again is my time as head of a college. There were, it is true, aspects of it that I enjoyed, and I certainly enjoyed getting to know Cambridge for the first time, and being involved in the government of the university, something that I had never experienced in Oxford, but the relations between the head of a college and the Fellows are always complicated, sometimes definitely hostile. At Girton there was a sharp division among the Fellows between the scientists and the rest. Because of the distance of Girton from the centre of town, the scientists seldom came in to college for lunch, not wanting to spend time away from their laboratories in the middle of the day. The arts Fellows, on the other hand, usually lunched in college, and had time then to talk about their pupils, plan joint strategies, and generally gossip. Accordingly, the scientists, though not all of them, had an arrangement that they would dine on Tuesdays, and talk to each other in the Combination Room after dinner. This was a sensible enough plan; but no one told me about it. And so on one Tuesday in my first term, feeling guilty about how seldom I dined in Hall (I loathe dining as early as 7.15 p.m.), I decided one Tuesday that I ought to dine. It was an exceptionally embarrassing occasion, and when I went along to the Combination Room for a postprandial cup of coffee, and saw the chairs drawn up close round the fire, apparently for the conspirators to meet, I fled. Most heads of colleges have enemies, but few can have enemies so open in their hostility. There were friends, too, and especially those who did not take sides, but were prepared to argue for their views. There was one Fellow of whom I was especially fond, who had come to my room when I was staying at Girton to be interviewed, and with whom I soon found the bond that we had both been in love with the same

Latin teacher, I at St Swithun's, she years later at the Perse School in Cambridge. It is impossible to say how that topic of conversation arose, but we were friends from then on, though she often opposed my views.

There are, I suppose, some people who seem to take naturally to being head of a college, and, if they have difficulties, do not suffer greatly from them. I think Geoffrey was one of these. He was certainly successful, and almost universally liked and admired. I put my own difficulties down, at least in part, to my coming to Cambridge from Oxford, and not at first realising how different the two universities were, both in detail and in general ethos. Geoffrey was fortunate in that he came to Hertford when the college was in a low state, and whatever he suggested was almost certain to be an improvement on the past. At the same time, he knew Oxford inside out, and was not likely to make basic mistakes. He also had some extremely able Fellows, whom he had not known before, and who quickly put their talents to what they saw were his benign purposes. Even so, when I went to Girton he warned me that if I really wanted to get any measure through the College Governing Body, I must make sure that I concealed the fact that I wanted it.

Rachel, unlike Geoffrey, though she knew Oxford well enough, also knew the Fellows all too well. She had to make the subtle and difficult move from being their colleague, to being, while still their colleague, also their permanent chairman, and the person on whom responsibility for decisions ultimately fell. I do not know the full story of her election. I know that there was at least one other internal candidate, but I do not know how many external candidates there may have been, nor how strongly they may have been supported. In the run-up to election, I was still at the Oxford High School for Girls, no part of the college or the university. After I left the High School, I went to Lady Margaret Hall, as a

Research Fellow, and did not return to St Hugh's, as a Senior Research Fellow, with a seat on the Governing Body, until 1974.

It seemed to me that Rachel, with her warm sympathies, and her instinct for close friendship, and of course for gossip, found it hard to discipline herself to be visibly fair in the distribution of her sympathy and her understanding, and indeed her desire for laughter. Justice rather than love has to be the chief virtue of a head of college, and Rachel's natural bent was for the latter rather than the former. I do not know whether she started with some who had been opposed to her election, who would perhaps have preferred someone more orientated towards science and technology (it was the days of the 'white heat of technology'); but certainly I formed the impression that she was quite often at odds with the younger members of the Governing Body, and especially a group of youngish and fairly radical scientists who, no doubt greatly to the advantage of the college, had been quite recently elected. The composition of the Governing Body was very different from that of the old days. For one thing, though the college was still single-sex at the undergraduate level, men had started to be eligible for election or Fellowships. This meant that the doctrine of total commitment to the college, day and night, had finally died out. Almost all the Fellows, male or female, were married, and only a tiny minority lived in. Expectations of undergraduate behaviour had inevitably also changed, the era of the Pill having dawned, and the Swinging Sixties having wrought revolution. Rachel was, I think disconcerted to find herself so very much on the side of conservatism, both academically and in matters of morals and manners. She was also deeply against the admission of men as undergraduates, though she was still able to say of herself that she was 'torn' between the arguments, in her interview with Alistair Hetherington in 1980. I found meetings of the Governing Body, when I attended them, quite difficult, and sometimes embarrassing. We quite often disagreed, especially over appointments, and I hated the feeling that she, like Kathleen Kenyon before her, might expect 'loyalty' from the Fellows, and especially from her close friends. On the other hand the last thing in the world the college needed was a return to the old emotion-driven days of Miss Procter. So I became a rather sporadic attender.

I felt a certain nostalgia for the old days, when Rachel and Susan and I used to sit together, passing one another notes, or composing elaborate doodles of our own to while away the tedious hours. (Susan used to do beautifully elaborate geometrical drawings. Rachel used to write sad lines of verse in various elegant scripts. I remember a whole page, in one especially tedious meeting, covered with the words: 'The dawn breaks not; it is my heart'.) But that was another world. In any case by 1974, when I rejoined the college, I was exceedingly busy, standing in for a Fellow of Somerville and doing her teaching, and involved in a totally new subject, the education of children with special needs, as chairman of the four-year long committee of enquiry, which involved, among other things, several protracted journeys to America and to Norway. In addition to that there was a lot to do at Hertford, of which Geoffrey had become Principal at the beginning of 1972. So I had plenty to occupy me apart from St Hugh's, and I was not much good as a support for Rachel, if she had difficulties. All the same we continued to see a lot of each other, with long evenings of talk; but the talk was about our private lives, not about college matters.

Rachel was greatly involved in a relatively new but very deep friendship with the designer and engraver, Laurence Whistler, whom she had first met at David Cecil's house, and whom she later often had to stay at the Principal's Lodgings. She commissioned from him both the redesign and redecoration of the elegant little Chapel in college, and also some splendid iron gates for the entrance to the grounds from Canterbury Road. She thought of these as solid monuments to her term of office. And they are thoroughly typical. Although often impatient with what sometimes seemed like egocentric follies in her colleagues, she had a grand conception of what being Principal of a college entailed. I do not mean that she was boastful; but that she was expansive in her hospitality, and recognised that she had a status both in the society of Oxford and beyond. Above all, she had a sense of occasion. Being a natural orator, deploying rhetoric in the proper sense of that word, she never failed to strike the right note for her audience when speaking on public occasions, whether at Gaudy dinners, memorial services or at the formal opening of buildings. One always knew with absolute certainty that what she said was going to be all right, and much more than that: appropriate, witty, light, but with a hint of a proper and sometimes intense emotion, with never a cliché to be heard. It was like the feeling I had, in my headmistress days, when some girl who was a real musician started to play at a concert. I could, with complete assurance, relax and enjoy. Not one of her colleagues, whatever they may have thought of her judgement on other matters, had any doubt whatever of the judgement with which she chose and delivered her words on these quite frequent occasions. One could call it a sense of style.

Style, however, as Rachel well knew, could never be considered apart from matter. She had a sense of her life as a whole. As I have suggested, she thought of her life as a story, a series of chapters each leading to the next. And I think her inner life was, to a great extent, given up to this story, with its varying attachments and varying characters contributing to the plot. In the unfolding of this plot, she saw a large role for the element of luck, which meant that in the end nothing was wholly predictable. She hated all forms of determinism, God-centred, physical or psychological. The creative imagination after all cannot be wholly predictable in its workings; and for her, the imagination was the centre of life. Love, friendship, literature and religion were all crucial to her, and were all linked through imagination.

When asked, in her 1980 broadcast, which of them had been most important to her, she replied that they were inextricably bound together. She could not separate them. Religion, which was undoubtedly important to her, was essentially a way of looking at and interpreting the world, through the imaginative framework of the Christian story. She was devoted to the Church of England, which she had joined as an adult, as a deliberate commitment to a continuous tradition. She detested the new forms of Anglican service, and especially the belief which lay behind their invention that the words of religious worship must be plain and intelligible and everyday. For how could religion be made intelligible? It was at best a metaphorical striving to say something that could not ever wholly be said. It needs the imagination both to construct and to interpret the texts. In this it was a part of literature. She could not take the dogmas of the Creed literally. She wrote to me once, in the early 1970s, when Marcus Dick, who had become the first Professor of Philosophy at the University of East Anglia, died suddenly, that she could not believe in a literal life after death, but she could not believe either that the life of someone who had been loved could be completely snuffed out and become without significance. The future would continue, in some sense, to contain this person. The past is not over and done with; it stretches out into what the future promises to be, forming the whole story.

She was therefore naturally a religious traditionalist, holding on, as far as was possible, to the continuity of the church. In the 1970s, she and I were part of a small group, apart from us entirely composed of college chaplains and Canons of Christ Church, who used to meet on Mondays for lunch, starting with the short service of Sext, with a reading from Psalm 119, which we used to take it in turns to lead. We then had lunch in one or other of our colleges, and settled down to gossip. Rachel and I used to enjoy the Holy Lunches, partly because they were a way of meeting every week, though she used to have to go off punctually to meetings of the Hebdomadal Council which met that day. But the ritual was somehow comforting, making religion unembarrassing and also unchanging; and for me at least it was agreeable to get to know quite well some very remarkable people whom I would not otherwise have met.

Rereading Rachel's letters to me, covering twenty years, there is no doubt that we *got on.* One year, in 1969/70, we were both candidates for the Principalship of LMH, having been asked to stand by different Fellows. Most fortunately, in the event, neither of us was elected. The Fellows were at pains to conceal from each the candidature of the other. We, on the other hand, filled each other in with every detail of our conversations with our sponsors, who our likely supporters were and the rigours of our final interviews. We had agreed from the beginning that each would be happy for the other to be elected and that, if some third person were chosen, neither of us would grieve. We had never felt very warmly towards LMH, and did not now. The outcome was fortunate, and perhaps an illustration of the benign operation of chance, because, if I had been elected, it might have inhibited the Fellows of Hertford from electing Geoffrey as Principal two years later; and Rachel, equally, turned out to be far better off at St Hugh's, where there was a beautiful house as Lodgings, with a garden that she loved, and where she could have her mother living with her until her death several years later.

I think Rachel was capable of jealousy, and certainly of envy. She was envious, I suppose, of Iris Murdoch, whose first novel was published in the same year as her own, and whose novels enjoyed such worldwide success. She was disappointed that her own novels did not succeed, never appearing in paperback, nor being published in America. But she was glad she had written them. She had enjoyed it, and was pleased to think that they had been published at all, and were to be found on the shelves of the Bodleian. I do not think she was either jealous or envious of me, nor I of her. There were many things that we did not do together: we did not go for walks, nor to concerts (though she loved music and was a much better pianist, in a rather impressionistic and romantic style, than I); we never went to the cinema nor the theatre together, we never went shopping or travelled abroad. But we loved writing to each other, and above all we loved talking. This represents just one of the many forms of friendship Rachel experienced, understood and enjoyed.

Peter Shore and the Development of the Labour Party

I have had an interest in or, more accurately, a curiosity about Peter Shore for a long time. I started to be interested in him because I knew his wife, or at least his wife's family. He married her when they were both quite young, and I shall return to her below. I have never known him at all well, but for a long time he was almost the only person I knew at all who was a real politician, and who was completely committed to the Labour Party. The Labour Party itself was a puzzle in which I was interested but which I could not understand, a problem I could not solve.

I knew of myself, from the age of about fifteen, that I was a natural Tory. All my instincts and all my loves were Trollopian. I loved the thought of a landed aristocracy, though I would never be a member of one (I did not, even in my fantasies, believe that I should marry a duke). I loved hunting; I loved time-honoured hierarchies; I loved cathedrals. I wanted to become an old-fashioned scholar. Above all, perhaps, I loved the idea of accumulating, inheriting and passing on wealth to my family. Nothing could be further from the politics of the Left. Yet increasingly during the war I felt that to indulge my instincts was wrong. I must pull myself together, recognise the unfairness of my privileged and comfortable way of life, begin properly to aim for a classless society, think about politics, become someone who would go to what I vaguely thought of as Meetings. By 1945, I had talked myself pretty thoroughly round to the Left. Just about at the time when Peter and Liz Shore got married, in 1948, I had got to know Geoffrey, whom I married the next year. He was much more wholeheartedly Left than I, and finished my conversion. He had won a prize, when at school at Winchester, for an essay arguing that the Public Schools must be abolished, if social equality were ever to be a possibility. And during his time in the army, as an officer in the Irish Guards which he joined before the end of his last year at school, though inevitably his friends were officers, he was by no means a natural officer-type. His task, towards the end of the war, was to explain the Beveridge Report to the troops, and he was completely convinced that it would need a Labour government to carry these reforms through. In any case it would have been very strange if he, or for that matter I, had not voted Labour in 1945. It seemed plain that that was where the future lay. So there we were, by 1949, a pair, a couple of Labour voters. And yet I think, and thought, that I was just as class-bound as before. I was prepared to argue with my mother about the merits of Socialism (though not quite so fiercely and implacably as Geoffrey argued with his). But I had no knowledge or understanding of those whom I thought of as proper Socialists, miners, for example, or Trades Unionists; nor, so far, of any Labour Members of Parliament. Peter, who at least stood as Labour candidate for St Ives in 1950, was about the nearest I could get; and I knew a little about him because he had married a Wrong. (My own commitment to Labour, such as it was, came to an end in the 1960s. I felt that I could hardly remain a member of the local party, which I had briefly become, while working as head of a Direct Grant school. These schools were opposed by Labour, and were shortly to be abolished. It was not, however, simply a matter of consistency. I was involved in, and admiring of, the newly-formed comprehensive schools in Oxfordshire; but I deeply believed in the Direct Grant schools with their mixture of fee-paying, part fee-paying and wholly state-financed pupils, nor do I think that anything has yet been devised to replace them.)

To return, then, to Peter Shore: two men from King's College, Cambridge, both having served in the RAF during the war, married two Newnham College sisters, of whom one, Imogen Wrong, is, as I have said, my greatest friend. When she married Brian Rose, an economist, who joined the staff of the International Monetary Fund after he left Cambridge, he and Imogen went to live in Washington. Imogen's younger sister, Liz, a medical student, married Peter Shore. Brian and Peter did not know each other well at King's (where Peter read History) but they had a common friend, George Clayton, who became Professor of Economics, first at the University College of Wales, Aberystwyth, and then at Sheffield, and with whom Brian put me in touch. I owe George Clayton a debt of gratitude for entertaining me in Sheffield, and sparing time to talk about Peter Shore. He is, however, in no way to be held responsible for the opinions I express in what follows, or for mistakes I may make.

These two friends, George and Peter, had met when they were still at school in Liverpool. They did not attend the same school, but met at a local boxing club, curiously enough. (I find it hard now to imagine Peter as even an embryonic boxer; but for all I know he may have been a brilliant exponent of the art.) The two families, Claytons and Shores, became friendly, George and Peter being particular friends. They shared an interest in politics, and used to go for long walks together, with endless talk. Peter was already a passionate Socialist. His father, who had been a Master Mariner, was an old-fashioned Tory, but too little interested in politics, according to Peter, to be prepared to argue with his son.

Peter married Liz Wrong in 1948. It is said that she and Peter met at the same party at which Brian first set eyes on Imogen, but this may be myth. She was the youngest of the six Wrong children. Her father, Murray Wrong, a Fellow and Tutor in History at Magdalen College, Oxford, died when she was still a baby. Theirs was one of the great, spreading Oxford families, part of what Noel

Annan refers to as the Intellectual Aristocracy (see *The Dons*, 1999). Rosalind Wrong, her mother, was the sixth daughter of A.L. Smith, Master of Balliol; and the family was connected by the marriages of these dazzling daughters with families such as the Hodgkinses and the Cairnses, and in the next generation, Liz's and Imogen's generation, with the Mitchisons and thence the Haldanes. It was a formidable family to marry into, but in some ways, Liz was quite detached from it. After the death of her father, when Liz was nearly four years old, the three youngest Wrong children, Imogen, Oliver and Elizabeth, were sent to Canada, to be looked after by Murray Wrong's father in Toronto. George Wrong was a notable historian of Canada, and seemed well enough off, with other members of the family, to take charge of these three children and pay for their education. Their mother, Rosalind, was far from well-off, earning what she could by teaching history in Oxford for various colleges, coaching candidates for scholarship examinations, and correcting School Certificate papers. She was a brilliant teacher, and a brilliant companion. I can never think of any word but 'brilliance' to describe her character, or perhaps 'vivacity'. She was small, with bright chestnut brown hair and brown eyes with an amazing shine, when she was excited or interested in some topic. She was a great, rapid, caustically witty and reckless talker, an endless source of knowledge about things she was devoted to, like medieval churches, Roman Britain, wild flowers, roses and many other things. For a short time, in the 1950s, she lived next door to us, in Fyfield Road, close to LMH and the University Parks, and I used to see quite a lot of her. Once, when a friend of mine, whom Rosalind also knew a little, called while she was in my house, she said afterwards: 'I always thought she was neurotic, and now I know. Stockings wrinkled round the ankles are a sure sign of neurosis.' I said something vaguely defensive about its being more difficult to keep one's stockings up when one is eight months pregnant. But she would have none of it. Since then, I have always been on the lookout for confirmation of her generalisation (though as most people wear tights these days, it is harder to find anyone displaying wrinkles). I have to say that I have found the rule for the most part confirmed. On another occasion, I was talking about another common acquaintance, and she said, 'Are there sparks?' I did not at once understand what she meant, so she explained a bit impatiently: 'You must know. There are some men who send out electric sparks and you send them back. You may not like them best, but you can't avoid returning the sparks'. I think this was true of her. She was a flirt. And this was probably partly why her family arranged that she send the three youngest children to Canada. They thought she was flighty and not to be trusted. She certainly picked up sparks from my younger son, James, who was two or three years old when we were neighbours. He was a clever, solemn little boy, and she liked asking him to tell her the makes of all the cars parked in the road where we lived, and was endlessly patient and encouraging with his rather slow, though always accurate responses. To me she used to say, 'He has the most beautiful eyes of any child I've ever seen. That's why I love talking to him.' But all this was later. When I first met her, while I was still at school, I was completely terrified of her sharpness and her speed. One time when she was talking to me in her garden, then in Museum Road, I was so nervous that unconsciously I pulled the heads off some flowers and rolled them up in an agony of anxiety. She said nothing at the time, but was unforgiving (not surprisingly) when she talked to Imogen afterwards about her ghastly friend.

In 1930, before Imogen, Oliver and Liz went to Canada, their grandmother, Sophia Wrong, died. George was lonely, and eager to have the children to cheer him but he soon married the woman who had been sent over to Canada to look after them. Imogen at least detested this woman, always had, and particularly could not stand her in her new role. Liz, on the other hand, who was much younger, and could presumably remember little or nothing about life in England, was fond of her, and of her grandfather, and was very much their favourite, being, in conspicuous contrast to Imogen, biddable and anxious to please. It was difficult for all of them to adapt to their new life when they finally came back, Imogen first, in 1935, and the other two in 1938. But it must have been worst for Liz. She had been away for seven years, and was now flung among a family who were virtually strangers, and like all the descendants of A.L. Smith, fiercely critical, sharp and endlessly talkative. She was sent to St Swithun's School, where Imogen was already a pupil, and in her first term made a pathetic attempt to run away, hoping to join her grandfather and his wife, who had been staying in England, believing that they had promised to take her back with them to Canada, if she wanted to go. She got less than a mile from school when she was picked up and taken back by the police. But the school was a place of torment for her, as, in a different way, it was for Imogen.

When Liz went up to Newnham, I remember thinking, when I occasionally met her, that she was one of the most beautiful people I had ever seen. She was, in fact, what would once have been called 'a Beauty', with an extraordinarily clear skin, and a delicacy and grace unique in my experience. Imogen was still in Cambridge doing research at this time, and they used to see a lot of each other, but I do not imagine that they ever talked about their childhood in Canada. There must have been endless sagas about both of their admirers. Liz's admirers who were, understandably, numerous used to call on Imogen, in various stages of hope or despair, two of them dropping in and lolling about her room when she was once virtuously giving tea to our old Latin teacher, now working at a school in Cambridge. This must have been a remarkably awkward social occasion.

When now I hear Liz and Imogen talking about their childhood, I get the impression that Liz has, or affects to have, a very patchy recollection of it, or perhaps does not think it worth recalling in detail. At any rate, it seems that when she got to Newnham she put it all behind her; and when she met and married Peter, she started a totally new life. She did not want to suck him into the great Smith clan more than she could help. Equally, she did not want to become part of his earlier life. Liz was still a medical student when they married, and they must have been painfully short of money, she so far earning none, and he earning a pittance in the research department of Transport House. But they became a new entity together, a unit which expanded as soon as Liz began to earn, and they had children, but which, on the whole, excluded others. They were a close and devoted family, living in astonishingly child-dominated squalor, their friends mainly political friends and colleagues, and their aims on the whole Peter's aims. However Liz soon became a power in her own right in the General Medical Council and its various committees, and in the Department of Health, being particularly concerned with medical education, and especially that of women. She was authoritative and confident, as a professional. She is a marvellous and imaginative gardener and cook, and, last time I met her, was engaged in an Open University degree course in History. A friend of mine who met both the Shores for the first time some years ago at an enormous lunch-party, was surprised and touched by Peter's pointing out Liz across the room, when he and my friend had been talking for some time, and saying, 'Isn't she amazingly beautiful?'

George Clayton had gone up to King's College a year before Peter Shore, and had strongly urged him to take the scholarship and entrance examination the following year, in the winter of 1941, to join him at King's. This he successfully did, and had four terms, as I did in Oxford at exactly the same time (though mine were five), before leaving for the RAF. He and George continued both their friendship and their intense interest in the politics of the Left, while they were together in Cambridge. After the war, therefore, when he came back, he was a slightly elderly undergraduate, with an already developed commitment to undergraduate politics, the Labour Club and the Union. He never joined the Communist Party, though even while he was at school he had a great admiration for Russia, and many of his older contemporaries had joined, however briefly. According to George Clayton it was not so much Communism that attracted him as a schoolboy, far to the Left though his opinions were, but more the idea of Russia itself, a country which seemed actually to have done something, and be doing something for its own people. Communist Russia seemed like Holy Russia in a new guise. Moreover, whatever was actually happening domestically in Russia in the 1930s, *something* was happening; and the peculiar strength and fascination of Marxist philosophy was that, as Sartre noted, you could not just read it; if you read and understood, you had to act. From that beginning sprang the feeling that to embrace Socialism was more than simply to adopt a theory of political economy. It was to commit yourself to a cause.

Peter was, from an early age, personally committed to this cause. His family had been much affected by the Depression and he was familiar with the effects of poverty and unemployment. I, though I wrote endlessly in my diary about the Socialism that was bound to come after the war, and which, as a matter of moral theory, I increasingly welcomed, was, by contrast, wholly theoretical in my approach. I never thought of taking any active part in politics, even at an undergraduate level. This was partly because I disliked political undergraduates, and had a particular horror of the Union, a horror I still retain. I loathe the posturing, show-off self-importance and facetiousness of the debates. (And incidentally, now that the House of Commons can scarcely be thought of any longer as a place for serious debates, the role of the university Unions as the nurseries of politicians is presumably diminished.)

Nevertheless, I think that Peter Shore and I, radically different though we were, were both lucky to have been born when we were, in 1924. It meant that we were too young to share, in any practical sense, the anxieties and deep uneasiness of the 1930s. People ten years our senior, if they were perceptive about what was happening in Europe, if they loathed dictatorship, if they were aware how disastrously ill-prepared Britain was for a war that seemed increasingly inevitable and increasingly justified, if they were shocked by the government's attitude of complacency especially with regard to Germany, had to live through genuine despair about what was to be done. Some of them felt compelled to make the gesture of going off to fight in Spain; some of them joined the Communist Party, all of them were pessimistic about both the short- and the long-term future. For Peter, strongly though he may have felt the wrongs of government policies, there was nothing he could actually do, before the war, except get on with his education, and then join the forces until it was over.

By 1945 our generation had the vote for the first time; the mood of the country had radically changed, and it was pretty clear even before the election that Labour would get in. The great new reforming documents, the Beveridge Report and the Butler Education Act, had been published or already implemented. Loyalty to an ageing wartime leader would not be a match for the egalitarian sentiments of the new generation of voters, or of those who had so much hated the 1930s. For anyone interested in the politics of the Left, there was every reason to be optimistic.

As early as 1950, as I have said, Peter stood as Labour candidate for the constituency of St Ives. He stood again for Halifax in 1959, and was finally elected as MP for Stepney in 1964, where he stayed through two boundary changes until he retired in 1997 (his constituency having been transformed into Tower Hamlets, Stepney and Poplar from 1974 until 1983, and then into Bethnal Green and Stepney in 1983). It was a constituency that suited him perfectly and one in which he could see at first hand the social evils which, despite the optimism of the 1940s, still beset the country. Meanwhile, before his election to Stepney he had spent five years as head of the Labour Research department. He was becoming an authoritative political thinker and writer.

In 1958 a book of left-wing essays by young authors was published, entitled *Convictions*, to which Peter Shore (and Iris Murdoch, among others) contributed. His essay was called *The Room at the Top*. The title of the essay is a reference to John Braine's bestselling novel, *Room at the Top*, published the year before. John Braine was part of a group of writers including Kingsley Amis, John Osborne and John Wain, known collectively as the Angry Young Men, who wrote radical, anarchical novels and plays, left-wing, and highly cynical about what came to be called the Establishment, including institutions of high culture and learning, as well as of government. They caused considerable outrage, especially as they had no seriously thought-out political views, and were offensive especially to the high-minded pre-war left-wing intellectuals, such as Stuart Hampshire and Isaiah Berlin. (In fact virtually all of these authors, especially Kingsley Amis and John Braine, moved to the right with astonishing rapidity as they grew older, which their detractors treated as proof that they had never had any political principles in the first place.) The 'room' of Shore's title was a physical space, on the top floor of a typical corporate headquarters or large manufacturing company, where the newly rich class of managers did their managing in style and comfort. On the lower floors in hierarchical order were grouped the workers, hands-on in their various ways.

The argument of the essay is that with the growth of larger and larger corporations (not yet seriously multinational, but large nevertheless, and growing) the managerial class had also grown immensely, and had access, through the salaries they allotted themselves, as well as the perks and hidden advantages that were taken for granted as their right, to the wealth of the companies for which they worked. Shore compares this class to bishops in the Church, who do not own the property they enjoy, but control it, and can amass wealth from their position, which they can hand on to their children. It is the ability that the managers possess to make life better for their children, through education and other advantages, that justifies describing them as a 'class', rather than merely as an elite, to which others might have access in their turn. The working class in these corporations is looked after, paternalistically, and thus manipulated into corporate loyalty; but there is no serious movement towards industrial democracy. Whether such a corporation is nationalised or privately owned makes no difference. The new managerial class remains the same in either case. Socialism in the sense of the equalising of wealth, opportunity and power is lacking. Shore ends with these words: 'I do not want a society in which one [class] viewing the world through Board Room windows, makes the big decisions, collects the big rewards, while the mass of men, deprived of power and responsibility dig their gardens or watch the telly. I want instead a society which shapes its institutions so that men may become self-determining, their own masters. For we are in the end what society allows us to be: adults or children, masters or slaves, apathetic or involved. Humanity can develop only if we have faith in its innate capacity, if we refuse to believe that men are what they are because they can be no different. This is to me the start of democratic socialism, and the basic case for social change'. This was his far-Left credo. He failed to be elected at Halifax on the strength of it; but he was adopted as the candidate for Stepney in September 1964, before the General Election in October, when he was elected. Labour won by a considerable majority, and Harold Wilson became Prime Minister after what was described in the Labour catch-phrase as 'thirteen years of Tory misrule'. Peter Shore's insight into the rise of the new managerial class had a considerable impact later on the fierce arguments about whether or not the Labour Party should aim, above all else, at the nationalisation of the great companies, the notorious Clause IV arguments.

Harold Wilson was Prime Minister from 1964 until 1970. Peter Shore was his PPS for a year from 1965, when he moved, after the February 1966 General Election, first to being Joint Parliamentary Secretary at the Ministry of Technology, then, in August 1967, to the same rank in the Department of Economic Affairs, before being given sole charge of that portfolio in September 1967. The Department, brought into being by Wilson in 1964, had a wide scope. It was supposed to concentrate on the general allocation of resources, on investment policy and import replacement, and on coordinating the work of all the industrial departments. It was supposed at the beginning to be a counter-force to the Treasury, headed by a Senior Minister, George Brown, the Party's Deputy Leader, with the specially created title of First Secretary. He was supposed to be able to stand up to the Chancellor of the Exchequer. Whatever it actually did, it sounded formidable. We learn from Richard Crossman's diary that Peter was widely regarded as a 'satellite' of Wilson, though generally also regarded as very clever. However, there is a good deal of muttering in the diaries that the papers produced by the Department of Economic Affairs were sloppy and badly drafted, and that 'Peter Shore, who is a brilliant draftsman if he wants to be, seems to have done nothing himself ...; Here is Peter, promoted far beyond his station by the PM ... too grand to do the drafting that would make the

White Paper [on Prices and Incomes] tolerable' (*The Diaries of a Cabinet Minister* volume II, 1976 p. 738). Perhaps Peter was not thought to have made himself enough of a professional economist to do much good at this department; at any rate, in a huge reshuffle, not just of Ministers but of Ministries, the DEA was abolished in October 1969, and Peter became Minister without Portfolio and Deputy Leader of the House of Commons until the Labour defeat in 1970. In opposition for four years, Shore was spokesman on Europe. When Labour won the election in 1974, and Wilson became Prime Minister for the second time, he was Trade Secretary for two years, and then Secretary of State for the Environment, both of these being Cabinet posts. Then followed the long spell in opposition, from 1979 until 1997. He did not stand again for Stepney in 1997, but with some hesitation, no doubt, accepted a peerage and joined the House of Lords as Lord Shore of Stepney, soon after Labour came back into power.

So how does this long, useful and prominent career in politics, useful and prominent both while Labour was in power and while it was in opposition, reflect or throw light on the nature of the Labour Party itself? There is no doubt that Peter Shore was, or at least became, a thorough politician, as well as a much-loved constituency MP, and extremely well-known. He, like many politicians, had a look and a style which made him instantly recognisable, his pale straw-coloured hair, with a long hanging lock in the front constantly in his eyes, unless swept to one side for a moment. He also had a recognisable loose-mouthed way of talking, almost spitting out his words, and a recognisable and consistent angle at which he held his head. And to this was added emphatic gestures with his hands. Such characteristics, part natural, part exaggerated, perhaps never recognised clearly by the protagonist himself, are important for politicians as they are for schoolteachers. It must be useful for a politician to be an easy subject for cartoonists; and television manifestly makes gestures and mannerisms into natural symbols. Some members of his extended family complained that Peter always spoke to them as if addressing a full House of Commons, and especially as if they were the dimmest of the benches opposite. On the other hand, when he spoke from the front benches in the first Wilson government, Dick Crossman took a very low view of his performance. After a party Crossman gave in November 1967 he wrote this in his diary: (*The Diaries of a Cabinet Minister* volume II p. 547) 'This evening we gave dinner for Barbara [Castle] Wedgy, [Anthony Wedgwood Benn] and Tommy [Thomas Balogh]. Peter Shore and his wife, Liz, came later on ... Listening to Wedgy and Peter I became a little worried about the future of the Party. Wedgy is brilliant at public relations and has enormous drive and ambition but he refuses to face the real difficulties because he has a second-rate intellect. Peter is infinitely more intelligent but he completely lacks Wedgy's power to put himself across. He has made a very poor appearance on the front bench this week, reading aloud a dull script dully, and getting a bad response from our back-benchers, poor man ... but as private friends we must give him time and work closely with him'. Whether or not Crossman's assessment of Peter's performance at that date is accurate, it is very difficult to relate it to his performances now in the House of Lords, thirty years later, where he speaks with brilliance and passion and with a script he hardly looks at.

In 1993 Shore published a book entitled *Leading the Left* which, in my view, very well analyses some of the inbuilt contradictions of the Labour Party, and incidentally betrays quite a lot of his own attitudes towards recent leaders, though the book is not even remotely autobiographical. Of course, the paradox of the party is in a sense easily explained, and totally inevitable. Shore sets out the two main causes of the continuing divisions within the party (and thus of the virtual impossibility of leading it) in the introduction to his book. The causes are closely linked. The first lies in the origins of the party. Since the Industrial Revolution, increasingly throughout the second half of the nineteenth century, there came into existence groups and projects aimed at enabling the needs of the working class to be met by means other than charity. The logical outcome of universal male franchise should be recognised, it was argued: Labour must be given a voice of its own. Charity, even if properly organised and distributed, was increasingly seen to be paternalistic and derogatory of working men and their families, both inequitable and inefficient as a way of improving the lot of the workers. Marxism and any form of Socialism is naturally at war with the concept of charity. This was the conclusion of Beatrice Potter, later Beatrice Webb, who, when she was young, worked for the Charity Organisation Society. This was the conclusion, too, of Leonard Woolf, when he came back to London in 1912 from serving in Ceylon with the Indian Civil Service. He was the kind of high-minded and morally high-principled person who was central to the Labour Party in the early days. After having responsibility for the life of communities in Ceylon, he felt drawn to exercising similar responsibility at home, but recognised quite soon that organised charity might be fitting for the natives, but not for the British working class. He pulled out of charity, therefore, describing himself as halfway to being a Socialist, and was soon drawn into the Fabian Society, by Beatrice and Sidney Webb. The Fabian Society had been dominated by the Webbs since 1890, and they were convinced that State Socialism must be the ultimate goal of all the different Labour movements that were springing up. But they were equally convinced that any attempt at swift change would damage the workers, not help them, whether the change took the form of revolution or legislation. The Fabian aim was to start at municipal level with as much Socialism as possible, and gradually permeate central government with Socialist ideas. In fact the Webbs believed that the best way forward might well be for the Trades Unions and the employers to bargain with the Conservative Party, who might enshrine the agreements they reached in legislation.

This cautious policy formed one important element of the Labour Party when it emerged. It was wholly opposed, however, by the Independent Labour Party, founded by Keir Hardy in 1893, and by the more broadly based Labour Representation Committee which was finally transformed into the Labour Party in 1906. And besides these elements there were also explicit Marxists and revolutionaries who were represented in the Social Democratic Federation. From the very beginning, then, the new party could be divided into Left and Right, from Marxists to Fabians.

It could also be divided between pacifists and non-pacifists. Part of the reason for the strong strand of pacifism in the party was, I suppose, its connections with Marxism, according to which, world wide, workers must unite to overthrow capitalism, wherever it existed. Capitalism was to be the only enemy against whom violence could properly be used; and capitalism itself, according to this pure doctrine, was the cause of war. War was a phenomenon which worked in the interests of capitalism, and capitalist competition encouraged it. Thus there was a strong link between anti-capitalist, left-wing Socialism and pacifism; and the later campaign for unilateral nuclear disarmament was on the whole supported by the far Left of the party, though there was not a complete overlap between these factions (Bevan, for example, though strongly Socialist, was not a unilateralist) But the connection was much strengthened after the First World War, when, alongside the slaughter of millions of working-class men (among others), capitalists got ever richer and more capable of exploiting the workers. These, then, were some of the deep disagreements which formed part of the baggage carried by the Labour Party, contentious ideas that entered permanently into its conceptual framework and its political vocabulary.

The second and related cause of the continuing difficulties of the party, was, as Shore lucidly sets out, its extraordinary constitution. He makes clear that, because of its late birth compared with that of the other two parties, a constitution had to be established that would seem suitable for an era of mass democracy. 'While all parties now have mass membership and annual conferences,' he writes, 'control over policy in the two older parties has remained firmly in the hands of the parliamentary leadership. In the Labour Party, however, the struggle for control over party policy between the parliamentary leadership and the Annual Conference has had to be waged continuously' (*Leading the Left* p. 9). And since the Conference cannot sit all the time, a committee of it, the National Executive Committee, sees to the day-to-day business of carrying out policy for the party as a whole. Membership of the NEC is therefore highly prized, and carries enormous power. Indeed, with hindsight, it looks as if the constitution had been expressly designed to bypass Parliament and its elected members altogether, or at least to reduce them to mere ciphers (perhaps an early manifestation of the withering away of the state). No matter what combination of Trades Union leaders, constituency party members and Ministers made up the NEC, the fact would remain that it was a committee of the Annual Conference, and to the Conference and the Conference alone was it answerable. It seems a recipe for disaster. I suppose at first it was assumed that because the leader of the party, who would be Prime Minister when Labour was in power, would be in broad agreement with the party at its conference, there would not be a conflict. Nowadays, anyone who has witnessed students elected by their colleagues to take their statutory seats on, as it might be, the Council of Senate in Cambridge will know that being part of Government (or even, though to a lesser extent, part of the official opposition) brings a totally new sense of what is possible, a realism, and an understanding of how things actually work, which is often far from popular with those who elected them. The student body as a whole can make demands and express bright ideas about changes that ought to be made without restraint. Their wretched representatives, though they may carry the messages faithfully, may recognise at once that these demands, for excellent reasons, cannot be met. Then of course they, the elected members, are denounced as traitors, accused of having turned gamekeeper, and of betraying the student cause. So it must be for a leader of the Labour Party. 'Conference', as they call it, has no responsibilities, and can decide on whatever policy it likes, the more ideologically extreme the better, or the more concerned solely with the demands of the Trades Unions. (For example, in the case which I have followed most closely, policies adopted at 'Conference' which are concerned with school education seldom seem to bear much relation to current educational legislation.) Only Government (or Opposition) has the task of seeing from the inside whether the policy is practicable or even widely desirable. As Shore says, no single one of the leaders he discusses has avoided the accusation of betraying Socialism, apparently abandoning the ideology of extremists at 'Conference'.

These deep and inbuilt divisions within the party go a long way to explaining my own uneasiness, my feeling that I should never really understand the Labour Party. It is very easy to forget the genuinely revolutionary Marxist origins of some of the ideas of the Left; and it is easy to be bewildered by the fact that the Annual Conference may seem to be at odds with the parliamentary Labour Party, and that in theory its powers are superior. It would seem to be a miracle if any leader could do more than try to hold the party together. All such difficulties had been obscured during the war, at the time of the Coalition government, and during the first great Labour government, when it was a question of passing legislation that had been anticipated for years. Then the Labour Party was, apparently, speaking with one voice, and basking in its own popularity. After Attlee it began to fall to pieces, or at least to speak with discordant voices.

I want, therefore, to ask how Peter Shore stood with regard to these divisions, and to suggest that on the whole his has been a perceptive and unifying presence, his career a thread running through the dramatic and often traumatic course of Labour history. One must first remind oneself that he did not enter Parliament until 1964, after Gaitskell's election to the leadership in 1955, after his great victory over the National Executive Committee in 1961, and after his death in 1963. However one must also remember that he was, as head of the Labour Research Department, not only knowledgeable about, but enormously influential in the formation of Labour policy before this time. For example, Gaitskell managed to defuse the issue of the ownership of industry, the great Clause IV controversy, for several years in the mid-1950s, by arguing that the central Socialist war against capitalism, the private ownership of the means of production, had lost some of its urgency, now that companies were bigger, and the huge division was not between capitalists and workers, but between managers and workers, the very argument expounded in Peter Shore's 1958 essay, mentioned above. It is more than probable that Peter was responsible for this idea, which turned out to be useful, in so far as it showed how Marxist simplicities increasingly looked like mere rhetoric, in the changing industrial facts of society.

The other great divisive issue, that of disarmament, came to a head when the Conservative government announced in 1960 that the only long-range nuclear missile that was produced wholly in

Britain, Blue Streak, was to be discontinued. The National Executive Committee and many of the Trades Unions in their own conferences took this as an occasion to vote for the policy of abandoning nuclear arms altogether, and unilaterally. This brought into the open the constitutional chaos of the Labour Party. It seemed that there was a complete impasse, since only a few months before, when the government abandoned Blue Streak, Gaitskell, as Leader of the Opposition, had pledged that Labour would not join the 'pacifists, neutralists, unilateralists' but would seek to maintain British defences, relying on the Nato alliance, that is, on the technology and manufacturing capability of the USA. During the following year, 1960/61, Gaitskell, with enormous skill, managed to increase his own reputation, above all with the press and in Parliament, so that at the autumn conference the unilateralist decision of the year before was easily overthrown, and the danger of an absolute split of the party into two was averted. But it was clear that Gaitskell's vision of the Labour Party was far from the old orthodoxy. In the follow-up to the election defeat of 1959 he had spoken of the social changes that had come about since the war, which had changed the nature of the working class itself. To become electable the party must present itself, he said, in a new way. They must be seen to be 'a modern party, looking to the future not the past'. New Labour, in fact: the speech could have been written by Tony Blair himself.

The last great issue that Gaitskell had to face as leader of the party was that of the Treaty of Rome. Terms of possible entry were being worked out in the summer before he died, and at his last conference he presented a statement, *Labour and the Common Market*, which had in fact been drafted for him by Peter Shore. Though the arguments both for and against entry were rehearsed in the statement, the conclusion was that we should not enter, and Gaitskell's speech against entering was not only powerful, but extremely popular. There can be no doubt that Peter's influence was strong, on this issue. But I doubt whether he had fully made up his mind on what was the right thing to do before working all the summer, with Gaitskell, over the details of the Treaty of Rome. As often happens, it was in deciding, during that summer, how to balance and present the arguments that what appeared to be the right solution emerged. The real issue was national sovereignty. In his speech, Gaitskell foresaw that what Europe really wanted was federation, a United States of Europe: 'That is what it means; it does mean the end of Britain as an independent nation state; it means the end of a thousand years of history. You may say "let it end", but my goodness it is a decision that needs a little care and thought.' These were Gaitskell's words. But they could have been Shore's. The idea was shared.

On the matter of Europe, then, Shore and Gaitskell thought as one, and probably reached their position together. Yet, had Gaitskell lived, and had he won the General Election in 1964, the year when Peter entered Parliament, it is not certain whether or not Britain would have entered the Common Market in the end. Nor is it certain how Gaitskell and Peter would have got on, or whether his rise in the parliamentary party, and in government, would have been as meteoric as in fact it was. He would undoubtedly have done well, being clever and ambitious as well as a very good MP. But I doubt whether he and Gaitskell would ever have been particularly close, or necessarily in agreement except about Europe, on which subject, of course, Peter has never changed his mind.

There was something about Gaitskell's own attitude towards the party that contributed to my personal sense of unease about Labour. He was posh Labour; and this was something that Peter Shore never was. This was partly because Gaitskell and his friends, whether in Parliament or outside, were too overtly to the right of the party to suit Peter. After all, when he first became a Member of Parliament, he and Benn were often linked together, frequently, for example, by Crossman in his diaries. But it was partly, I suspect, a difference between Oxford and Cambridge, however absurd it may seem to say so.

It has often been remarked that Oxford is an altogether more worldly place than Cambridge, and this has never been more true than in the 1950s and early 1960s. Never have Oxford and London seemed so close. This was the time when, academically, Oxford was at its height, especially perhaps in the fields of Philosophy, Politics and Economics. The very existence of the joint school of PPE and the newly instituted B.Phil. courses in all three subjects drew good students from all over the world; and there was no shortage of outstanding teachers. Senior members of the University were supremely confident, and were therefore wooed by the BBC and felt at home there, as well as in 'the corridors of power'. We were all, comparatively speaking, affluent, and could supplement our income by journalism and broadcasting and extremely well-paid semesters in America. We could spend money, within reason, on clothes (which we bought, as a matter of course, in London), parties and holidays, mostly in Tuscany. And we were of the generation who had first voted, and voted Labour, in 1945, having tacked ourselves on to the pre-war left-wing intellectuals, Isaiah Berlin and Stuart Hampshire, for example, who had been so much horrified by Conservatism before the war. There were many such people, of course, in Cambridge as well, but their links with Westminster were not, on the whole, so close. The Oxford left-wing dons seemed to take it for granted that they would advise Labour, and seriously influence policy. I remember Stuart Hampshire saying, in 1963, when he was about to go off to a Chair in Princeton, that though he looked forward to it, he bitterly regretted that he would not be on hand to 'help Labour' in the next election.

Among the post-war PPE people, a central character was Ian Little, an economist, and a friend of Geoffrey's from New College days. He and Geoffrey had shared tutorials in philosophy, and their tutor, Herbert Hart, newly appointed after the war as Fellow and Tutor at New College, having been a barrister, and never having taught philosophy before, used to teach them early on Monday mornings, so that he could pick their brains, and use their tutorials as the model and a crucial resource for the rest of the week, or so he claimed. As an undergraduate before the war, Ian had been conspicuously idle, and spent a great deal of his time playing cards and driving fast cars, having pursued much the same course at Eton. But in the RAF, where his driving skills were put to use as a test pilot, he found himself stuck in Egypt, and, being bored, he more or less on the spur of the moment decided to start to read. He knew he would be returning to New College if he survived, so he wrote to his former philosophy tutor, H.H. Price, later Wykeham Professor of Logic, and asked for a reading list. Here his academic career started, and when he came back he had no doubt that he would remain in the academic world if he could. Besides being clever, he was quite seriously rich, his grandfather having made his money in the railways. He was, as an undergraduate, someone of amazing charm. He already had a lizard-like, wrinkled face, and he had a kind of wit that essentially went with his physical appearance and his elegant way of doing things, such as playing golf, and driving his Jaguar. His manner was far from over-confident, and in some matters he was anxious to seek advice. Geoffrey and he, with his wife, Dobs, whom he had met in his RAF days, saw a great deal of each other. Geoffrey used to stay with them for weekends, play golf with Ian and take Dobs to the opera, where they both sat and sobbed. I never met them until 1948, when I was just beginning to get to know Geoffrey, and we were both taking our final examinations. Ian asked us both out to lunch after Schools finished. In fact my examinations had not, strictly, finished; there was a Greek Prose examination in the afternoon of the day we were invited. But by then the Greek and Latin Proses were more or less optional, and I had done the Latin Prose, and thought that that would do. I was not going to refuse what seemed to me the most glamorous invitation imaginable, and which gave me extra pleasure in that I was being treated as Geoffrey's 'girl', as I very much hoped to become. So Ian and Dobs picked us up outside the Examination Schools, where we sat (at that time still more or less legitimately) in the car drinking champagne, and then drove, at what seemed to me fantastic and thrilling speed, to Woodstock, to the Marlborough Arms. I was dazed by the fact that Geoffrey and I, still in our black and white subfusc, and carrying our gowns, were sitting together at this perfect lunch party, and that exams were over. I was, as was he, totally exhausted, and exceptionally short of sleep, sleep having become progressively more impossible as the week of the exams went on. But I was still capable of eating a vast lunch, smoked salmon, mixed grill and apricot tart, an absolute feast for those post-war days, drinking more champagne, and brandy with our coffee. I immediately adored Ian, he and Dobs representing an unknown way of life which I longed to discover.

When Geoffrey and I got married in the following year, his parents came to live in Sutton Courtenay, a village on the Thames not far from Oxford, famous as the home of Asquith in his years in power. The Littles also lived there, and so we came to see a great deal of them; we went out to Sutton Courtenay for many week-ends in term, and for longer stays in the vacations. The Littles' children were much the same ages as our eldest two, and we often entrusted our pair to their nanny, while we went and played golf. (This, in retrospect, seems rash: the nanny had had a pre-frontal lobotomy, a fashionable cure for depression in those days, but known to diminish the patient's moral sense.) It was in their house at Sutton Courtenay that we first met Anthony Crosland, who had been an economics tutor at Trinity College, but was now an MP.

Soon Ian and Dobs moved to a larger, grander house at Clifton Hampden, still beside the Thames, which ran past the bottom of their garden. Here they used to give dances in the summer, on a magnificent scale, and posh Labour was to be seen in force. Besides Crosland, there were Dalton, Douglas Jay, Crossman and Gaitskell, and, as of right, the ubiquitous Thomas Balogh, who as seemingly perpetual adviser to the government was inseparable from them. One of the dances was in fancy dress, and Balogh, who was in fact Hungarian, but who had extraordinary oriental-looking eyes, which in normal circumstances gave him a not misleadingly sinister appearance, came as a Chinese grandee with a drooping moustache attached to his upper lip (for a bit) and a splendid yellow silk coat. These dances were not particularly well-behaved. There was a great deal of talk, and not very much dancing; but every room in the house was open, and one would sometimes wander into a downstairs room and find someone who had passed out on the floor. It was unwise to venture upstairs, for fear of finding Gaitskell or Douglas Jay in bed with the girl of his choice. Balogh was exceptionally predatory, not only at these dances but at other parties in Oxford. (These were the 1950s equivalents of the Labour Luvvies, thirty or more years later; the Pinters, the Mortimers, the Bishop of Oxford and his wife, and others.)

It was among these people that the Common Market as a first tentative adumbration was endlessly discussed. There were those who loved the idea of becoming part of Europe, on purely cultural grounds. They were prepared to put up with anything (though they did not know what it might be) to have the privilege of joining the world of Racine, Voltaire, Proust, of great vintages, and international chefs. These sentimental pro-Marketeers were more often than not passionate francophiles; they did not think so much of the rest of Europe, especially not of Germany, there being less talk about the joys of becoming members of the world of Bach, Mozart or Strauss.

On the other hand there were those, among whom Geoffrey and I were numbered, who thought that the Common Market must be, fundamentally, an economic concept, and so we wanted to be told what the economic advantages or disadvantages would be if we were to join (but no one could tell us: or rather, everyone told us, but they told us different things). These were the endless conversations of the Chattering Classes of those days.

I could never see how Douglas Jay persuaded his victims to go upstairs with him; but Gaitskell was the greatest seducer, and I could feel, though never at very close quarters, his charm, and the force of his personality. Sometime in the early 1960s, when Geoffrey was away in America, I was invited to lunch by the then editor of the *Daily Telegraph*, who had known my brother Duncan at Winchester. The only other guest was Gaitskell. On that occasion I experienced what I suppose made him so irresistible to women, his power to turn his whole attention on them, and speak as if for their ears alone, even though what he was discussing was foreign policy or the obstinacy of the Trades Union leaders. As we were going down in the lift after lunch, our host said to Gaitskell: 'Did you know that Mary is Duncan Wilson's sister?' Gaitskell turned to me with an intense and piercing smile, and said: 'I don't need to know whose sister you are'. I cherished that remark for months, and thought of it sadly when, a short time later, he died.

I do not believe that this charm, felt by men and women equally, should be underestimated as an element in Gaitskell's success. He was, after all, successful in at least temporarily smoothing over some of the great divisions in the Labour Party. But would it have answered in the long run? There seems to me no doubt that if he had become Prime Minister, and especially if he had won more than one election, it would have been New Labour he led to victory. He understood very well, as did Peter Shore, that the working class was changing rapidly, and that old-fashioned Socialism was becoming irrelevant; but it may well be that 1964 was too soon to accept the kind of revolution that we have seen since 1997, when the old working class could simply be written out of the script. I believe that he might have proved too intolerant of his colleagues, too much of an intellectual, too much tarred with the Oxford brush, perhaps even too frivolous to have been 'the best Prime Minister', if he ever had become one. Benn, in a diary entry for 1981, quotes Chris Price (then MP for Lewisham, and later head of Leeds Polytechnic) as saying, 'What really happened to the Party was that when Gaitskell became leader in 1955, there was a plot to put in an elite of Oxford Right-wingers to take the Party over. They were pro-American, pro-European, anti-Communist and they got all the jobs in later Governments. I never had a chance'. Twenty-five years on, he obviously still felt resentment, the use of the word 'plot' betraying him. There was no plot; but there was undoubtedly a deep affinity between Gaitskell and the smart and self-confident PPE set in Oxford, and it is doubtful whether someone capable of stirring up such deep feelings of hostility could have made a wholly successful Prime Minister.

It was when Harold Wilson became leader of the party in 1964 (Prime Minister until 1970, and again from 1974 until his retirement in 1976) that Peter Shore, now an MP and soon a Minister, exercised most power in the party, and somehow mirrored its progress. I personally, for what it was worth, lost my sense of confusion about the party, which I left in 1965, so that, thankfully, I could now observe it without any commitment. But in any case Harold Wilson seemed in a remarkable way to obscure the deepest causes of division, though they did not go away. It may have been partly that, though not a real member of the working classes, and though in some sense an intellectual, he seemed a very plain down-to-earth person, and he certainly recognised that the world was changing, and that socially the nature of industry and employment within industry would change, with the new technologies beginning to emerge, the cloth cap replaced by the white laboratory coat. It was his insistence that the first task for the Labour Party must be to exploit these new technologies, through education and investment, that made him seem, at least from the outside, an original, even an imaginative voice. He had no charm, but he had competence. Again, his newly formed Department of Economic Affairs promised to bring together the needs of industry with those of the unions, and generally to oversee the distribution of resources in a way that was never really part of the task of the Treasury. Even the intensely tedious Regional Economic Planning Councils (of one of which I, on the invitation of Peter, was a member for a time) seemed part of a properly democratic move, by which differences might be reconciled, and old hostilities forgotten. It was a remarkable feat for Wilson to win a second election, with an increased majority, in 1966.

In Wilson's third term of office, however, after the 1974 election, when he replaced Heath as Prime Minister, all the old divisions within Labour seemed to have broken out again. The period in opposition had given them time to resurface and intensify. The left wing of the party, with Benn very much in charge, became far more demanding. It is of interest to note that Tony Benn records in his diaries that his wife gave him a copy of the *Communist Manifesto* in his Christmas stocking in 1976, and that he then read it, surprisingly for the first time, and was fired with a new enthusiasm for Marxist Socialism. It is perfectly true that, when Benn was an undergraduate in the late 1940s, one could read PPE without ever reading a word of Marx. And it may well be that Benn had read a lot of Marx, but had not read the *Communist Manifesto*. Speculation is pointless. In 1977, Benn remarked (also in his diaries) that Peter was moving sharply to the Right. It is possible; but much more likely that Benn, on the wings of his belated enthusiasm for Marx, moved fairly sharply to the Left. Peter himself believes that a change came over Benn a decade earlier, in 1964 or 1965, when Peter first became a Member of Parliament. It was probably then that the deliberately devised persona began to emerge: the revealed braces, the huge mugs of tea, the 'working man's' jollity. In any case, his interventions in favour of the strikers who were increasingly disrupting industry in the 1970s, his insistence on the primacy of the NEC's decisions over those of Cabinet, and his genuine belief that capitalism could not recover and must be replaced made him an awkward and a very high-profile member of the 1974 government, both when it was led by Harold Wilson and when Callaghan had taken over. By the next election, in 1979, not only the Labour Party but the whole economy was in disarray. In the winter of 1978/9, the 'winter of discontent', the unions and the Left of the party appeared to have total control. There was no question of being able to impose a pay policy. Huge demands for increased wages came from every side. Strikes, both official and unofficial, were on a scale that we could none of us remember. No one emptied the dust-bins, patients could not be taken to hospital; grave-diggers refused to carry out burials of the dead. It was no surprise that Labour lost the election in the May of 1979. They proceeded to lose three in a row; and then to everyone's amazement they lost a fourth in 1992.

Even the Conservatives seemed totally taken aback by this fourth victory. They had no very coherent and certainly no new policy in place. John Major, in his months as Prime Minister after the fall of Thatcher and before the 1992 election, had had on the whole a bad press (though nothing like what was to come). It was one of the cases where a one-word description (the word 'grey') seemed to have taken hold of the public consciousness, and defined what they wished to see as his character. It was impossible to dislodge. It is true that he got great credit for the concessions he had won to the Maastricht Treaty at the end of 1991 but that did not seem to be enough to win a second term, especially in a period of recession. Yet it was plain that Labour, itself still in bad shape and deeply divided between Left and Right, and perhaps even more divided over Europe, still failed to convince. And if there were waverers, as I at any rate thought at the time, some must have decided to vote Conservative when they heard Neil Kinnock's hubristic and premature triumphalism, in his speech at Sheffield, shortly before polling day.

There followed five years in which the Labour Party had time to become stronger, at least one of its causes of dissension, namely the power of the unions to dictate policy and to determine the quality of day-to-day life in the country as a whole, having more or less been forgotten. Meanwhile, the word 'Socialism' dropped out of the political vocabulary. And while the Labour Party became less divided, the Conservative Party increasingly tore itself to pieces, the idea of cabinet loyalty becoming a dream of the past. They became more and more arrogant; they drove through legislation, often carelessly drafted, regardless of public opinion. It was increasingly clear that there had to be a change of government, and the sooner the better, if for no other reason than that we had had one party in power for so long that they had ceased to give a damn about what anybody thought of them. I for one could never understand why so much thought and agonised analysis of causes was devoted by the Tories to the question why they lost the 1997 election. They had to lose; and most people voted simply for a change, regardless of policies or manifestos.

After the much lamented death of the Labour leader John Smith, in 1994, Tony Blair had been elected leader of the Labour Party and in 1997 he became Prime Minister with a vast majority. John Major, in his autobiography, described him as a 'political kleptomaniac'. It is true that he has taken over most of the Tory policies, developed, for good or ill, over the last decade. The difference between his New Labour and Conservatism is that New Labour shows an astonishing ignorance of, or disregard for, the historical continuity of politics, and especially of the development of the constitution over many years. Looking towards the future cannot make sense if the past is disregarded, and such disregard is the major fault of the present party.

The other new factor in New Labour is the reliance of members of the party, especially of the parliamentary party, on the services of so-called spin doctors, professional presenters both of people and of policies, so as to display them to the public in the most favourable light. The consequence of both these factors is that a deep cynicism has grown up among the general public about politicians. They seem to assume a difference between themselves, who are in the know, and the rest of us who are suckers, and do not know that we are being manipulated by puppet-masters behind the scenes. We are not, on the whole, such fools: we know that we would prefer to hear from politicians themselves rather than being presented with a story constructed by someone else, made up for a particular purpose. We would rather be told what people believe, even though we may disagree with it, than what it is supposed would be most attractive. What we get now is rather like what one gets if one asks an Irishman how far it is to the next village. The answer is always what will be most agreeable to hear. 'Oh not very far at all.' The news sounds nice but in the end it does not satisfy the basic demands of human communication. It is for this reason that the young have an increasing affection for Tony Benn who seems, however dotty, to be endearingly sincere, and for Ken Livingstone who again appears to say what he himself means rather than what he is told to say. Being young they have little sense of what damage these new-found heroes have done. They do not fear the consequences of Socialism, nor of an allegiance to Marxism, or the other bogeys that frightened us in the past. However, I find it hard to believe that the style of New Labour, being based on marketing techniques, can convince for ever. And Europe may yet be its downfall.

For there is an absolutely central source of potential instability in the present political scene. We do not know, even after all this time, what to think about Europe, or how far our commitment to complete membership should go. This is by far the most important issue, a cross-party source of division, more than any other at the present time. It is here that Peter Shore has been steadfast and unmoved. His opposition to the European union, thought out, clarified and defended in his long-ago drafting exercise for Gaitskell, has never wavered. And increasingly, day by day, his fear for the erosion of British sovereignty is justified. Do we or do we not want to be part of a federal Europe, with a common currency, and subject to laws which emanate from Brussels? The Conservative Party has not definitively answered this question. New Labour has answered it, but has not yet quite clearly publicised its answer in case it is too profoundly unpopular. There may still be some people who believe, as Tony Blair wants them to, that we can join as, somehow and miraculously, dominant partners, and also as retaining our national sovereignty.

Some people have expressed surprise that Lord Shore of Stepney is so much at home in the House of Lords. But it is not really to be wondered at. At last he is free to speak his mind without having to think of the political consequences of doing so.

He has no inhibitions about speaking against his party's received view. Thus he is free to attack, in reasoned but passionate terms, his party's attitude to the salaries of those who teach in the universities, or, even more tellingly, the erosion of British sovereignty under the increasing domination of Brussels. It is a delight to hear him speak. He is rational, emotional, articulate and manifestly sincere. He is a voice of the best of 'Old Labour'. It is not possible to think of him as remote, in the manner of the Oxford Groupies of the 1950s and '60s; but nor has he ever, I should suppose, worn a cloth cap.

Compared with him, much though the honesty of his diaries is to be admired, Tony Benn is a made-up character. As I remember him, in undergraduate days, he was deeply ambitious, and determined to be a notable politician, whatever it cost him. This was not necessarily a characteristic to be despised. But it made him into a very disagreeable young man, at the time. He weighed people up, almost visibly, to test whether they were worth or not worth cultivating. I remember a particular occasion when, having very properly disregarded me, as of no possible use to himself, he said he must rush off from the party we were at, to go to the Romanes Lecture, to be delivered in a few minutes in the Sheldonian Theatre. I could not prevent myself from saying (because I very much disliked him) that I too was going, because it was my cousin who was giving it. His eyes widened, his manner visibly changed, he suggested we go together. He suddenly saw a window he had not suspected.

He had begun to make himself up into a figure, potentially a figurehead, even then. Peter Shore could never, in one's wildest imaginings, have become 'Pete'. It has been his role to cast light on the aspirations, but also the troubles of the Labour Party in the second half of the century, and for that we should, permanently, be grateful. As to my puzzlement with the nature of Labour, with which I started, it has withered away. Under Tony Blair, the Labour Party, to all intents and purposes, no longer exists. New Labour is something else.

Margaret Thatcher

Missis Thatcher
    Stick her in the bin
        Put the lid on
            Sellotape her in.

(skipping rhyme *c.* 1985)

Considering for how many years the topic of Margaret Thatcher was more commonly discussed, more guaranteed to fascinate than any other, not in this country alone, but in much of Europe and the United States, it may seem absurd to write just one chapter about her. But part of the reason for the universal obsession with her in the 1980s and early 1990s was that nearly everyone had their own story to tell, and her impact on individuals was astonishingly strong, and also varied. It may therefore be worth trying to recall what that impact was like on one person, myself.

I first met Margaret Thatcher in March 1977, when she was already Leader of the Conservative Party. We, Geoffrey and I, had been asked to a pre-lunch party by Janet Young (now Baroness Young) who was a Conservative city councillor, and at that time a close friend of Mrs Thatcher. She used to come down to Oxford quite often to 'unwind', we were told, in the Youngs' large house in North Oxford. Janet's father, Councillor Baker, had been a prominent figure in the City of Oxford. Her mother lived with her and her husband, Geoffrey, a nice, quiet scientist in the university, in one of the most beautiful parts of North Oxford, close to the Dragon School. Before Geoffrey (my husband, that is) became

Principal of Hertford College we had been near neighbours of the Youngs, though never exactly friends. I was rather frightened of Janet, with whom I had had some sort of a brush at an earlier date, when I was headmistress of the Oxford High School, and she a governor and a parent. Also, she was always immaculately turned out, with neat short-cropped hair, and wearing a very great deal of make-up. I have never felt entirely at ease with women who use a lot of make-up (unless they are young and making some kind of aesthetic statement about themselves). I feel as if they were not made of the same material as I, not wholly flesh and blood. It is impossible for me to imagine becoming an uninhibited friend of such a person. This formed, I suppose, and still forms part of my reaction to Mrs Thatcher.

At any rate, whether or not Margaret Thatcher was 'unwinding', there was little sign of relaxation at this party. Like royalty, she had been well briefed. The guests were lined up, and she walked past them, again like royalty, shaking hands and uttering a word or so to each. I was at that time chairing a committee of enquiry which she had herself set up, in the previous administration, when she had been Secretary of State for Education and Science. The committee was concerned with the education of children with special educational needs and had been continued by the next government. So she asked me how we were getting on, and when we hoped to report, and, without waiting for a reply, said 'SO important, I always think' and moved on. I had the chance to notice what I thought was a total absence of warmth, and also that the back of her stiffly bouffant hair (nevertheless not as startling then as it later became) was less impressive than the front, indeed quite ragged. She seemed mildly discontented with North Oxford society, but doing her best.

I did not meet her again until December 1980, when she had been Prime Minister for over a year, though of course I had seen her often on television, and watched her with fascination (and considerable admiration) for the way she handled interviewers, such as the snakey and clever Brian Walden in his Sunday lunch-time show. I was also beginning greatly to admire her determined outfacing of the Unions, and even her down-to-earth housewifely attitude to the British economy. Our meeting this time was over lunch with the Independent Broadcasting Authority, of which I had then been a member for six years or so.

1980 was a time of considerable stress within the IBA, because of the reallocation of the television broadcasting licences, the incumbent companies being in competition with new applicants. We were also about to have a new chairman, as Bridget Plowden was coming up to retirement age. The Authority itself was widely suspect, being thought, both by the broadcasting industry and by the government, to be incompetent to carry out the reallocation, and we were, individually and corporately, constantly wooed by the companies, old and new, to get us on their side. We had laid down strict rules for ourselves that we should accept no hospitality, no present, scarcely even a Christmas card, from any interested party. Moreover we were on the brink of setting up two wholly new channels, Breakfast Television and Channel Four. There was a great deal of work to do. In normal times we met on alternate Thursdays, and were accustomed to have guests to lunch in the middle of our meetings, politicians, advertising people, people from industry or the creators of programmes. These lunches were lavish and usually very enjoyable; members of the Authority and the senior staff were present. About halfway through the meal, a predetermined topic would be introduced, and from then on the conversation would be relatively formal, like a kind of seminar. But it was the custom for people to contribute fairly freely. However at this particular time, towards the end of 1980, we had given up inviting guests, and we met much more frequently than before. We had invited Mrs Thatcher more than once to our Thursday lunches, but she had never been free to accept. But suddenly, one Friday when we were having one of our extra meetings, the Authority was rung up by the Prime Minister's office to say that she was unexpectedly free, and would like to have lunch. We had a meeting in the morning and had put aside lunch-time to say goodbye to Bridget Plowden. However, there was nothing we could do but accede to the request.

Mrs Thatcher arrived late, and at our pre-lunch standing-about drinks time she behaved rather as she had at Janet Young's party, bustling about, shaking hands with members of the Authority and senior staff, though this time she had a press secretary with her. As soon as we sat down to lunch, and while the dishes were still being served, she started to speak. It must have been before she was taught, by those responsible for her packaging, to drop her voice by nearly an octave, and there were no dulcet tones. There was not even the air of the exasperated primary-school teacher, with difficulty keeping a grip on her patience, to which we were becoming accustomed on television. Instead, she spoke loudly, in a high-pitched and furious voice, and without drawing breath (or so it seemed, though she was able swiftly to eat up her lunch at the same time). Her theme was the appalling left-wing, anti-government bias of the independent television companies, and of the Authority itself. She spent a lot of time inveighing especially against *Panorama*, and there was no time, nor did it seem much to the purpose, to point out that this was a programme made and broadcast by the BBC. Indeed, all the specific programmes she mentioned were BBC programmes, but it was possible, we judged afterwards, that she never watched anything except the BBC, and in any case we were perfectly used to people who never noticed who made a programme, or on what channel it was shown. Her new plan, she stated, was to curb the media, and compel them to present news and current affairs in accordance with government wishes. The Director General at this time was Brian Young, a former headmaster, given to stuffing his handkerchief into his mouth when either acutely embarrassed, or overcome with unseemly laughter; and at this point he withdrew his handkerchief and managed to say that perhaps such a policy would be damaging to the freedom of the press. It was the first time that any of us had spoken, and it sounded, and was, banal. In any case, she swept it aside, and declared that the People were not interested in the freedom of the press, but only in having Choice (it was the first time I had heard this formula); and choice meant having available a variety of channels, all of which were truthful and encouraging. Nobody mentioned Stalin, but he was in everyone's mind. The only other intervention from our side came from the Director of Radio, who was having success at the time in setting up independent radio stations all over the country. He said that people seemed on the whole to like the kind of news they got on radio, biased or not. He managed to sound quite cheerful, but his intervention was not thought worthy of serious attention, and the flow continued. At last, at nearly 4 o'clock, Mrs Thatcher grabbed her shiny handbag, leapt to her feet and bustled out. Her press secretary lingered just long enough to opine that she had been rather tired, before following her, leaving us dazed. Bridget Plowden who had not uttered a word since coming into the dining room was in a state of near-collapse.

In the evening there was a different party for Bridget, given by Christopher Bland, the deputy chairman of the IBA (later chairman of the BBC Governors) at the Beefsteak Club. Bridget crept in with her husband, looking pale and ill. I was fond of her, and felt deeply for her, with her last day at the Authority ruined as it had been. She was sad enough to be leaving anyway, in the middle of such exciting new developments. When I said something vaguely sympathetic about the afternoon, she dissolved briefly into tears.

When I got home the next day, I tried to convey to Geoffrey the horror and outrage of this lunch, the barbarous battering we had had, the sheer rudeness and bad behaviour. He thought I was exaggerating and, as usual, making a great saga out of nothing, a mode of conversation he did not much like. In any case he had no love for commercial television, and was inclined to argue that anyway Mrs Thatcher was probably right. Within a year he had become Vice-Chancellor of Oxford, and was instrumental in setting up a lunch for the Prime Minister, along with the other Vice-Chancellors and Principals of the universities, in their headquarters in London. It was the beginning of the reforms in university financing, the end of the University Grants Committee. The future looked bleak, both in terms of the actual government money to be made available, and in terms of the freedom of the universities to determine their own policies and set their own priorities. A full discussion of future needs had been planned as the agenda for the discussion over lunch. It did not happen. The IBA pattern was repeated exactly. Almost as she hurried in with her little partridge steps, the Prime Minister began to rant against the universities, their arrogance, elitism, remoteness from the People, their indifference to the economy, their insistence on wasting time and public money on such subjects as history, philosophy and classics. Again, she did not stop for more than two hours; again no single one of her hosts could get a word in. Keith Joseph, then Secretary of State for Education, and who was also a guest, spoke not at all. Geoffrey came back to Oxford much shaken, both by the content of her tirade, and by the very fact that it had happened, exactly as I had described.

My last encounter with Mrs Thatcher was indirect and took place in the mid-1980s. There was a freelance journalist called

Graham Turner who lived in Oxford and wrote mostly for the *Telegraph*. He had written an extremely perceptive and fair profile of the motor works as they then existed in Cowley. I first met him on the train between London and Oxford, and we fell into conversation and got on very well. He told me that he had become a born-again Christian, and was exceedingly funny on the subject of his attempts to track down and make amends to the various people whom he had treated badly in the days before he discovered God. I thought that this was just the kind of thing that the Chaplain of Hertford (also Chaplain to Oxford United Football Club) would like as a Sunday sermon; and so it was. Indeed, Graham Turner became a frequent and popular preacher in College Chapel, and, though we did not much care for the born-again aspect, Geoffrey and I came to like him very much. He was engaging and funny and a great gossip.

He had asked whether, one weekend, he could interview us both, separately, about our views on the Prime Minister, and the present state of the universities (I was by now working in Cambridge during the weeks). It so happened that, for the weekend in question, we had an American journalist staying, George Will, who wrote a very right-wing, syndicated column, and who had been a pupil of Geoffrey's at Magdalen, his father being a philosopher, and an old friend. It seemed a good idea to ask Graham Turner to lunch to meet George, and then he could conduct his interviews afterwards. George was over in England partly to try to answer a question which fascinated him. The question was why did so many of his British friends loathe Mrs Thatcher, while in America she was adored? And how was it possible that, while being so widely disliked in this country, she was nevertheless voted for, often by the very people who disliked her? Such a thing, he alleged, could not happen in the States. If you were going to vote for someone, you had to make some sort of pretence that they were not only good at the job, but nice. We thought this an interesting question, and one worth analysing, and we thought that Graham Turner would enjoy discussing it. So I made it clear (as I thought) that we would talk off the record over lunch, for George's benefit, and the formal interviews would be afterwards. In the chatter that followed, just such a mixture of analysis and gossip as makes up the very best conversations (that which has given rise to the concept of the chattering classes) with quite a lot of wine and a great deal of hilarity, Geoffrey and I tried to pursue the details of what it was precisely that made us detest Margaret Thatcher, though in many ways still admiring her. He would continue to vote for her; I happily, had lost my vote, having become a life peer, so I had no choice to make. Geoffrey concentrated mostly on what had so much struck him at the Vice-Chancellors' lunch, namely her deep philistinism, amounting not just to a failure to understand but a positive hatred of culture, learning and civilisation. And of course we both spoke with eloquence on the subject of her appalling rudeness. We expanded this into a discussion of her style and taste (as shown in her gaudy clothes and her now rampant hairdressing), and I ended by saying, I think, that she simply did not know how to behave and was in some way LOW. Graham Turner said, 'You mean she is not a lady?' and I half-agreed, though this involved a good deal of further analysis, for the benefit of George Will, about what one could possibly mean by such an assertion, towards the end of the twentieth century.

Well, of course, when Graham Turner's article came out, all the measured words I deployed after lunch about the future of the universities were omitted; even Geoffrey's were given short shrift. The main point to emerge was my apparently frivolous and equally apparently snobbish objections to Mrs Thatcher's taste, and her well-publicised grocer's shop origins. I should have known.

Fortunately, our remarks came among equally hostile comments from many other people, among them 'intellectuals' such as Jonathan Miller and John Mortimer whom Mrs Thatcher particularly detested. All the same, the hate mail I got was prodigious. My poor secretary at Girton, already used to accusations against me of murder (because my committee of enquiry on embryology had condoned the – regulated – use of live human embryos for research) now had to put up with even more hysterical denunciations of my snobbishness. I never spoke to Graham Turner again, nor, I think, to Margaret Thatcher.

But was I wrong? Of course, if I'd had my wits about me I would not have expressed my views in the presence of Graham Turner or any other journalist. In this sense I was undoubtedly wrong. Yet I still think the question raised at that lunch party was worth discussing (and was indeed endlessly discussed at the time). What was it about Margaret Thatcher that made her so detestable to us and many of our contemporaries and friends? And this leads to a much more important question. What is it about Thatcherism that makes it so detestable and, even now, so difficult to shake off?

Before coming to that question, however, it is necessary to say something about the part that gender, or rather sex, plays in such issues. Although it is true that many of the people who wrote reviling me for my snobbishness were women, I think many women, nevertheless, found Margaret Thatcher peculiarly hard to bear. There were several reasons for this. In the first place, though basking in the glory of being the first woman to be a British Prime Minister, and much adored as a woman abroad, at home notoriously, she did not really like women very much, and certainly did not like having them around her. (She had long ago got rid of her erstwhile friend, Baroness Young.) Everyone knew this of her, and it is a characteristic hard for women to like, while men can, understandably, more easily forgive it. Women may be conscious that, to their shame, in similar circumstances they might react in the same way. There is, and has long been (though this may, I hope, be dying out), a certain excitement about being, not so much the first woman to do this or that, as the only woman. In the old days of the 'token woman' on boards and committees a woman did not always feel unmixed pleasure at being joined by another woman. Would that other dilute what she had come to think her right, the kind of courtesy and consideration and half-jokey admiration accorded her by her male colleagues? Would the other be cleverer, more attractive, better dressed, more articulate, more successful in combining femininity with power than she herself? To take a lowly analogy, I even remember that, when I first examined in the Final Honours School in Oxford, I had to be extremely careful not to be unfair to any woman who looked likely to get a First. My immediate reaction was to feel that I did not like the idea of others joining the club. Age, as well as a greater interest in seeing my own pupils do well, fortunately overcame this extremely disagreeable emotion.

Another reason for dislike, at least among women of Margaret Thatcher's own generation, and those older, was that they found her behaviour often offensive. They were conscious of certain social demands made of them simply as women, demands which she disregarded: it was a matter of deeply ingrained habit for them not to interrupt, not to monopolise a conversation, to allow other people to have their say, and to listen to what they said. I am not suggesting that men do not have this kind of sensitivity. Of course many of them do. But it is not so essential to their way of engaging with the world. It may be objected that this is simply no longer true of women: it used to be all part of 'being a lady', and therefore of no possible relevance to the world of this century and beyond. I am not so sure. Certainly, very young girls read in their comics that if they fancy a boy, they must not be too aggressive.

If they know the answer in class and he doesn't, they must keep quiet. If he wants to explain something to them, they would be ill-advised to let fall that they know all about it already. And so on. Not to be too pushy is something we have all learned, one way or another. I do not especially wish to defend this attitude; indeed I deplore it, in so far as it may make girls hide their talents or fail to develop them (and this is one of the great arguments in favour of single-sex schools). But to see the rules so flagrantly broken as by Margaret Thatcher at least took some getting used to, for many women. There is, or perhaps was, a feeling that rudeness befits a woman even less than it befits a man. Nor is it a trivial fault. I believe that the ruthless overriding of other people was a real moral defect in a Prime Minister, and of course was, in the end, her undoing, as she became more and more monstrously interventionist and disloyal to her Ministers. To link this with more ordinary lack of manners is not absurd, for this lack is perhaps a sign of the egocentricity that finally destroyed her judgement.

Again, I believe that women are more observant of and affected by the clothes that other people and especially other women wear than most men (unless they have a specialist interest). It is hard for many women to avoid taking not just clothes but possessions in general as the signs or expression of the inner person. This explains why women are generally so much fascinated by being invited into other people's houses, and tend, at least mentally, to poke about among the furniture and objects that are in it, and observe the details of the decoration and of the food that is served. The people whose house it is are 'placed', not merely socially but on some cultural scale which includes slavery to fashion, or its opposite, the aesthetic, the intellectual, the creative. Thus what sounds like, and indeed is, in some sense of the word, snobbishness, is not therefore trivial. I still cannot think of Margaret

Thatcher without thinking of a particular electric blue suit with fitted jacket, metal buttons and big lapels, a memorably vulgar suit of which she wears a version to this day. This suit is not a symbol, it is not like a flag whose meaning one has to learn. It actually expresses directly, like a language one has always known, the crudity, philistinism and aggression that made up Margaret Thatcher's character.

And yet (and perhaps this was the most irritating fact of all) this suit and the candy-floss hair, and the lately acquired deep, vibrant voice, to say nothing of the amazingly elegant legs with which nature had endowed her, all added up to a sexual image that worked. Once when Geoffrey and I were visiting an American university and we were, as usual, being questioned about Mrs Thatcher we expressed, with moderation I think, some fairly negative opinions. We genuinely shocked our hosts. There could, they said, be no possible reason for such opinions except jealousy. How could someone who was so lovely otherwise fail to be loved? One of those present half-seriously declared that he was in love with her. And both in this country and in Europe there were people who again half, or more than half, seriously claimed to love her. One such was the admittedly susceptible Alan Clark, who in his memoirs spoke of her romantically as 'the Lady'. And I cannot forbear to quote an entry for April 3rd 1984: '... the PM came in. She sat next to me (first time ever) and ... I radiated protective feelings – and, indeed, feeling of another kind(s). She has very small feet and attractive – not bony – ankles in the 1940 style. (Julian Amery will nod his head sagely, and say in a gruff voice, "There's blood there, you know, no doubt about it, there's blood." And I see what he means.) The Prime Minister's foot twisted and turned *the entire time* although her eyes were closed, and her head nodded at intervals. The back of her hair is perfect ... it can't be a full wig as the front is clearly her own. But I suspect it is a "chignon".' It was the proneness of some men to talk of her as if she were a horse that was hard for women to put up with. Later, when she had joined the House of Lords I remember sitting beside a very ancient peer who pointed to Lady Thatcher sitting on the front bench opposite (crossbenchers, having too little room on their own benches, regularly share part of the Labour benches) and said: 'I come in nowadays only in the hope of seeing her. Look at those legs'. He was drooling.

These are some of the aspects of Margaret Thatcher that made it impossible even for one moment to forget that she was not just a Prime Minister, but a woman Prime Minister; and this in turn may explain why she was even more hateful to women, some women at least, than to men. This, as I have tried to explain, was not a matter of jealousy, or envy, but because of her own attitude to other women, and her somewhat tasteless exploitation of a certain kind of femininity. But obviously there was much more to it than that. There were aspects of her policies and her tastes which were shocking to anyone, male or female, who had, as Geoffrey and I had, first voted in 1945 and had lived their whole adult life with the welfare state; who had, moreover lived this same adult life in a university, not even having to raise the question whether higher education and research were valuable, whether learning was worth having for its own sake, and whether the universities themselves should determine their own priorities. We had both, with some difficulty, switched our political allegiance from Labour to Conservative in the mid-1960s, Geoffrey rather earlier than I, and we were prepared to be reasonably loyal to our leader. But we found it impossible. It was not Conservatism but Thatcherism that was too much for us, and many like us.

I am not certain when the concept of 'Thatcherism' gained currency. It is undoubtedly a useful and intelligible idea, for the policies, priorities and values it denotes all stem not merely from the particular period when she was in power, but directly from Margaret Thatcher's own personality and value-system, even though Thatcherism has long outlasted her time in office, just us the term 'Augustan' denotes not just the temporal reign of a particular Roman Emperor, but features which characterised the man himself. As we discovered in the conversation with Graham Turner, it was far more than a matter of style. Geoffrey Howe, for long her loyal Minister, when he finally came to resign was sometimes accused of differing from her only in style. In his memoirs, *A Conflict of Loyalties*, he wrote 'The truth is that in many aspects of politics style and substance complement each other. Very often they are two sides of the same coin'. And so it is with Thatcherism.

Before Margaret Thatcher became Prime Minister, the Conservative Party, or its th nking members, were looking round for some philosophy to embrace. I remember one day towards the end of 1978 sitting next to Keith Joseph at a lunch party in Oxford. He said that hitherto Conservatism had not needed a philosophy. The Left had always had the monopoly of philosophers, not just Marx but others who could infuse a sense of idealism and high aspiration into party politics. Conservatism, he said, had always been a matter of common sense combined with decent and deeply-rooted feeling, to both of which philosophy or theory were antipathetic. But now, he thought, Conservatism had need of a specific theory with which to counter Socialism, to justify the overriding value of individual choice and to minimise the power of the state. I recommended the American philosopher Robert Nozick, whose *Anarchy, State and Utopia* had been published a year or so earlier, and who argued for a truly minimal state, its functions confined to protection against force, theft and fraud, and to the enforcement of contracts. He certainly read this book, but I doubt if he passed on its contents to the Prime Minister, though it is possible that he did. She is said to have been most influenced by the political economist and anti-Marxist Friedrich von Hayek, whose theories Nozick discusses in some detail, and to whose writings Keith Joseph undoubtedly pointed her. But the fact is that, however much the intellectual Joseph may have hankered for a philosophy, Margaret Thatcher herself did not need one. She was a doer, not a thinker; and she would pick and choose among theories to suit her tastes. Thatcherism was born of such a hotchpotch: it was not a philosophy so much as a set of policies, not all consistent with each other but all founded on passionate conviction.

Geoffrey and I personally saw Thatcherism at close quarters mainly in the field of higher education. Almost as soon as she took office in 1979, the Prime Minister, with considerable reason, began to demand that the universities, all of which except one (Buckingham) were heavily subsidised by government, should be accountable for the money they were given, and should give evidence that they were managing their affairs without waste. Hitherto, they had been funded by a quinquennial grant, their needs presented to the Treasury through the University Grants Committee, a body of academics, set up to be an impartial, 'arms-length' mediator between the Treasury and the universities themselves. Universities, of course, did not always get all they asked for. But the concept of need was nevertheless understood. And because applications were for grants covering five years, universities could set realistic targets for building up departments, or introducing new subjects for undergraduate teaching. Within the framework of what the Treasury could be persuaded to grant, universities were free to go the way they wanted. The number of universities had, however, greatly increased since the early 1960s, as a result of the Robbins report, and it may well have seemed that costs to the government were becoming unsustainable. Certainly at the beginning of the 1980s the cuts to university grants were severe, and all universities had to make economies, often, no doubt, such as to improve their efficiency, but in some cases bringing them to near bankruptcy.

It was possible, however, at this time to remain reasonably hopeful about the future of higher education. Geoffrey was Vice-Chancellor of Oxford from 1981 until 1985, and even in his last Oration, he managed to sound, if not cheerful about the future, then at least cautiously optimistic. Nevertheless the universities as a whole were deeply hostile to Margaret Thatcher's apparent disregard of their educational and research needs. In Oxford she was notoriously refused an honorary degree, proposed by Hebdomadal Council, but turned down by Congregation, the body to which all senior members of the university belong, the opposition led by the scientists. This was a deeply mistaken move. Every Oxford-educated Prime Minister has automatically been given an honorary degree in the summer after he was elected. It is completely unclear why Margaret Thatcher was not given one in the summer of 1979, and her college, Somerville, was understandably angry that this did not happen, especially as being the first Prime Minister from a women's college made her achievement more remarkable. By the time the matter was raised again, at Geoffrey's insistence, though backed by many other members of Council, it was too late. The financial cuts had enraged enough people for the argument to prevail which held that it would be a disgrace to appear to accept them. Not only Margaret Thatcher herself, but other members of Government were deeply offended, their hostility not just to Oxford but to the universities in general greatly reinforced.

It was not until 1987 that it became clear quite how drastic the changes were to be. In 1986 Kenneth Baker, an enthusiastic Thatcherite, had become Secretary of State for Education, replacing the highly academic Keith Joseph, and in the following year the White Paper *Meeting the Challenge* was published. By this time the UGC (still made up of practising academics) and the universities themselves had shown that they were able to make radical cuts in expenditure and live with the results, even though this had meant a great many redundancies among academic staff, the closure of some whole departments, and a freeze on salaries, so that junior lecturers were being paid less than policemen on the beat. In the White Paper, and in due course in the 1988 Great Educational Reform Bill (known to teachers as Gerbil), Kenneth Baker's magnum opus, the UGC was replaced by the University Funding Council, a body numerically dominated by people from commerce and industry, with only a sprinkling of academics. Its first chairman, Lord Chilver, head of the Cranfield Institute of Technology, was a great admirer of Margaret Thatcher who firmly believed that the purpose of higher education was to satisfy the requirements of industry. The function of the new UFC was not to distribute resources according to the needs of universities, as perceived by themselves. Instead it had the task of telling universities what they might or might not do, to satisfy the needs of industry. If students wanted to study, say, history or philosophy at university, rather than science or technology, that was too bad. The White Paper made it clear that what subjects students should pursue was a matter for Government: 'The Government considers student demand ... to be an insufficient basis for the planning of higher education. A major determinant must be ... the demands for highly qualified manpower'. It was assumed without argument that 'the world of business', to serve whose needs the universities were now seen to exist, wanted more and more theoretical scientists and technologists, such as those who read for degrees in these subjects. (The passion for degrees in management and business studies had not yet become widespread; indeed they were still thought of as a bit suspect and transatlantic.) The White Paper went on to declare that 'if evidence of student or employer demand suggests subsequently that graduate output will not be in line with the economy's needs Government will consider whether the planning framework should be adjusted.' The 'planning framework' was now that to be imposed by the UFC, who would decide what courses were worth retaining and which should have their finances withdrawn. All grants were to be for one year only, and the performance of every department in every university would be subject to monitoring, to check the quality of its teaching and research. ('Quality' here meant quantity. Research was judged by the criterion of the number of publications, or even citations of publications, that could be counted as emanating from a department; and individual academics had their performance judged by the same criterion. The criteria for good teaching were less easy to fix, though an attempt has been made more recently by a new body concerned with 'Quality Assurance'.) It was presumed that when students began to see that unless they followed a course in the sciences, they would be unemployable, their demand for the humanities would tail off; they might also be frightened by the possibility that the humanities department within which they were studying might close while they were in mid-course. Things did not turn out quite like this; but there can be no doubt that after 1988, the status of the universities changed, their supposed purpose radically altered.

Baker himself took much of the initiative in these changes. He almost out-Thatchered Thatcher. Indeed in her memoir, *The Downing Street Years*, she claimed (p. 6) that her policies had always been especially opposed to the nature of government since 1945, which, she said, represented 'a centralising, managerial, bureaucratic, interventionist style of government'. Yet how much more centralist and interventionist could any government get than that which imposed the 1988 Act on higher education? Later in the same book she stated that her policy with regard to education (and it might be supposed that this included higher education) was directed towards 'the extension of choice, the dispersal of power and the encouragement of responsibility' (p. 618). Specifically with regard to the universities she wrote 'Universities were developing closer links with business and becoming more entrepreneurial. Student loans had been introduced: these would make students more discriminating about the courses they chose, with greater sensitivity to the market.' She went on to speak of those who criticised these policies. Some criticisms, she said, were 'predictable' (as though this made them necessarily invalid). 'But undoubtedly other critics were genuinely concerned about the future autonomy and academic integrity of the universities ... It made me concerned that many distinguished academics thought that Thatcherism in education meant a philistine subordination of scholarship to the immediate demands of vocational training. That was certainly no part of my kind of Thatcherism' (p. 598). So perhaps it was Kenneth Baker's kind; or, as it now seems, New Labour's. But it would not have existed without her support. Baker showed himself totally indifferent to the widespread fear within the universities that their freedom was being eroded, and that they were in danger of becoming simply arms of government policy, the choice of what they might teach and research dictated from outside. (However, in June 2000, he suggested that the only hope for universities might be to become privately funded.)

What seemed so extraordinary to me at the time was the supposition that Whitehall would send in 'experts' to judge the 'output' of departments headed, in many cases, by people who were the most distinguished in their field, uniquely qualified to judge the value of what their departments were doing. It was like the Stalinist cultural experts, sent in to 'evaluate' the compositions of Shostakovich in the 1950s. The House of Lords, through the medium of a powerful intervention by Lord Jenkins of Hillhead, Chancellor of Oxford, managed to get an amendment accepted to the Bill modifying the 'contracts' Government would make with universities. These were the contracts according to which Government would pay universities for services they wanted; but they were contracts in name only: they were really conditions in accordance with which Government would fund approved university projects, and only those. The amendment laid down that the contracts would be drawn up so as to 'ensure that academic staff have freedom within the law to question and test received wisdom and to put forward new ideas and controversial or unpopular opinions, without placing themselves in jeopardy of losing their jobs or privileges'. This amendment was accepted by the government only with extreme reluctance. As Simon Jenkins commented (*Accountable to None*, 1995 p. 147), 'It is remarkable that a modern liberal government should have found this so unpalatable a clause'.

In 1993 the change in university status was completed in the new Education Act. This may be regarded as the apotheosis of Thatcherism, though Thatcher herself had already been replaced. Under this Act virtually all institutions of higher education became entitled to call themselves universities. The new universities of the early 1960s could truly be called universities, modelling themselves as they did on the ancient seats of learning, and respecting, as they tried to, the standards of learning and research exemplified not only in the ancient foundations of Oxford and Cambridge, Edinburgh, Glasgow and St Andrews, but in the great nineteenth-century provincial universities, founded by industrialists with a real respect for what they had often themselves missed, but wanted others to have, the Universities of Liverpool, Manchester, Leeds, Hull. Some of these 1960s foundations have now taken their place among the best universities, by all standards, in the country (I think, for example, of Warwick and York). The new universities, former polytechnics, already gave their own degrees, validated by a standard-setting body called the Council for National Academic Awards (CNAA) whose task was to ensure that the degrees awarded came up to the standard demanded of an undergraduate degree, rather than a certificate or diploma. There had already been a government enquiry on the status of the polytechnics, under the chairmanship of Sir Norman Lindop, which had recommended that polytechnics could apply for university status, and free themselves from the CNAA if they met certain criteria. But in 1993 the CNAA was abolished, and the former polytechnics could all claim to be full degree-awarding bodies.

The motive for this new move is not entirely clear but it has to be remembered that the polytechnics had been controlled and financed up to now by Local Authorities; and one of the passions animating Thatcherism was a detestation of Local Authorities, and a strong desire to strip them of their powers. By transforming the polytechnics from being local institutions, funded locally, into institutions designed to serve the whole nation, Thatcherism in effect nationalised, or at least centralised, the whole of higher education, bringing it now under a single funding Council, the HEFC, with powers to monitor and to distribute funds using the same criteria over the whole range of institutions.

I blame myself and other like-minded academics for not speaking up against this change, when the 1993 Bill was before the House of Lords. For the first time in my life, however, I felt total despair. I knew that the response to anything that I or any other peer from the old universities might say against the move would be, roughly, 'She would say that, wouldn't she?' The charge against us would be snobbishness or elitism, a wish to retain the title of university for those institutions of which we had always been a part. It seemed useless to protest. The polytechnics, at their outset, had always been supposed to be close to industry, and to prepare people for careers which used the latest technologies. That they did not do this, or did not always make it their first priority, was due to a phenomenon known as 'academic drift', which made them aspire to university prestige, concentrating on the theoretical rather than the practical, and insisting on the inclusion of the humanities among their courses. This in turn may partly be laid at the door of the CNAA, whose role was to show that degrees from these institutions were roughly comparable with degrees from universities. For them to become universities may be seen as the inevitable next step. The aim now, according, as I remember, to one of the education Ministers at the time, Gillian Shephard, was to treat virtually all institutions of higher education, all that were now called universities, as of equal status, and they would be funded by the new body using uniform criteria across the board. Of course everyone knew that the new university of, say, Bournemouth or Huddersfield was not of equal academic status with, say, Cambridge or London; but this was to be the new mythology. All equally were there to serve the needs of industry, and 'turn out', as it said, people fit to seek employment in the business world.

The universities themselves were partly to blame for all this. They feebly gave in to one after another of the government's demands, fearing that their fate would be worse if they resisted; and of course they were largely dependent on government money.

At any rate the condition to which higher education was reduced was, I think, one of very worst effects of Thatcherism. Margaret Thatcher's denial that it was 'her' Thatcherism does not exonerate her from the greatest blame of all. The concept of learning, the respect for higher education for its own sake, as something intrinsically worth having, an essential part of any civilised society, had been thrown out; and this largely because of her own detestation of academics. Oxford may have been wrong, and spiteful, to deny her the honorary degree she undoubtedly merited; she was equally spiteful and short-sighted in her treatment of the universities. Moreover she did not even get the facts right. By amalgamating the polytechnic and the university sectors, she blurred an extremely important distinction. Even if we were to accept the broad hypothesis that only employers' needs are to be taken into account when setting the goals for higher education (and I do not accept it) Thatcherism did not understand what the needs of employers actually are. For even at the level of 'vocational' higher education, there are needs which must be met: needs for teachers, for example, and for Civil Servants with a broad vision of what there is to be done by Government and what is possible. Nor does the world of business, to which Thatcherism increasingly looked not only to employ graduates but to help to finance educational establishments, supposedly in their own interests, necessarily want people educated only in science and technology, which may well be out of date when the time for employment has come. It is equally important for this rather mysterious world that they employ graduates who can communicate, write coherently, understand a wide range of subjects, and know how to work alongside other people, abilities which may or may not be fostered by working in theoretical physics, applied mathematics or computer sciences. The throwing together of all the universities and polytechnics has simply made this kind of confusion of aims easier, and less amenable to remedy.

I personally was equally concerned in another aspect of the Great Educational Reform Bill of 1988, and this was in the matter of the education of children with special needs. The consequence of the 1988 Education Act in so far as it was concerned with school education was to introduce the ideas of competition between schools, and choice for parents. The league tables showing the academic achievements of schools alongside one another were supposed to enable parents to choose the best schools. The free market would operate. Schools which performed badly would not be chosen by parents, and so would ultimately wither away. This was the original idea. (No one gave thought, apparently, to what would happen to children who were pupils at these bad schools while they were in the process of withering away.) This part of the 1988 Act was derived largely, like the part concerned with higher education, from a personal vendetta of Margaret Thatcher's, this time against the teaching profession. Teachers could be judged, she thought, by the academic results of their pupils; the operation of the free market would succeed in the end in eliminating those schools where the teachers were bad; or market competition would cause those schools to get rid of their bad teachers and employ good ones, so that they would become good schools. This was the theory, enthusiastically propounded by Kenneth Baker, and close to Margaret Thatcher's own heart.

There was a certain basis of reason in her detestation of teachers. There had been in the late 1950s and 1960s a strong move among educationalists towards a Rousseauesque theory of education, according to which children must be given an environment in which, like plants, they could flourish naturally; they must not so much be taught as allowed to learn, and learning was best accomplished through discovery of the world (including the worlds of literature and numbers) by the child himself. This image of school as a garden of natural plants became an orthodoxy perhaps most potently expressed in the Plowden Report, *Children and their Primary Schools*, published in 1967. Here it was stated at the outset that 'at the centre of every educational process lies the child'; and the aim of teachers must be to facilitate a process by which children must learn to be themselves and develop in the way and at the pace appropriate to them. Combined with this essentially Romantic view of education there came from America, at about the same time, the doctrines of the philosopher John Dewey, who held that education must essentially be education in democracy. It should not be hierarchical or authoritarian. Instead teacher and pupils should work side by side in an enterprise of joint discovery and experiment. The result should be a kind of consensus, an equal and democratic method of discovering what was useful, what actually worked and so what was true. The idea that teachers were hired to know more than their pupils and explain to them what they knew, or how to do things which they could do and their pupils couldn't, was anathema to Dewey. This kind of theory was, by the 1970s, entrenched in the teacher-training colleges, and was therefore firmly lodged in the consciousness of most teachers by the mid-80s. Child-centred education sounded good, but it was disastrous for all but the most outstandingly intelligent children. The bogey at that time was 'rote-learning', so no one, except perhaps those taught by the oldest teachers, learned their tables any more, or were given lists of 'spellings'. It was out of a desire to stop this rot that Callaghan when he was Prime Minister inaugurated the Great Debate on the school curriculum, in 1977; out of it finally arose the National Curriculum, and the notion that schools must compete against each other in their measurable results. Each of these moves was strongly opposed by the teachers, unions, and those responsible for training. It was no wonder that Margaret Thatcher regarded the profession as a whole as subversive, silly and incurably incompetent.

But, from 1988 onwards, the government's educational imagery switched dramatically from the horticultural to that of the factory floor. Children, far from being encouraged to flourish and blossom, were to be turned at school (and indeed at university) into tools for the improvement of the economy. A school would be judged by how many of these useful tools could be 'turned out'. Every stage of the manufacturing process should be laid down by the State, and the new inspectorate should monitor both the process and its outcome, as a means to provide 'quality assurance'. The outcome of the process was to be judged by the criterion of examination results, which in turn would lead to employability. Parents would choose the schools with the best results, and schools would be encouraged to compete against each other to secure a high place in the league tables. Education as a good in itself was forgotten. Parents, it was assumed, wanted their children educated to form a workforce, on which national prosperity depended. If they did not find a school efficient in producing this end result they would take their custom elsewhere.

Of course in real life, as opposed to theory, there remained numerous good schools which steered a course between these two kinds of metaphor, and the best of them, though they accepted, even welcomed the National Curriculum, continued to teach children with a view to their enjoying their work, and personally benefiting from it. In real life, too, the market could not possibly function as intended. Parents could not be sure of finding places for their children in the schools they judged good, withdrawing them from the 'bad'. More important, there were many children who needed and indeed were legally entitled to education who could not be treated as tools for improving the economy. These were the children with disabilities of different kinds who might never become competent enough to get a job, but for whom education was an essential lifeline making the difference between an enjoyable and independent life, and a life of dependency, totally without pleasure or purpose.

In 1981, the Conservative government had passed an Act laying down the framework of education for children with special needs, ensuring that their entitlement to education was observed, however severe their disabilities, and advocating that, as far as possible, they should be educated alongside other children in ordinary schools, as opposed to special schools. This Act can be regarded as the last gasp of welfarism; for it was specifically the needs of children that were to determine the special measures required to give them access, as far as possible, to the curriculum which other children followed. But of course the concept of educational needs, that is of the needs of children, was incompatible with the new theory of the purpose of education, which was to satisfy the needs of the economy, not of the children themselves. Schools which in the spirit of the 1981 Act welcomed children with disabilities and took pains to give them access to the curriculum were not following the supposed demands of the market. They were not going to be placed high in the league tables. They could not be judged by the sole criterion of examination results. The incompatibility between the purpose of the 1988 Act and that of 1981 showed clearly that it was impossible to treat education as a commodity in the marketplace which could only improve by competition, and where market forces might drive some products off the shelves. The Thatcherite attempt to apply the language of the free market to education (and one may think, to health) not only could not work, but was intensely damaging. The true purpose of education was lost in the commercial jargon of cost-effectiveness, value for money and quality assurance. The fact that children need education, and that their needs are different, was simply overlooked.

In the field of education, then, Thatcherism has been both long-lasting and disastrous. But it is only one field within which the Thatcherite values became predominant. Any government must attempt as far as possible to eliminate the waste of resources, spending, as we are frequently told, taxpayers' money on things that do them no good. But perhaps of all the legacies of Margaret Thatcher the most pervasive was the assumption that nothing matters except the non-squandering of money, and that no positive value exists except to save and prosper. The worst effect of such a scale of values was that people began to adopt it not simply with regard to the state, but with regard to themselves as individuals. Thatcherism increasingly, as the 1980s went on, became associated with the yuppie culture, the admiration for the upwardly mobile. But 'upwards' meant 'richer'. Increasingly, people talked about 'offers they could not refuse'. And these, of course, were offers they could have refused, but did not want to, because they were offers that would enrich them. In such a culture it becomes increasingly easy to cross the line between honest and dishonest means of becoming rich. If personal wealth is generally seen as the highest value, then the means to attain it may gradually become a matter of indifference. The erosion of moral standards in the City and the Stock Market illustrates what may come to seem inevitable. And once such a scale of values is adopted within a society, it is very difficult to see how to change track. The legacy of Margaret Thatcher, then, is still pervasive and harmful to society as a whole. The idea of the common good, which genuinely lay behind the welfarism of the 1940s and 1950s, has simply got lost.

I certainly would not condemn all that Margaret Thatcher did. I don't think anyone could. Nor would I deny that her brisk insistence on good-housekeeperly virtues such as thrift and individual self-reliance was timely and bracing. Yet out of her character and her tastes arose a kind of generalised selfishness hard to reconcile with the qualities of a truly civilised society; and since Thatcherism is by no means dead, even under a Labour government, the damage is widespread indeed.

Duncan Wilson
Diplomat and Master of Corpus Christi College, Cambridge

There was no time when I consciously encountered Duncan Wilson, because he was my brother, thirteen years older than I and, when I was born, the only surviving male member of our household, a remote and mysterious figure. He remained more or less remote for far too long. Indeed it was not until the very end of his life that I really began to know him and feel at ease with him, though I had always admired him. I shared the nursery with my sister Stephana, two years my senior, and to both of us Duncan was an object of alarm though she, being braver and more open and talkative than I, may have been slightly less afraid of him.

He did not, I think, mean to frighten us. Nor was it that he had taken on the responsibilities of head of the family. Our mother certainly did not so regard him. Indeed I think she treated him rather as she had treated her husband, as someone essentially to be shielded from the responsibility and bother of domesticity and children, so that he might be free to devote himself to masculine pursuits, work, that is, and his chosen recreations. She thought of men as essentially defined, first by their profession and then by their sporting or leisure interests. So, when enquiring from me in later years about some undergraduate friend, she used always to ask 'What does he do?'; and as he had not yet got a profession, the expected answer was something like 'shooting' or 'tennis'. 'Nothing' was not a satisfactory reply.

She had always attended to the running of the household, a considerable task when my father was a housemaster at

Winchester. In those days a housemaster and his wife were like the proprietors of a hotel; they had to see to the comfort of the boys, but also cause the house to run at a profit. She kept the accounts and made all the decisions. My eldest sister remembers an occasion when she and Duncan, two years younger than she and both in their teens, were travelling somewhere with our mother and Duncan offered to carry the suitcases. She refused to countenance it and struggled along the platform with them, leaving Jean and Duncan shuffling shamefacedly behind, exposed to the disapproval of everyone who saw them.

Though Duncan was not expected to take responsibility, nor turned to for help, my mother regarded his opinions as of enormous importance, and his taste as constituting an absolute standard. This was largely because he was male; but also because he was by this time manifestly clever, well-informed and musically talented. The year that I was born was his first year at Winchester, top of the Roll of Scholars.

I had a highly romantic view of College, feeling from my earliest youth that we were exiles from what should have been our birthright. It was, I suppose, Paradise Lost. Our Nanny was full of stories about life in Kingsgate House (Beloes), which had been our father's house, and from which my mother had had to hustle out in the summer in which he died. Stephana and I used to be asked back sometimes to children's parties, there and in other houses, as outsiders, objects of pity. We used to go quite often to Chapel on Sunday mornings in term, and on Christmas Day, when there was a special service for college dons, their wives and children. I loved the Sunday services because of the extraordinary musty smell of the gowns worn by members of College, and the loud exuberant singing. The sermons, too, were mercifully short. Then we used to go to the Eton Match in the alternate years when it was held at Winchester, and for this we had special dresses, hardly ever worn on other occasions, made of pale coloured voile over coloured petticoats, worn with straw hats from Hayford's in London. The white-flannelled cricketers, the open space of Meads, the background of school buildings and the strawberries and ice-cream were all sources of the excitement of College.

Soon after I was born we had moved to a large house some way from the school (Kelso House) and Duncan used to bring his friends to lunch on most Sundays. This was another source of pleasure to us. They discarded their gowns, long-sleeved waistcoats and top-hats to play games with us, or show us conjuring tricks, or came into the nursery to talk to Nanny. I think all boarding-school children, however grand their status at school, love occasionally consorting with children, having an excuse to revert to childhood themselves. These College men seemed to us much easier to talk to than Duncan himself, and they put themselves out to please. We were not afraid, with them, of making fools of ourselves.

At least once Stephana and I were asked, by ourselves, to have tea in Duncan's Chamber and I remember being carried round Chamber Court in a huge waste-paper basket. (This memory came back to me with overwhelming vivacity when, twenty years later, I was crossing Chamber Court in my uncomfortable shoes to be married in College Chapel.)

Duncan was important to us in our early years as one of our sources of music. He played the piano for hours on end in the holidays. The piano he played was in the schoolroom, a sitting room used by the older members of the family, but we could hear it faintly from the nursery up above. In the summer we could hear it better from the garden because the schoolroom had large windows reaching almost to the ground and we could sneak up to the windows and listen. When I was very small I used to be put to rest in the afternoons in my pram outside the schoolroom and I think the habit must have lasted well beyond babyhood, because I can remember the cool green of the pram with its summer shade and the sound of the piano.

We would never have dared ask Duncan to play something we particularly liked, but we had our favourites. I liked best a piano version of *Jesu, Joy of Man's Desiring* and we both loved the Mozart Piano Sonata in F Major K132, which I believed was called Snorter. In his last year or two at school, and when he was an undergraduate, Duncan was a great collector of records and he donated some of his cast-offs to the nursery to be played on our tall wind-up gramophone. So we acquired parts of Handel's *Acis and Galatea*, the Mozart Quartet in B flat (The Hunt), played by the Busch Quartet, and a record of the soprano Elisabeth Schumann singing, on one side, Handel's aria O *Hatte ich Jubal's Harfe* (known to us as Happy Schubert), and on the other side the real Schubert's *Hark, Hark the Lark*. Even writing the names of these pieces of music sends shivers down my spine. These records were played over and over again, along with songs such as *Olga Pullofsky the Beautiful Spy* and *The Daring Young Man on the Flying Trapeze*.

Duncan was not the only source of music. There was a drawing-room gramophone as well which had records of Harry Lauder songs, something known to us as 'The Haydn Trio', Weber's *Invitation to the Waltz* and Bach's Third Brandenburg Concerto, for long my favourite piece of music of all. And there was Sunday hymn singing round the drawing-room piano, our mother playing in her curious clumsy style, every chord slightly broken, where we sang hymns to her favourite tunes, Abridge, Martyrdom or Winchester Old, mostly metrical versions of the psalms, for she was at this time still in what we later thought of as her Scottish Period, romanticising the Scottish aspects of our father's family.

Duncan was nevertheless held to be the authority on music. It was perhaps his air of being an authority that intimidated us. It is certain that, despite all the benefits he brought us from the world outside the nursery, he made me familiar with the terror that I might not have understood what he said, or especially not have seen whether or in what way it was supposed to be funny (a problem I have encountered with other Wykehamists, though mercifully not with Geoffrey), and, secondly, with a terror of 'not being able to think of anything to say', a terror that has never entirely left me. There was the related anxiety lest one should 'say the wrong thing' especially the thing that would mysteriously excite ridicule. Later, when I went to boarding school myself, I realised, as I have already said, what a delight it was to get away from this fear of ridicule, not just from Duncan, but from his more or less contemporary sisters, 'the big ones' as they were known to us. I could show myself to be as silly and as ignorant as I liked. Ever since those days I have always had a horror of laughing at children, my own or other people's, and making them feel fools.

Duncan had an impeccable undergraduate career, the top scholarship at Balliol, followed by an apparently effortless First Class in Classical Mods and Greats, and several university prizes. Apart from the not very serious mishap of failing to win a Fellowship by examination at All Souls (on which in any case I doubt if he had wholly set his heart, being always slightly dubious, as he later told me, about entering the academic world), his first major setback was that, having spent a year abroad improving his modern languages and having passed first on the list in the examination for the Foreign Office, he failed the medical examination. His chest was apparently too narrow. I was old enough by now to enter into the terrible sorrow and outrage at this result, especially as from the time that he was at Winchester, our mother hoped that he would become a diplomat. She too disliked and rather feared the academic. It was all the more of a blow to him, because he was now anxious to get married, and very much needed to settle in a job.

He was going to marry a girl he had met at Oxford, a classicist from Lady Margaret Hall called Betty Fleming.

My mother had reservations about Betty, reservations which later hardened into near hostility on both sides. Betty was, I suppose, too careless of convention, too critical, too open and perhaps too inclined to the Left to be acceptable to my mother (not that she herself was exactly conventional in some ways). She may have had another candidate in mind for the post of Duncan's wife, as our Nanny certainly had. She wanted Duncan to marry a Scottish girl, but even so Betty did not quite fill the bill. We, on the other hand, the nursery party, had no reservations at all. We loved Betty's soft Scottish accent, her energy, her easy accessibility and her laugh, a marvellous laugh of pure enjoyment, which was frequent and flatteringly easily provoked, but with no hint of our being made fun of, or having made fools of ourselves. On her first visit to Winchester, in 1933, she brought us as a present a plush elephant with a particularly amiable and foolish expression on its face, and kid tusks. Although we had given up our toy animals by now, we loved this elephant and it went everywhere with us until it became limp and bald. We called it Betty Velvet Fleming and made it speak in a particular, strange accent all its own. This irritated our mother very much, partly because, as she told me, we were too old for such follies but partly, I suspect, because our fondness for the toy reflected our fondness for the real Betty.

After the disaster of the Foreign Office, Duncan took a job teaching at Westminster School and, in his holidays, he walked and sailed and played golf with Betty, seeking to remedy his weediness. Betty was large-boned, healthy and full of energy, an essentially outdoor person, and the effect on Duncan was obvious. I later met some of the clever people he taught, at least three of whom became philosophers in Oxford. They recalled with pleasure the eccentric, rambling, sometimes unintelligible manner of his teaching Latin and Greek, but I doubt if schoolmastering would have suited him. In any case, after a year he was advised to get a job in the Civil Service to make it easier to transfer at some stage to the Foreign Office, where he still wanted to be. So he became an Assistant Keeper in the British Museum, in the Department of Western Manuscripts, a job he enjoyed and found unexacting. He never had to apply for a transfer, or face another medical examination, though by now he would certainly have passed it, because war broke out and he was at once sent to the Ministry of Economic Warfare. From there he was transferred to something called the Political Warfare Executive, responsible for disseminating propaganda to Europe, including Germany, and thence, as soon as the war in Europe was over, he became part of the Control Commission in Germany, where he and his family lived for four years. Finally, in 1949, he was transferred to the Foreign Office where he remained until he retired in 1971, becoming an expert on the Communist countries, Yugoslavia, China and the USSR.

During all this time I saw little of him. He could not come to England in 1949, as he would have hoped, to give me away at my marriage to another Wykehamist in College Chapel. There was however a time in 1940 and the beginning of 1941 when it was dangerous to live in London and Betty came down to Winchester with her child (another soon expected) and lived in my mother's house, helped by our old Nanny. Duncan came at weekends. This was a terrible time, as I remember. My mother and Betty could not get on and each used me as a confidante and recipient of complaints. I, on the whole, sympathised with my mother, whose household arrangements were disrupted and who already had several evacuees in the top floor of the house, and had the unenviable task of keeping her elderly cook and maid from leaving. She was subjected to unceasingly scornful lectures from Betty about how she ought not to have a cook or a maid anyway, and how she certainly ought not occasionally to accept extra food from loyal tradespeople, some of whom had had her custom since the days of Kingsgate House and with whom she was a favourite. I understood Betty's righteous indignation, but I enjoyed the luxuries all the same, as Betty did, and much as we loathed the cook and the maid, I could not really see how my mother could get on without them. She was terribly incompetent, a total non-starter as far as cooking, or the simplest household tasks went. I remember Geoffrey's astonishment, soon after we were married, to hear her say, 'I will get them to open a new pot of marmalade' (the pot being in her hand). 'They' by this time were a pair of almost non-English-speaking Russian peasants, a man and wife, who had replaced the cook and the maid.

At any rate, during Betty's regime I was absolutely thankful to escape to school. Sadly, but understandably, Duncan also turned against our mother at this time and relations were never wholly easy between them again. Even so, he was, according to my sister Jean, deeply upset by her death in 1953 and wrote movingly about it. And in any case, our mother continued to want his opinion of every phase of the war and the aftermath of war.

I am ashamed of one time when I did have contact with Duncan during the war. This was before the time I have described, early in 1940, when Betty was in hospital giving birth to their first baby. For some unintelligible reason my mother decided that it would be a good idea for me and Imogen to go to London for a week and stay with Duncan in the flat they had temporarily rented in Tavistock Square, to cook for him and look after him while Betty was away. (I suppose in fact it was readily intelligible. She simply wanted to get us out of the way, with our ceaseless talk and our large schoolgirl appetites.)

We had never cooked so much as an egg before, we had never done anything in the house except make our beds, nor had we ever been in London for more than a day, still less on our own. It was the last week of our Easter holidays and we had not met since the previous term when, as usual, we had undergone extremes of trouble and drama at school and we could think of nothing but how it would be when we got back.

The week started with a terrible row between me and my mother who thought it essential, in London, to have a hat. (How astonishing this seems today.) I refused to wear a hat because, although I had one which I hated, I knew Imogen did not own such a thing and would, so I thought, be put to shame if I conceded that no one could go to London without one. In the end I took the hat onto the train from Winchester and, after a minute or two, threw it out of the window. This was the beginning of a week of liberation such as we had never known.

We were quite incapable of cooking the bacon that poor Duncan liked for his breakfast. It was always either raw or burned. We never even thought of cleaning the flat. It was the week of the British disaster at Narvik, the Norwegian port where two battles were fought and a British retreat was actually under way. We did not understand, nor did we try to understand, Duncan's anxiety and we took as little interest in Betty and her new baby, Catherine, as we did in the Norwegian campaign. All day long, while Duncan was at work or visiting the hospital, we tramped the streets in an ecstasy of excitement. We went to the cinema, where we saw the new Walt Disney, *Fantasia*, and to the theatre for *How Green was my Valley* and *King Lear*. We looked in the shops and ate at Lyons Corner House. Finally, on our last day, Duncan, with great forbearance, took us out to lunch at a Spanish restaurant, the like of which we had never seen, and Imogen disgraced herself by raising in loud tones the question whether or not the waiters' accents were assumed.

This was the day we were to leave and Betty and Catherine to come home. Duncan must have been profoundly thankful to see us go.

We were in fact amazingly uninterested in the war. It seemed to have been grinding on uneventfully for ever. At school we had been accustomed to listen to the wireless only on grand occasions, such as Edward VIII's abdication speech. We had no access to newspapers. Even day girls, who presumably knew more, seemed uninterested. When we had been back at school a little while that summer term of 1940, I had a letter from Duncan telling me that I must not despair; that despite all evidence to the contrary, he knew we could defeat the Germans in the end, even though they had at present such a huge advantage over us in equipment and training. He even set out the ways in which he thought we should ultimately prevail. I wrote back, thanking him kindly, but I privately thought he was being absurdly pompous. Of course we would win the war; that was simply what we did. I showed this letter to some of my friends and they all agreed with me; they were astounded that anyone should write in this way. These were the days leading up to Dunkirk.

I learned that the Germans had entered Paris only because I had a dental appointment in the town that day, and was let off games to keep the appointment where, my mouth propped open and full of cotton-wool, I heard from the dentist what had happened. I remember that I got back to school and flew to the tennis courts, interrupting a game, to recount this terrible news. Even I was shocked. After that, for a little while, we had more of the wireless, including de Gaulle's great speech to the rallying Free French. It was conceded that we might have some interest in the future, and shortly after that the school closed down for fear of invasion.

My other contact with Duncan during the war was that he rang up LMH in my first term there, Michaelmas 1942, to say that he would be in Oxford to see someone and wanted to take me out to dinner and, there being no way I could communicate with him, he would simply come to college and pick me up at a stated time. I had no means of putting him off, nor would I have dared to do so, but it put me in a terrible difficulty. Every year in the Michaelmas term, the two Miss Denekes, who lived in Gunfield, next door to LMH, gave something called an African Party. All the new scholars were invited, along with anyone, scholar or commoner, who was reading Music.

It was particularly important that the senior scholar of the year should be present because there was a ceremony at which she would have to make a speech of thanks to the Miss Denekes and also, much more important, to the aged composer Dr E. Walker who lived at Gunfield and was an object of worship and veneration to the Deneke sisters. The party was held to celebrate a trip to Africa, undertaken years before, by Dr Walker and Marga Deneke who had travelled the continent collecting African music which, on return, Dr Walker had put together as a long symphonic work, somewhat in the style of Brahms, for four hands. This was played each year by him and Marga on the great Steinway in the galleried music room attached to Gunfield. It lasted, I was told, one and three-quarter hours. My sister Stephana, who had gone down from LMH the term before I came up, had been to the African party, though not a scholar and not studying music, but because she was known to be a keen musician and Marga Deneke had heard her play the cello in a quartet that sometimes rehearsed at Gunfield, so that she had become a favourite. It was all the more shocking, therefore, that I, the senior scholar of the year, should be obliged to creep up to Marga and tell her that I would not be present because my brother was taking me out to dinner. Now, of course, I would have begged an invitation to the party for Duncan as well, thus killing numerous birds with one stone, but such a course of action never entered my head at that time. At any rate, Marga was absolutely outraged. Such a thing had never happened before. Thereafter, when she came round the dining hall at lunch-time on Sundays to distribute to favoured undergraduates tickets for the Balliol concerts, she never gave me a ticket, nor for years acknowledged my existence. I was not sorry to miss the party, but I felt guilty all the same and it weighed on my mind during the far from easy dinner at the George with Duncan. I, as usual, was paralysed by the thought that I was going to run out of things to say.

After two years in the Foreign Service in Berlin, during the Russian blockade of the city, Duncan had a spell in Yugoslavia as Counsellor in the early 1950s. He was back for two years in London as Director of Research at the Foreign Office by 1956, the year of the Suez Crisis. This was the most extraordinary time for us at home, division of opinion being on the whole split according to age, those under forty deeply hostile to Anthony Eden, the Prime Minister, and ashamed of the British role as apparently unprovoked aggressors. The leading article in the *Economist* for November 3rd 1956 began with these words: 'Sir Anthony Eden has isolated Britain, except for the company of France. On Tuesday having addressed an outmoded and questionable ultimatum to Egypt and Israel, he got a majority in a deeply divided House of Commons, observing "Honourable Gentlemen may if they like impugn our judgement. I hope they will not impugn our motives". But that is precisely what must be done. Was it to stop the fighting which Israel had started by moving faster than the Security Council could move? Or was it to carry out a project cherished since July, the seizure of the Suez Canal and the forcible overthrow of Colonel Nasser?' Having analysed the dire consequences of alienating the USA by these goings-on, the article ended as follows: 'On the best allowance, there are too few conceivable advantages to measure against the dead-weight of clear loss. Even if the Eden-Mollett technique achieves what it is intended to achieve, which is, presumably, a shock sharp enough to bring about the end of fighting, the fall of President Nasser and the recovery of some permanent Western authority over the Suez Canal traffic, the damage still promises to be out of proportion .... These thoughts force sober men in Britain to the conclusion that French Ministers, stung to fury by the Egyptian support of Algerian rebels are not the best counsellors for a British Prime Minister smarting at a betrayal by an Egyptian President whose advocate he once was. To attack Egypt against the reasoned urging of the world and under cover of a smoke-screen of obfuscatory statements can arouse no confident support in the country. The manner in which this crisis has been handled suggests a strange union of cynicism and hysteria in its leaders.'

This leading article reflects exactly the views of those passionately opposed to Eden. Duncan was certainly one of those 'sober men in Britain'. Asked, indeed virtually ordered, to act as spokesman for the government on the BBC, presenting the unfolding of events every evening in as favourable a light as possible, and in particular aiming to damp down the hostile reactions of the USA, he refused the assignment and offered to resign if this became necessary. Someone else was found to carry out the task and Duncan's resignation was not called for; but there may have been a black mark against his name.

There was certainly a black mark on our domestic front. With the worst of timing, Geoffrey and I had just bought a house in North Oxford large enough to accommodate us and our then four children and his mother, recently widowed and unable to face living alone. When we moved in, in the autumn of 1956, the alterations to what was to be her part of the house were not yet complete and for two miserable months we had to share a sitting room. I was in any case less than overjoyed by the new arrangements, unfairly contrasting Geoffrey's mother with mine, who had shown no inclination to live with any of her children after they grew up and who had, in her own way, intellectual interests.

The Suez Crisis made the situation practically intolerable. Geoffrey's mother would not leave the subject alone. When she heard about Duncan's threatened resignation, reported in the *Daily Telegraph* (we having been prepared, naturally, to conceal the facts), she took Geoffrey aside and told him that she had always known that Duncan was a Communist. What else had he been doing in Yugoslavia? Why was he now looking forward to going to China? We must be very careful not to get too close to him and his suspect colleagues, and Geoffrey must realise that I was tarred with the same brush. It made me feel an identity with Duncan I had never felt before.

Britain was not 'recognised' by Communist China in 1957, so Duncan went out as Chargé-d'Affaires rather than as Ambassador, but it was his first virtually ambassadorial posting and it suited him perfectly. During his first year there the Chinese, though officially hostile to the British, were to a certain extent prepared to put themselves out, for example to organise 'foreign tours' for diplomats involving long journeys and extremely energetic sightseeing, mostly to admire new factories and new bridges up and down the country. Duncan and Betty, indefatigable walkers wherever they went, even managed from time to time to go for long walks, sometimes starting by train (an unpredictable form of travel) by themselves, and these they much enjoyed, though they sometimes got into trouble and were told that their visits to this place or that would be 'inconvenient'. They managed to arrange piano lessons for their youngest daughter Lisa, now aged ten, from a fearless old professor who did not mind coming to the Embassy compound. For a time an equally fearless young cellist used to come and give cello lessons; but then it became 'inconvenient' and he stopped coming.

The compound was a walled enclosure occupied by all the foreign diplomats, recognised or not, each family in its own box-like house with a bigger box surrounding it where the Embassy staff lived. Duncan described his own house, the innermost box, as 'Works Queen Anne, and reasonably comfortable.' The compound was an ideal safe play area for children, and there was an international school where Lisa made friends with all nationalities, and they could rush around with the dog, left behind by Duncan's predecessor, a friendly and stupid animal called Barnaby, which went well into Chinese as Bar-la-bee. But even though there was a great deal of jollity within the compound, Duncan was oppressed, even in the first year, by the extent to which the Chinese whipped up hatred against foreign critics of the regime and seemed more and more motivated simply by the love of exercising power rather than by ideological considerations. As usual, when he was abroad, he became sympathetic to the original motives of the presiding government, but feared they would be corrupted beyond redemption.

After the first year, sure enough, things became much more restrictive. Though Betty and the young Lisa were able to enjoy wonderful skating in their first winter, by spring they could not venture outside the compound. Betty and Duncan must have found themselves increasingly claustrophobic, especially as no Chinese were allowed into the compound any more (though the old piano professor was sufficiently distinguished and indifferent still to come). However, as the anti-British demonstrations increased, in one case leading to their being completely besieged in the compound for a week, with paper darts bearing anti-British slogans thrown over the walls (to the delight of the incarcerated children), so Duncan and Betty's characteristic calm stoicism obviously asserted itself. My eldest sister, Jean, went to stay with them towards the end of their time there and one of the Embassy staff told her how reassuring it had been, at the height of the riots, to see Duncan walking down to the Embassy chapel on a Sunday morning to take matins, 'for all the world like the squire crossing the village green'.

It was at this time, too, that the somewhat incongruous practice grew up of organising Embassy music. They started to give concerts for staff from all the missions, partly of live, partly of recorded music. They found an excellent pianist among the staff, and the Ministry of Works representative, out there to oversee the maintenance of the buildings, turned out to be a very good bass-baritone who had never hitherto sung in public except at the dinners of Aldermen and their wives at home, and whose repertoire consisted mostly of such well-loved favourites as 'I Love You Only'. But under ambassadorial tuition, not to say ruthlessness, he became an enthusiast for classical music, as did the members of the missions from Afghan and Cambodia. Betty organised Scottish country dancing and there was an Embassy cricket match from time to time, of a highly international nature. From the distance, I had the impression of a kindly and paternalistic colonialism in which everyone became loyal to Duncan and regarded him as carrying out an essentially British role. All his staff loved him and Betty, but they were both glad to get away.

Duncan's next major step was to become ambassador to Yugoslavia. Both he and Betty had loved Belgrade and were delighted to go back. Now they could throw open the doors to whoever was willing to come and offer the use of the swimming pool to both grown-ups and children. Though the Embassy was bugged and though, wherever they went, they were followed by Tito's Secret Police, in fact they felt remarkably free, especially after their experiences in China. They made many Yugoslav friends and became deeply interested in what was happening in Tito's Yugoslavia (about which Duncan later wrote a book). They had learned a good deal of the Serbo-Croat language when they were there before, but Duncan now became fascinated by the language, its development, and the early development of Serbia. While he was there this time, he started work on a book on the life and times of Vuk Stephanovic Karadzic (known in Yugoslavia simply as Vuk) who had lived from 1787 until 1864 and who had been, in effect, the founder of the modern (or I should say then) Yugoslavia, and of the Serbo-Croat language. This book was published by Oxford University Press in 1970.

It is an impressive and fascinating book and it demonstrates, I believe, the characteristic qualities of Duncan's mind, and of his scholarship. As he explained in the preface, the book is not based on primary sources. These were being extensively studied by Yugoslav scholars and the archive in Vienna had already been much used. It was on this work that he mostly relied. In any case, as a working diplomat, he simply had no time to pursue original research. He was greatly helped by new friends in the University of Belgrade and elsewhere, who also helped him to extend and deepen his knowledge of the Serbo-Croat language.

The fact that he was using secondary sources perhaps made it easier for him to take a wide view of Vuk's achievement, and his place in the history of ideas, ideas which had an effect on politics and on history itself. It was in this kind of what might now be called 'joined-up' thinking that Duncan excelled. I sometimes wonder whether, if he had gone to All Souls, he would have become a close friend of Isaiah Berlin. In many ways they thought in the same way, essentially historically, though Duncan's learning could not be compared with Isaiah's. As things were, though they knew each other, they were never friends. I felt that Isaiah perhaps despised Duncan for being too respectable, too English, too much tarred with the Foreign Office brush (though this did him less than justice); and this even though they shared a passion for music. At any rate, when Isaiah and I spoke of Duncan he always employed tones of more than his usual irony, or so I thought.

In 1824 Vuk published the first book of his 'Leipzig Collection' of Serb popular songs. In the introduction he included a review of one of his collections by the great grammarian and linguist Jakob Grimm, published the year before. In the review, Grimm spoke of the effect these publications would have on the whole of Europe, but first and foremost on Serbia itself. Vuk had already, in 1818, published a dictionary of the Serbian language, separating what he regarded as the purest form of the language from the Russian form, which was used especially as a liturgical and highly literary language, regarded jealously by the Russians as a sacred possession of their own. Vuk had himself heard all the popular songs he collected, sung according to the oral tradition, and he transcribed them in the new alphabet he had produced for the dictionary, an alphabet designed to produce one pure orthography, to bring together all the dialects of the Slav languages current at the time. His motto was 'Write what you hear'.

The popular songs of his collection were of a particular heroic form, telling sagas from mythological or remote historical times up to the time of quite recent battles, such as those fought in the Serb uprising against the Turks in 1804. They often contained absurd or comic elements as well as more properly heroic ones. They had, until now, been passed down in an oral tradition, usually sung by blind men, in true Homeric style, though there were also so-called women's songs whose metres were different.

Vuk's collection of songs came at a time of immense enthusiasm for the primitive, the distant and the sublime, an enthusiasm which swept Europe in what may roughly be called the Romantic Age, and which had an enormous influence on the romantic imagination, insofar as that was broadly anti-intellectual, or consciously irrational. James Macpherson's fake heroic poems, *Ossian* and

Fingal, were embraced as authentic and became central to the craze for the Gothic, but were exposed as mostly Macpherson's own invention by such sceptics such as Doctor Johnson. This exposure hardly diminished the enthusiasm. Whatever their origin, they expressed the spirit of the age as much as did Gothic ruins in the garden or the novels of Sir Walter Scott. Seen as part of this movement (and Vuk was received with respect by Goethe at Weimar, who asked for literal translations into German of some of the songs), Vuk may be regarded as someone who succeeded above all in getting his version of the Serb language accepted, by employing it in a highly popular literary form. But he did more than this.

Vuk, like Goethe, was profoundly influenced by Herder. At the centre of Herder's political philosophy was a philosophy of history, according to which a 'native' voice is productive of, or perhaps an integral part of a 'national' voice and must be discovered if a nation is to exist as a political entity, with its own powers. Speaking of Herder, Isaiah Berlin said 'What I find valuable in Herder is the very idea of cultural diversity as intrinsic to human history; that history does not move in straight lines; that between different cultures there is an interplay, sometimes of a causal kind; but there is not a single key to the future or the past'. And again 'Herder discriminated between Greece, Rome, Judaea, India, Scandinavia, the Holy Roman Empire and France. The fact that we are able to understand how people live in the way that they do, even if they are different from us, even if they are hateful to us, and sometimes condemned by us, means that we can communicate across time and space. When we claim to understand people who have a different culture, very different from our own, it implies the existence of some power of sympathetic insight, Einfühlen, a word invented by Herder. Even if these cultures repel us, we can by an effort of empathetic imagination conceive how it can be possible that men think these thoughts, feel these feelings, pursue these goals, commit these acts.' (Ramin Jahanbagloo *Conversations with Isaiah Berlin*, 1992 pp. 36-7). It was the discovery of a cultural identity for the Serbs, as a huge group of Slavs in Europe, that was Vuk's most important achievement. But as a result of his unrelenting efforts, often against strong opposition, to unify the language, he brought the Serbs and the Croats closer together and so laid the foundations of a Yugoslav state, albeit perhaps inevitably an unstable and, as it has turned out, an impermanent entity. At the time that Duncan was there, this seemed a great achievement.

Duncan loved Belgrade, and loved Yugoslavia, experiencing increasingly the Einfühlen of which Herder spoke. He would have been sad, I think, but not astonished at the breakup of Yugoslavia. He would have understood it. He, like Isaiah Berlin, rejoiced in the thought of cultural diversity and could understand the motives and aspirations of other regimes, even if he did not approve of them. His understanding of the life and times of Vuk displayed, but also strengthened, this basic philosophy of differing cultural identities, to be understood across time and space. It was no wonder that among his masters in Whitehall he was often thought to be 'going native'.

Duncan's next and final diplomatic assignment was to Moscow as British Ambassador, starting in the autumn of 1968. It was a fraught period in British-Soviet relations. The Russian invasion of Czechoslovakia had taken place on the night of 20th/21st August 1968. Duncan's predecessor as ambassador had left Moscow on 25th August. Duncan was not due to arrive until the end of September; meanwhile the Embassy was in the hands of a temporary Chargé-d'Affaires. But there was much to be done in London. There were conversations with the Foreign Secretary (Michael Stewart) and with the Soviet Ambassador in London, to prepare a general strategy and to see what could be salvaged from a period when, on the whole, relations had been thought to be slowly improving. However, there was no doubt that, inevitably, Czechoslovakia had made a huge difference. British attempts to 'build bridges' with Eastern Europe were seen by the Soviet press as an encouragement to subversive activity and were deeply mistrusted.

It was in Moscow that Duncan's Einfühlen, his sympathetic understanding of another culture, even one that was hateful to him and to the British government, had probably its fullest and most beneficial expression, though many people at home thought him too optimistic, and when he came to leave he felt that he had failed. Things were worse than they had been when he arrived. Years later, Betty told me how impressed she had been, and yet how familiar and characteristic it had seemed, when on one occasion she was complaining of some apparently pointless restriction by which she found herself inhibited, and Duncan had said, 'They have their own problems too, you must remember'. And at this time there were dissensions within the party, which had as far as possible to be concealed from the outside world, in case they should be seen as a sign of weakness. He had to tread extraordinarily carefully and put up with a great deal of blustering abuse from the Russian side if he were to pursue the general long-term policy of keeping discussions open. All this is clearly shown in the dispatches and telegrams he sent home, many of which are now published in *Documents on British Policy Overseas Series III* volume I *Britain and the Soviet Union 1968-1972* (1997). Though generally neither party put a foot wrong, yet from an ironic twinkle in his eye, I believe many of the Russians began to recognise that each knew the games the other was playing, and that this form of cryptic communication might on the whole be trusted, and allowed to continue. But one could never know when suddenly things might break down, people who were personae non gratae expelled, arrangements arbitrarily cancelled.

The establishment at the Embassy was in some ways unusual in Duncan's day. For one thing, Lisa, his youngest daughter, had been living in Moscow for some time, studying the cello at the Conservatoire under Rostropovich, and now she could begin cautiously to bring some of her fellow students to the Embassy, an otherwise unheard-of thing. Then Betty, who had learned Russian before her marriage, on an adventurous trip, mostly by herself, to the USSR, was a good Russian speaker and had embarked on making an up-to-date English-Russian dictionary. She had enlisted the help of a distinguished academic at the University of Moscow called Olga Akhmanova to construct a corresponding Russian-English part. Akhmanova, known to generations of British ambassadors in Moscow and their staffs, was regarded as useful to the KGB, and could probably be deemed a spy. She was a loyal Communist, though probably with a good deal of ironic contempt for the theory of Communism, but she certainly struggled as far as possible to keep up the standards of the English Department at the University, and to protect it from too much political interference. Her particular relations with the Party and the University meant that she and Betty could spend hours together over the dictionary. It was through her that Betty was given a part-time job, taking a seminar once a week in the University of Moscow for postgraduates studying English language and literature. Again, it was an unheard-of thing for an ambassador's wife to have even a modest job. Her teaching was, if anything, more useful to her than her pupils. She simply went through the dictionary word by word, alphabetically getting their suggestions for translations, their critical assessment of what she had written and bringing it up to the minute. Since the dictionary was designed to be as far as possible non-literary and informal, with examples drawn from everyday speech, to be useful to businessmen and tourists, these young students were invaluable to her.

Early in 1971, Duncan's last year as ambassador, I was invited to spend two weeks at the Embassy with my elder son Felix, then in his first year as a student at the Royal College of Music and on vacation when we were to go. This was the only time I experienced Duncan and Betty in ambassadorial action. I was astonished, never having stayed in an embassy before, by the impeccable planning of our programme, every hour of every day (though things did not always work out as planned). The Embassy, though extraordinarily grandiose, having been built for a sugar merchant in the nineteenth century, with a splendid dining hall, its ceiling painted with cupids, nevertheless had very few bedrooms. I had the best spare room for most of my stay, a large room with its own bathroom, rather inconveniently opening out of the drawingroom, and looking straight out over the river to the Kremlin. Felix, on the other hand, had to sleep in a kind of alcove off the corridor of the servants' quarters above. But even his alcove had a warning reminding him that every room was bugged. I remember only two occasions when the bugging made any difference. One was when Betty wanted to fill me in with the gossip about the alleged sexual peccadilloes of Duncan's predecessor, which she wrote on the back of an envelope and pushed conspiratorially into my pocket. The other was a time early on in our stay when about forty Russians had been asked to a formal lunch and little round tables, each with a vase of flowers, had been meticulously prepared by Ron the footman, the food all ready, when a message came through to say that all forty Russians had 'flu and would not be coming. They were due in about two minutes. Betty was understandably furious and stood in the middle of the room to shout, 'I'll never entertain another bloody Russian again in my life! There! Unscramble that!'

Duncan had, with great difficulty, and many threats of cancellation, arranged some Days of British Music for that April, with which our visit partly coincided. He had asked for and received permission from Madame Furtseva, the Minister of Culture, almost a year earlier, when she had agreed that the Days could go ahead, provided that 'worthy examples of British music could be provided'. Duncan assured her that he planned to invite Benjamin Britten, William Walton and the whole London Symphony Orchestra, among others.

Britten was held in very high esteem in Russia, largely because of his friendship both with Shostakovich and, especially, with Rostropovich. However, as the year passed, Rostropovich fell increasingly out of favour with the Party because of his denunciation of the treatment of his friend, Alexander Solzhenitsyn, and the fact that he had given Solzhenitsyn a safe haven in his dacha did not improve things. Britten declared that he would not come unless Rostropovich were allowed to play, and after a good deal of vacillation the Ministry of Culture had reluctantly given in, presumably fearing the adverse publicity should negotiations break down. Rostropovich was therefore allowed to perform both in Moscow and in Leningrad, in exchange for undertaking numerous concert tours up and down the country (for example, as Duncan put it, to 'the music-loving Eskimos in Kamchatka').

The Days of Music were splendid and memorable days for Felix and me. We heard a great deal of music, and were welcomed to rehearsals as well as the concerts themselves. We had gone with Lisa to Leningrad, in one of the lesser Embassy cars, on a sightseeing trip, spending one exceedingly uncomfortable night in Novgorod, in the course of a drive through sleet and snow. I found the sightseeing depressing because I loathed going into churches used as either museums or nothing at all. We were delighted to arrive in Leningrad to a more comfortable hotel, and to the prospect of concerts beginning next day. On the first day we spent the morning on a VIP tour of the Hermitage (of course with nothing like enough time) with Sir William and Lady Walton, the former rather grumpy, the latter elegant and charming, seeing, among other wonders, the Scythian golden jewellery from the tombs in the middle of Siberia, of which Herodotus had heard tell, some of it dating from 3,000 BC. That day there was a concert in honour of Britten at the Conservatoire Hall, including a rather terrible performance of the *Serenade for Tenor, Horn and Strings* which caused Peter Pears politely to wince, and a superb performance by the strings of the Leningrad Symphony Orchestra, who played the *Simple Symphony* as a piece of chamber music, without a conductor, which reduced Britten to tears.

The climax of the music was on our last day in Leningrad, a concert in the Philharmonic Hall, where Britten's early piano concerto was played by Sviatoslav Richter, and his cello symphony with Rostropovich as soloist. This was the first time that Rostropovich had played in Leningrad in many years, though it was where he had started his musical career, because he had quarrelled with the Leningrad-based conductor Mravinsky. His welcome back was rapturous. The hall, built to seat 2,000, was said to have contained 4,000 that evening. That is doubtless an exaggeration but it was certainly overflowing, with students perched on the window sills, and even on the roof. The applause was deafening and apparently never-ending. We managed to get away just in time to catch the train back to Moscow. And we had an extremely jolly journey, Felix, Lisa and I joining Rostropovich and his wife, and one of the music critics from London, as well as, for a time, Britten and Pears, all in Duncan and Betty's compartment, where we drank whisky. Then Lisa, Felix and I went off to our own compartment, where we went over our experiences in Leningrad. We were sharing the compartment with a very small and understandably terrified Russian whom Lisa, in vain, tried from time to time to bring into the conversation. He simply turned up the volume of his radio, poor man, to try to drown our increasingly giggly conversation.

Felix and I had had a particularly bizarre lunch party with an academic linguist to whom I had a letter of introduction from one of the language teachers at the Oxford High School for Girls, where I was headmistress at the time. She, most unusually, had her own car and had come to pick us up from our hotel to see the sights of Leningrad, before she took us off to lunch. Luckily, we had already seen not only the Hermitage, but various other parts of Leningrad, and had both decided that Leningrad must be the most beautiful city in the world. Our hostess, however, showed us the war cemetery and the museum commemorating the Siege (both extraordinarily impressive, despite the piped Beethoven), we were taken round the new suburbs and post-war factories. She frequently lost the way and we, who were becoming hungrier and hungrier every moment, were less than riveted. But when we got to her house, and before we could have lunch, she had to explain to us the subject of her research. This was the issue (if such it could be called) of English words, many of foreign origin, used as technical terms in various sports and which had become incorporated in the French language. The sports most important to her research project were golf and cricket. She had never, of course, seen either golf or cricket played, so when she discovered that Felix was a keen player of both games she became extremely excited and questioned him relentlessly about the precise meaning of various terms she had come across, many of them out of date, such as 'mashie', 'clique', and 'spoon', to say nothing of 'silly mid-off' and 'leg-bye'. Felix was visibly wilting by the time we were at last led downstairs to the kitchen for lunch, where her mother, an ancient peasant, had boiled a huge chicken. We were plied with vodka and then fell on the chicken, than which nothing had tasted so delicious. The old mother immediately fell in love with Felix and, through her daughter as interpreter, showered me with compliments about him – 'Such a beautiful, healthy boy, such lovely curly hair, such perfect manners'. All the most succulent parts of the fowl were piled onto his plate, which must have almost compensated for his embarrassment at the stream of adulation. After lunch we had to go upstairs again for coffee while our hostess played us comic songs on the gramophone, the jokes of which had to be painstakingly explained. At last we were driven back, to change in a hurry before the evening's concert.

All this we recounted on the train, interspersed with Lisa's translating for us extracts from our fellow traveller's radio programme, all about the record output at various factories, and the early signs of a bumper harvest. We arrived back after an extremely hot and almost entirely sleepless night in time for a delicious long-drawn-out breakfast at the Embassy, feeling very much that we were coming home, even though I was now sharing a room with Lisa, giving up my beautiful room with its view across to the Kremlin to Britten and Pears. Lisa was extremely stoical and forgiving about having to share.

After the Moscow performance of the concert we had heard in Leningrad, with Richter and Rostropovich as soloists, there was a great reception for them and for the whole of the London Symphony Orchestra, in the Embassy. Shostakovich was present as well, looking old and haunted, with his son Maxim. I had met Rostropovich before, when he was over for one of the Edinburgh Festivals. He and Duncan were already friends and he had kindly suggested that he heard my daughter Fanny, then aged about nine, play the cello in his hotel bedroom. Getting the small cello into the lift from the station to the hotel was almost the end of it because Fanny would let no one carry it but herself. But at least we got there, and she played her very small repertoire among the plush furniture of the bedroom. After the performance, Rostropovich lifted her off her feet, kissed her warmly, and said 'Fanushka, promise me that you will practise for four hours every day'. Small hope. Even Lisa, his current pupil, got into severe trouble from Betty while we were staying, because in the time when she was supposed to be practising she and Felix sometimes preferred to play noisy duets on the white piano in the Embassy drawing room, clearly audible all over the house. That piano had been used by Duncan and Edward Heath when he was an Embassy guest; and now it was also used, with a great deal more subtlety, by Benjamin Britten, rehearsing with Peter Pears for a private recital they were to give in the Embassy, sadly after we would have left, of, among other things, Britten's *Winter Words*; but listening to their rehearsals, standing on the landing outside, was one of my pleasures.

To return to the reception; Felix and I were introduced to Shostakovich, who looked, as I have said, ill and old, and also apprehensive, or so it seemed. I just about managed to think 'We are shaking hands with Shostakovich' before we got swept into talk with members of the LSO, helping Betty to entertain as she rightly thought we might actually be useful for once. Felix was buttonholed by an old and much respected violinist, I think the leader of the second fiddles, who warned him solemnly and with many supporting anecdotes, that never in any circumstances must he become an orchestral player (which in due course he did). I, meanwhile, standing at the window, which like that of the best bedroom looked out across the Kremlin, was locked in the most inappropriate conversation with Peter Lloyd, the principal flautist, whom I had never met but had talked to over the telephone. He was a professor at the Guildhall School of Music and was teaching my goddaughter, a pupil at the Oxford High School and daughter of the same cousin Jenny with whom I had been at LMH, and who had introduced me to Philippa Foot. This girl was aiming (or rather Jenny was aiming for her) to enter the Guildhall as a student, and was to take the audition in the coming December. Peter Lloyd, who was not only her teacher but would also be an examiner, did not think she would get a place and had been trying to get my help in persuading Jenny not to push her into attempting it. I had failed entirely. So here we stood, in this unlikely environment, having all over again a painful conversation about Jenny's obstinacy, a conversation we might just as well have had in Oxford, or London, or anywhere else on earth.

After most of the guests had gone, Lisa, Felix and I, along with Betty's mentor Olga Akhmanova and several of Lisa's friends, music students for the most part, sat up far into the night, talking in what seemed to me a quintessentially Russian way, conscious of the precariousness of so talking, never saying anything directly political, indeed talking mostly about music, art and literature, but with a peculiar intensity, and therefore pleasure, drawn together by a kind of campaign spirit. It led me to wonder for the hundredth time whether such conversation and such pleasure could exist in a wholly comfortable easygoing liberal atmosphere, whether war or its equivalent, an edge of danger, were actually necessary for intensity of enjoyment.

As in any embassy where Duncan worked, there was, as a matter of course, an Embassy Choir, into which Felix and I were at once enrolled. At the rehearsal in our first week I was certain that this must be the most improbable experience of my life, such that I would never forget it. The choir was in the middle of a rehearsal, presumably for some later concert, and Duncan, as conductor, was having difficulty in getting us to sing a six-part sacred motet from the vast library he possessed of English Cathedral music. Felix was among the basses, standing next to Ron the footman, who was accustomed now to such music. My neighbour among the altos was the wife of the Pakistani Ambassador who was willing enough but, unsurprisingly, at sea. However I was wrong about its being the most improbable experience. Next week was still more peculiar.

We were conducted this time by Peter Pears (Britten having chickened out at the last minute with a well-timed headache), who both stood in front of us with the baton and sang the tenor line, or one of them. We sang rather better than we had the week before, but I was glad, all the same, to be missing the concert.

I came to like and admire both Britten and Pears very much. I felt with Britten that I was undoubtedly in the presence of a man of genius, burdened with acute and often agonising sensitivity and imagination. Pears, in contrast, who was very kind to Felix and me (indeed they both were), musical and sensitive though he was too, was a kind of nanny-figure, making things ordinary and bearable, remaining calm in the hectic atmosphere of the Days of Music. Duncan had to carry on the regular business of the Embassy at this time, while also trying to keep his guests happy. One of his tasks, whenever he had to make a speech, was to ensure that Walton was not left out of the welcome and adulation that was naturally showered on Britten by the Russians, partly because they were familiar with his music, and not with Walton's, but partly of course because of Rostropovich, whom they loved more, the colder the Party became towards him. I personally had known none of Walton's serious music until this time, and I began to greatly enjoy it, as did many of the Russians.

The other calming influence and attender to our needs was Ron, who was wonderfully good at seeing when it was time to bring proper drinks into the drawing room, to be enjoyed in peace by the visitors. I was quite amazed at how nervous Britten was before every concert in which he was performing, or in which his music was to be played. Among the Embassy guests, though staying at a nearby hotel, were Sue Phipps and her husband Jack, who were music agents working for Britten in Aldeburgh. I already knew Sue (her step-daughter, Jack's child by a previous marriage, was a pupil at the Oxford High School) and I did not much like her. She was not best pleased that Britten and Pears were staying at the Embassy. She would have preferred them under her eye in the hotel. One day, after lunch in the Embassy, Jack being elsewhere, she refused to walk back to the hotel alone on the grounds that it was dangerous. I was the only person to volunteer to accompany her (I having walked the streets of Moscow alone quite often by then), but she, understandably, did not like that plan. In the end, Felix and I and the Embassy dog, Fly, took her back, but this was little better.

Britten, at the first hint of trouble, had sensibly announced that he was going to bed to rest. He was all the time waging a private battle against the female 'escort' allotted to him by the agency Goskoncert, a Miss Sokolova, whom he detested and who, like Sue Phipps, felt cheated of her prey by his residence in the Embassy, to which she had no access. As Duncan recorded in his description of the Days of Music for the Foreign Secretary (Alex Douglas-Hume, *Documents* p. 336) 'This involved some near-storms and comedy', but, sadly he added 'which are better recorded elsewhere'. Sue, at any rate, was a fully-paid-up worshipper of Britten (and before a concert he needed not just admiration but worship). He liked to sit at her feet then, and have his hair brushed by her, to soothe his nerves. Betty was disgusted by these goings-on. One day, unmindful of the bugs, she said to me 'Well, I suppose you want to go and join in the hair-brushing, and you can if you like. Myself, I can't bear to have anything to do with it'. I, though I could easily imagine becoming a worshipper, kept well away.

One of the great benefits that I enjoyed as an indirect result of the Days of Music was that Betty, because she was so busy, handed over to me her weekly seminar at the University. As all the students were graduates in English language and literature, they spoke and understood perfectly so my total lack of Russian was not a problem. Very wisely, Betty had not told them that my subject was philosophy or they would have expected to have to talk about Marx or the theory of Communism. Instead, I simply went on with going through the alphabet, discussing words. By great good fortune, Betty was in the middle of the letter 'I'. I was just beginning to think about writing my book on imagination, a book which I started work on seriously in 1972, when I left the High School, so I had a wonderful time questioning them about images and icons (for which there seemed to be only one word, namely 'icon').

I had been terribly nervous before the first seminar and, when the day came, Betty was in bed with a migraine and I had to be driven by myself in the Embassy Rolls and find my way to the seminar room as best I could. I felt like turning back and telephoning to say I had 'flu, but the moment I got there, all was well. The students loved to be told to do things. 'Shut your eyes', I said, 'and see the Kremlin in your mind's eye. Now tell me exactly what you see'. It was a long time before I could get them to use the word 'image' or 'picture' at all. What pleased them most, I think, was the unstructured way we wandered from unearthing things they would actually say, in real life, and any possible theory of the nature of the image. At the end of this seminar they asked if, next week, they might bring a tape recorder, to which I had no objection. By the time of the second week's teaching, I was thoroughly looking forward to it. This time we started talking about 'immaterial', and the different opposites one could find to 'real' (such as 'imaginary', 'fake' and so on). By now they were well away, asking whatever they wanted to … the difference between 'real' and 'actual', for example, or, to my amusement, between 'peculiar' and 'queer'. At the very end they extracted from me the confession that I was a philosopher, and they were utterly delighted. 'Is this how you are allowed to teach in Oxford?' they asked. The idea of such freedom amazed them. Once again I was struck by the intensity of their pleasure in the conversations we had had, made sharp by their own restricted, rule-governed intellectual lives. And I sometimes now wonder whether our own concepts of political correctness may not before long lead us into the same plight. Even with the compensations, I would not want to go far down that road, yet I have seldom enjoyed teaching more.

When the time came to leave I was sitting alone in the drawing room, waiting for the car, and I picked up an out of date copy of the *Times*, and looked, as I always do, at the obituaries. There I saw that Marcus Dick, one of my dearest and saddest friends had died suddenly in Norwich. A moment after I had taken this in, Ben Britten came in to say goodbye. I looked at him, in tears, and said, 'He's dead'. He, knowing nothing of what I was talking about, embraced me and allowed me to weep briefly on his shoulder. He was a man of the most terrifying sensitivity, and therefore of sympathy. A few years later, when he died, I told Peter Pears this story, and he was not surprised.

Both Felix and I felt that we would not have missed our stay for the world. I was deeply grateful to Duncan and Betty for making it possible, especially when they were so busy, but I was conscious that we had been a nuisance. Negatively, we had been no help because of our linguistic incompetence but, more, we had probably behaved in some ways positively badly. There had been one day when I had preferred to go shopping with Britten and Pears (on the excuse that Ben had asked me to help him choose books for some children, including Jack Phipps' daughter, Polly) rather than meet with Betty and Akhmanova to talk about the dictionary (and it happened that this coincided with an especially exuberant performance of duets by Lisa and Felix, so that Betty was enraged and frustrated on all sides). We had taken up too much of Ron's time, who had, after all, better things to do than chat to the visitors. We both found ourselves asking, on the plane coming home, whether we had behaved well enough; what would our reports say after we had left? What I had learned, at any rate, was what a difficult job Duncan had and with what humanity, humour and grace he carried it out. But he did not, as I have said, believe that he had done altogether well, as his final dispatch reveals. In it he wrote (*Documents*, no. 72, p. 368) that he looked back with nostalgia on the days when his predecessor could write to the then Foreign Secretary that Russia regarded Britain as 'the sensible wing of the Western Camp, and that this was an image it was desirable to cultivate'. 'I am afraid', he went on, 'that our image in the eyes of the Soviet leaders is very different today, and I cannot congratulate myself on the results of my own mission here .... Anglo-Soviet relations are in poor shape, and may get worse before they can get better' (*Documents* no. 72, p. 366). In replying, Sir Thomas Brimelow, a man who probably despised Duncan's willingness to enter into the minds and purposes of Russians, just as he had of Yugoslavs, and who had come from the British Embassy in Poland to be Deputy Under Secretary of State at the Foreign and Commonwealth Office in 1969, a man, incidentally, for whom Betty had not a good word to say, wrote somewhat patronisingly, 'I think you did well in the circumstances which any ambassador must have found discouraging. I question whether any British Ambassador in Moscow has exercised a decisive influence on Anglo-Soviet relations. The forces in play are not accessible to his influence'. It did not much matter, he implied, that Duncan had wasted his time on cultivating personal contacts; nothing would have made things any better.

Duncan goes on in his letter, somewhat defensively, to explain both that he had had particular access to the world of artists and musicians, and had cultivated these private contacts, and that he found among non-official Russians an ironic acceptance of the regime, as something they could not change, but did not really believe in. On this second point, Sir Thomas Brimelow and, I suspect, most of his colleagues at home, strongly disagreed with Duncan. They held that Russia was still completely in the grip of Stalinist ideology, remembering too clearly the days when unless you toed the Party line, and believed in it, you faced your death. Characteristically, here, Duncan seemed prone to see things in less black and white terms, to detect irony wherever he could, and find evidence that ordinary people could see through the verbiage and blatant propaganda of the party machine, or at least partially shut their ears to it. On the first point, he writes (p. 374) 'Under present conditions a certain ... knowledge of the Russian language, some persistence and a modicum of tact can earn a number of private contacts for the foreign diplomat – perhaps most easily for Ambassadors, who are no doubt regarded as too stupid to be spies. The more fundamental question may be raised: Is it all worthwhile? The sort of contacts one can make are not likely to be typical, and have at best only a remote influence on Governmental or Party policies ... we should certainly not exaggerate the value of private contacts in terms of political influence (probably nil) or of sociological importance. But a little – even a very little value – is better than none'. It is a modest claim.

Generally, I should think the Foreign and Commonwealth Office was quite glad to be rid of this complex, subtle and certainly not stupid ambassador, and revert to someone more likely to think in ideological terms, who carried no risk of going native. Almost immediately after Duncan's leaving Moscow, relations between Britain and the USSR worsened considerably, over the huge growth of Soviet establishments in Britain, and the need to attempt to cut them down, expelling as many as 6,400 surplus hangers-on and spies who had somehow been allowed to proliferate. But this change in climate had really nothing to do with Duncan's retirement, and one may be tempted to agree with Brimelow that it really did not make much difference who the Ambassador was. One may nevertheless conclude that Duncan's regime was at least humane and intelligent.

When I went to Moscow in 1971, Duncan knew that he had been short-listed for the Mastership of Corpus Christi College, Cambridge. He, like most of those who retire from the Civil Service at the age of sixty, often at the height of their powers, was determined to get a job, and when duly elected he held this one until the end of the academic year 1980. He succeeded a much-loved Master, Frank Lea and his wife, who was also greatly loved, a fairly conventional pair, happy to rub along in a college largely controlled by its senior Fellows, some of whom were still there in Duncan's day.

He had really no idea what a university, or indeed a college, was like from the point of view of a senior member. His undergraduate days at Oxford were all he had to go on, but they were long ago. In any case, undergraduates are almost totally ignorant of the governance of their colleges, still more ignorant of the governance of the university as a whole. And Duncan was moving to Cambridge, not Oxford, and the extent to which, in occupying the Master's Lodge, they were occupying not their own house, but a part of the college, over which they had no real power, came as a shock to him, and to Betty. Power lay in the hands of the Fellows. Strictly, the Head of a House, whether in Oxford or Cambridge, is not even a member of the Senior Common Room (or, in Cambridge, the Combination Room) and goes there only by courtesy of the Fellows.

When, after Duncan's death, I followed in his footsteps to

become Mistress of Girton, Geoffrey, who had by then been head of a college for fourteen years, warned me, as I have said, of the potential obstructiveness of Fellows; for Fellows of colleges in both universities want desperately to show that they are autonomous, free agents, running the college, not to be dictated to like schoolteachers by 'the Head'. The Fellows are the college, and wish it to be known that they are. It is difficult, I suspect especially in Cambridge (probably because there are so many academics in the university who are not Fellows of any college, and therefore a Fellowship is an even more sought-after prize than in Oxford, and also less permanent), for Fellows to treat the Head of their House as an equal, as someone with whom things may be discussed openly, without falling into cliques or factions. On the contrary, the Head is a figurehead, to be manipulated in one direction or another. Duncan, used to the very different position of an ambassador and his staff, found this difficult to grasp; Betty found it outrageous. (After all, 'the staff' in a college are not the Fellows; they are the junior administrative and domestic employees of the college.) To be told by the Bursar whom she must have to stay in the Lodge for Feasts or Guest Nights was intolerable to her. She was frequently heard to say that she infinitely preferred the restrictions of Moscow to those of Corpus. Duncan at least had the consolation of contact with the undergraduates (which Betty also much enjoyed). They used to have parties of undergraduates to stay in Islay, which was now their permanent non-Cambridge home. They also encouraged the college music; and Duncan's major contribution to the university was his organising the fund-raising for the splendid new Music School which now stands in West Road. This involved setting up numerous concerts given by his old friends among musicians, such as Rostropovich. He never stood for the Council of Senate, the central university governing body, because he discovered that the Fellows had put forward his name only in the hope of keeping out a female Head of House, Rosemary Murray, the President of New Hall.

Duncan and Betty got on very well with all their staff. They had brought Ron with them from Moscow as a footman in Hall. He stayed on after they had left, and finally rose to the rank of Head Butler, the most senior of all domestic staff. When I got to Cambridge myself and was invited by Duncan's successor, Michael McCrum, to dine in Hall, I asked my host whether I might have a chance after dinner to have a word with Ron. McCrum said 'Ron? Ron? Which of the Fellows is called Ron?' When I enlightened him, he was shocked, still more when I went up to Ron as we left the High Table and we warmly hugged each other in Russian style. I had last seen him at Duncan's memorial service.

There were of course many things that interested and amused Duncan in Cambridge. I remember his particularly enjoying conversations with the college carpenter. When some new pews were commissioned for the Chapel and the question arose about how far the seats should be from the shelves in front, the carpenter said, 'I suppose, Master, that you will prefer the Shampoo Position'. On a different level, he enjoyed the occasion when he had to take the Augustine Bible from the college library down to Canterbury, for the installation of the new Archbishop, who has, by tradition, to take his oath on this Bible.

But the last five years of Duncan and Betty's time at Corpus was completely overshadowed by the death in an accident of their only son, David. David was a journalist, and had for some time been Industrial Correspondent on the *Observer*. He had written a good book about Dock Labour. He had just been promoted to be Washington correspondent and was bicycling to the office to clear his desk the day before he was due to leave, on a Sunday, and was crushed between two lorries and killed. Duncan and Betty were totally stricken with grief. They were a close family, and Duncan and David had come increasingly to like and admire each other. The college, including the undergraduates, was very supportive of them; but I do not see how anyone can get over the death of a child, and they never did completely recover. It seemed to confirm Duncan in the mild pessimism he always had, a feeling that, although there are great pleasures to be enjoyed, one must not expect much. The world is random and ultimately cruel.

All the time they were at Corpus, it was plain who the next Master would be. Michael McCrum had been Senior Tutor of the College in the past, and had then become Headmaster of Eton and was now eagerly awaited as the obvious heir. He used to come over to stay in the Lodge from time to time, not much to the delight of Duncan or Betty. Duncan's term of office ended on the August 31st 1980, but as soon as the Easter term ended, in the middle of June, the builders moved in to alter and redecorate the Lodge. Betty could go immediately but Duncan had to stick it out, so the last two months of his Mastership were spent in great discomfort, his bedroom upstairs and a small pantry downstairs being the only rooms available to him. He thankfully retired to Islay as soon as he could get away.

While he was in Cambridge, and while Betty was still slaving away at her dictionary, Duncan was commissioned, I think by the Hogarth Press, to write a book about Leonard Woolf, as a political rather than a Bloomsbury figure. After David's death, he urgently wanted work to do, and so he accepted the commission without great enthusiasm. He would have preferred, I dare say, to write about Virginia Woolf of whose novels and diaries he was an admirer. (One of my failures with Duncan in early days had been that he gave me a copy of *To the Lighthouse* for my sixteenth birthday. I doggedly read it, and thanked him for it; but when he questioned me afterwards, probably wanting a more enthusiastic or analytic response, I simply had not the nerve to tell him that I thought it pointless and boring, so I just muttered and went away. It was not until I was an undergraduate that I read it again, and it became one of my favourite books.) The book that Duncan wrote (*Leonard Woolf: a political biography*, 1978) seems to me successful in so far as it covers, through the eyes of Woolf's kind of dogmatic socialism, a number of major figures in the Labour Party of his time and also many of the major controversies of international relations, including the birth of the League of Nations. But Woolf himself, though pretending to rigorous philosophical and psychological thought about the foundations of politics, is such a confused and inconsistent thinker that weariness sets in before long. Duncan quotes at length, and with approval, a long and devastatingly critical article by Stuart Hampshire on Woolf's last political book, portentously, and after the manner of the Bloomsbury guru, the philosopher G.E. Moore, named *Principia Politica*. This article was published in the *New Statesman* on November 14th 1953. After that, Woolf turned to writing his autobiography. His autobiographical writing is far more interesting than his philosophical ideas, so perhaps Duncan concluded that his own book had hardly been worth writing. In the end I think he found Woolf to be not only a dull, but terminally confused dog.

Soon a far more attractive commission came his way, this time from the Oxford University Press, who wanted a life of Gilbert Murray. It was this which occupied Duncan from his retirement until his death two years later, and which in fact he never finished. However he had left enough notes for it to be possible for Betty to finish it for him, a task with which I willingly helped her as far as I could. The whole book, as published, forms a remarkably seamless whole both in style and in its basic conception.

Gilbert Murray was an ideal subject for Duncan. To write about him one would need to be both a classical scholar and someone with an interest in international affairs and an understanding of the ideals of the League of Nations. One would also need to be able to see the comic side of Murray's nature, his credulity, and occasional silliness, as well as to appreciate his own sometimes fey wit and charm. All these things Duncan's turn of mind could encompass. The result is undoubtedly Duncan's best book (*Gilbert Murray O.M.*, Oxford, 1987). There was a mass of archival material in Oxford, in the Bodleian Library, papers and letters, both official and personal (the latter somewhat bowdlerised after Murray's death by his daughter, Rosalind Toynbee). It was the sorting of this material and making notes on it which brought Duncan constantly to Oxford in the remaining two years of his life, staying with us in Hertford, conveniently across the road from the Bodleian. There was undoubtedly something of the goose in Murray's nature and it would have been tempting to write the biography wholly in the spirit of irony, or in the style of Murray's bête noire, Lytton Strachey. Duncan did not succumb to the temptation. His approach was genuinely historical. He understood very well, for example, the difference in the nature of classical studies that had come about in Oxford after the arrival of the great refugee scholars. (Murray, after all, belonged to a Victorian age of scholarship, having been appointed to the Chair of Greek in Glasgow in 1889, at the age of twenty three.) Duncan also understood the point and the appeal of Murray's popularising work, in his free translations of Euripides (much despised by purists) in the style of Swinburne. I, at the age of about fourteen, had found these translations profoundly exciting, and they still hold for me, as they did for Duncan, a nostalgic and romantic charm.

But equally, Duncan could sympathise with the liberal spirit and high-minded do-gooding which made up the political views and activities of Murray and his wife. He understood and wrote, in my view brilliantly, about Murray's thoughts on religion, manifested especially in his 1912 lectures delivered in Amherst, USA, becoming the book *Five Stages of Greek Religion*. He quotes from Murray's book: 'In religion, however precious you may consider the truth you draw from it, you know that it is a truth seen dimly and possibly seen better by others than by you. You know that all your creed and definitions are merely metaphors ... Your concepts are by the nature of things inadequate; the truth is not in you but beyond you, a thing not conquered but still to be pursued'. Duncan refers to this book as 'an intellectual self-portrait'. It represents a view with which he is uncommonly sympathetic. As well as all this, there were parts of his book which made me laugh aloud, especially those concerned with the spirit world, the dotty table-tapping and ghost-hunting of the Cambridge Verralls, founders of the Society for Psychical Research, with which Murray was associated.

I look back on Duncan's visits to Hertford with enormous pleasure. It is always satisfactory, in my opinion, to have a guest who is busy with his own affairs; and Duncan was quite capable of working for long hours in the Bodleian, letting himself in for a break and a sandwich at lunch-time and going back to work until it was time for a drink and dinner. He dined with Geoffrey in Hall once or twice a week, or with me in the Lodgings. Geoffrey had always got on well with him, and especially if we stayed in the holiday annexe to their house in Islay they were well-matched rivals on the golf course. Duncan usually won. Geoffrey was much more of a stylish player, and capable of much longer drives, but Duncan, in a characteristically ungainly way, was accurate, knew the course backwards, with all its 'blind' holes over the top of the sand dunes, and had developed a cunning old man's short game. Now they found a great deal to talk about, and Duncan became a well-loved and familiar figure in the Hertford SCR, a role he much enjoyed. He was a member of Common Room at St Anthony's College, which, with its mainly International Relations interests, suited him admirably and he sometimes took Oxford friends, or sometimes Geoffrey and me, to dine there.

Otherwise he and I and anyone else who was there used to have bacon and eggs (which I was now capable of cooking, and which was his favourite food) and settle down to watch television. It was a period of immense televisual richness. On Sundays there was the magnificent thirteen-part *Brideshead Revisited* made by Granada and partly filmed in Hertford, Evelyn Waugh's undergraduate college. And then there was the first series of *Yes, Minister* which Duncan loved so much that I feared that he, now rather overweight, would actually break the furniture, so convulsed with laughter did he become. These were the days when one had to make absolute rules to be in on certain days for the television. How different from now. He had always loved music with my children. Years before there had been a wonderful scene, again of convulsive laughter, when he had accompanied our younger son, James, about to take his Grade Five tuba examination, in *Rocked in the Cradle of the Deep*. They were joined by Felix, coincidentally ordered by the National Youth Orchestra to take his turn on the contrabassoon, which we had been to London to collect so that he could practise it. The floor shook with the vibrations, as well as the hysterical laughter, which of course ultimately made playing impossible. Now he enjoyed piano duets with our middle daughter, Fanny, when she came for weekends.

But best of all, he and I had plenty of time for conversation, either about current politics, the increasing awfulness of Mrs Thatcher, the prospects of the Liberal Democrats (he said he was one of nature's Liberal Democrats, only that he could never join a party led by David Owen, reportedly the most arrogant and insensitive Foreign Secretary imaginable, though he had never personally worked under him), or about our family. For the first time I felt totally at ease with him, and we could talk as equals.

We talked about his relations with my sisters, Jean and Grizel, and about my special (as he recognised) relation with Stephana. We talked about our parents' marriage, of which of course I knew nothing, and speculated about what would have happened if our father had lived. I have seldom enjoyed conversation more, and I felt I was making up for lost time.

His death in September 1983 came as a total shock. He suffered a mild heart attack while he was at home in Islay, about which Betty rang me up, without seeming too much alarmed. He came out of hospital after a day or two, but then relapsed, went back to hospital and died after a few days. For his funeral in Islay, Geoffrey was away on Vice-Chancellor's business. I managed, with efficiency that surprised me, to charter an aeroplane to take as many of the family as could manage it from Glasgow. Stephana, whose husband, also Duncan, had died a few months before, and I spent a night in a grim hotel in Glasgow, having driven up from her house in Yorkshire, and we flew over, the plane full of family, through thick fog and rain in the morning. Luckily we were able to land, in spite of the weather (it often happened that one could not land at the airport and had to turn back to Glasgow). The service was in the village church at Port Charlotte, and during it the rain lifted and the sun suddenly streamed in through one of the windows. I was reduced to helpless weeping by the hymn *Let Saints on Earth in Concert Sing*, set to one of our drawing-room hymn singing tunes from our childhood in Dundee. Afterwards the whole congregation processed for a few yards along the road, the coffin carried in front by men from the village; and then we went by car to a graveyard inland, surrounded by hills. There he was buried, all of us helping to lower the coffin, in a grave beside David, his son.

Duncan had earlier shown me a copy of the sermon he preached in the Corpus Chapel at the end of his last term there. (He had, I think, preached there only once before.) His theme was the relation between faith and academic knowledge. In it he attempted a reconciliation between faith, or hope, and his natural pessimism. He ended with these words: 'Joy does not cease to exist because there is so much evil under the sun. Neither our own personal experience nor the history of mankind is an arithmetical sum in which negative elements cancel or abolish the positive ones. For me the positive experiences have been best enshrined by the great composers with their direct attack on something deeper than the conscious mind. It is surely a truth about us that we can be so exalted, even for a short time. For long it was a truth thought to embody the truth about the structure of the universe. As Addison put it in his very eighteenth-century version of Psalm 19:

> What though in solemn silence all
> Move round the dark terrestrial ball?
> What though no real voice or sound
> Amid their radiant orbs be found?
> In reason's ear they all rejoice ...

I hope that the phrase 'reason's ear' for some of you stirs the memory of Britten's marvellous setting. Anyhow, the words lead me back to my main theme. They suggest a union of reason and instinct of faith; and surely reason rightly attuned by humility and sympathy is the best instrument we have for the apprehension of whatever the truth may be.'

Duncan was someone who used this complex instrument subtly and consistently. I only wish I had properly known him sooner.

Index